Holy Mavericks

Holy Mavericks

*Evangelical Innovators and
the Spiritual Marketplace*

Shayne Lee and
Phillip Luke Sinitiere

NEW YORK UNIVERSITY PRESS

New York and London

NEW YORK UNIVERSITY PRESS
New York and London
www.nyupress.org

Library of Congress Cataloging-in-Publication Data
Lee, Shayne.
Holy mavericks: evangelical innovators and the spiritual marketplace
/ Shayne Lee and Phillip Luke Sinitiere.
p. cm.
Includes bibliographical references (p.) and index.
ISBN-13: 978-0-8147-5234-0 (cl : alk. paper)
ISBN-10: 0-8147-5234-9 (cl : alk. paper)
ISBN-13: 978-0-8147-5235-7 (pb : alk. paper)
ISBN-10: 0-8147-5235-7 (pb : alk. paper)
1. Evangelicalism—United States—History. 2. Protestant churches—
United States—Clergy—History. 3. Church marketing—United
States—History. 4. Popular culture—Religious aspects—Protestant
churches—History. 5. Popular culture—United States—History. 6.
United States—Church history. I. Sinitiere, Phillip Luke. II. Title.
BR1642.U5L44 2009
277.3'083—dc22   2008047904

New York University Press books are printed on acid-free paper,
and their binding materials are chosen for strength and durability.
We strive to use environmentally responsible suppliers and materials
to the greatest extent possible in publishing our books.

Manufactured in the United States of America
c 10 9 8 7 6 5 4 3 2 1
p 10 9 8 7 6 5 4 3 2 1

Contents

Acknowledgments

In an academic profession that demands individual initiative and requires significant amounts of solitude for individual contemplation, it can be a pleasant change and fruitful experience to work collaboratively—especially across disciplinary lines. For a historically inclined sociologist and a sociologically oriented historian, such was the experience during the research phases and writing seasons of *Holy Mavericks*.

Just as the holy mavericks about whom we write depend on networks, associations, and connections, so too do scholars who conduct research and write books. To that end, we must first thank our wonderful editor, Jennifer Hammer, and her talented team at NYU Press for their diligence and expertise in the production of this book. We also happily acknowledge the great work of Susan Ecklund, our copyeditor. We also thank the University of Houston for allocating travel funds to conduct research and Tulane University for providing a generous grant to purchase photographs for our book. Additionally, we thank our California "cabbie" Mike Drago, an engaging and insightful high school history teacher from Orange County, who gave us a history of the area, accompanied us on our research excursions, provided transportation through the hills and valleys of Southern California, and offered delightful conversation over meals. We also thank the anonymous reviewers whose probing and insightful commentary and criticism of the manuscript strengthened our work. For additional insight on various parts of the manuscript and for unfailing encouragement along the way, we thank Edward Carson, Darren Grem, Carol Crawford Holcomb, Lauran Kerr, Vy Dao, Nadia Lahutsky, and David Sehat. We also thank those who provided time and perspective about our holy mavericks and their ministries: Stanley Hauerwas, Terrance Slaughter, David Daniels, and Tony Jones. Anthony Smith deserves a special note of thanks for introducing us to each other and for his fruitful consultation on the emerging church. Finally, we thank NYU Press for permitting use of segments of *T. D. Jakes: America's New Preacher* (2005) in chapter 3.

Phillip Luke Sinitiere thanks Virginia Commonwealth University historian and social scientist Andrew Chesnut (formerly of the University of Houston) for encouragement to pursue interdisciplinary thinking and research, for providing multiple opportunities to discuss religious economy and theorize about its various applications, and for his friendship. Phillip also thanks those who offered comments, questions, and observations on research presented at the Southwestern Region Meeting of the American Academy of Religion, as well as the American Historical Association; all helped to refine, revise, and clarify thinking about religious economy and the historical significance of holy mavericks. Phillip also expresses deep gratitude to Jenni, Matthew, Alexander, Madeline, and Nathaniel for patience, understanding, and love.

Shayne Lee dedicates this manuscript to Rodney Stark, the singular force behind his choice of sociology as a career path, whose monumental contributions continue to inform his theoretical perspectives on American religion. Shayne also thanks his family and friends for their encouragement and support.

Introduction

On March 12, 2006, the revivalist Billy Graham spoke in New Orleans as part of his Celebration of Hope evangelistic crusade. Graham came out of retirement to encourage New Orleans residents during the aftermath of Hurricane Katrina, one of the greatest natural disasters in American history. People packed the New Orleans Arena in record numbers as thousands more went to an overflow area to watch a videocast of Celebration of Hope. Cliff Barrows and George Beverly Shea, longtime members of the Billy Graham team, warmed up the crowd with a few songs. A captive audience turned out to hear this American icon deliver what most deemed to be his last sermon.

Although age and a prolonged bout with Parkinson's disease tempered the preaching of his earlier years, Graham still demonstrated an ability to connect with the crowd. For example, there was a special moment when he abruptly stopped preaching and proceeded to drink slowly from a glass of water. No doubt many in attendance speculated that Graham was taking a few moments to collect his thoughts. After emptying his glass, Graham took a deep breath and exclaimed, "Ahhhhh, fresh New Orleans water," a timely remark to residents struggling to get basic utilities just months after Hurricane Katrina damaged much of the city's infrastructure. Graham then commended the mayor of New Orleans for getting services back to the city and reminded his audience that "just like New Orleans is coming back, so is Jesus Christ, and you better be ready." The crowed cheered, suggesting Graham's tactical drink of water and appeal to the city's restoration struck a chord.

Fifty years ago, Graham captured the imaginations of many Americans and became the de facto pope of evangelical Christianity. He emerged at a unique historical moment when technological advances in travel and communication allowed him to crisscross the country and broadcast his sermons to the masses (Butler, Wacker, and Balmer 2003; Martin 1991). Graham's media savvy, marketing skills, and compelling message of salvation peppered with mid-twentieth-century, middle-class sensibilities helped him emerge out of the Cold War as America's leading evangelical voice. Graham, like many enterprising preachers before him, demonstrated evangelicals' unique ability to offer their contemporaries a relevant brand of Christianity. But as Graham recedes from public view, a younger crop of evangelicals draws millions of followers by reimagining Christianity in our postindustrial, hypercapitalist, postmodern age.

This book explores the extraordinary appeal of five evangelicals who make strong cases to replace Graham as America's leading preacher and evangelist: Paula White, T. D. Jakes, Rick Warren, Joel Osteen, and Brian McLaren. They pastor some of the largest churches in the nation, lead vast spiritual networks, and are among the most influential preachers in American Protestantism. They write best-selling books and draw thousands of people to their conferences. *Time* magazine included three of them in its 2005 list of the most influential evangelicals; and *Forbes, Fortune, Newsweek, Black Enterprise, Business Week, Christianity Today*, the *Atlantic Monthly*, the *New Yorker*, and many other popular magazines have featured stories about them. They are fixtures on the airwaves, appearing as special guests on television programs like *Nightline, Good Morning America, 60 Minutes, Oprah, The View, Religion & Ethics Newsweekly*, and *Larry King Live*. Newspapers like the *Washington Post, Los Angeles Times, USA Today*, and the *New York Times* report on their vast influence. Thousands of websites, blogs, and chat rooms dispatch their names throughout cyberspace, both praising and chastising their ministries. Through the power of their appeal, rather than the authority of ecclesiastical positioning, they assemble multi-million-dollar ministries and worldwide renown. With weak or no denominational ties, they are free agents who make their mark on contemporary American society.

Since religion is one of the most unregulated markets in our nation, few spheres teach us more about American consumption than the "faith industry" that churns out spiritual celebrities almost overnight. These five celebrity preachers have transcended unremarkable beginnings, and their unforeseen success leaves many curious observers with burning questions.

How did an unknown, frustrated English professor like Brian McLaren become one of the leading voices of Gen X evangelicals? How does a shy preacher like Joel Osteen attract 40,000 weekly attendees from various racial, ethnic, and socioeconomic backgrounds and draw sellout crowds for preaching tours in sports arenas and concert halls nationwide? How did a self-professed "messed-up Mississippi girl" like Paula White become a popular television host, philanthropist, and spiritual mentor to pop stars, athletes, and business tycoons? How did a poor country Pentecostal preacher from West Virginia like T. D. Jakes evolve into a spiritual celebrity who draws tens of thousands to his conferences, writes best-selling books, and produces edgy plays and movies? How did a chubby, unassuming Southern Baptist middle-aged preacher like Rick Warren write a best-selling nonfiction book and become one of the most influential Protestant preachers in the world? What does it mean that only one of these evangelical superstars attended seminary and three of them are college dropouts? How does a spiritual leader become a valuable commodity in our rapidly changing society? Answers to these questions shed much light on the vigorous intersections between contemporary religion and American culture.

With this study we join a growing cohort of religious scholars, sociologists, and historians who make the case for a supply-side analysis of religious vitality, contending that clergy (and their congregations or followers) hold the key to understanding why certain movements thrive while others decline. The popularity of American evangelicalism demonstrates that religious suppliers do not achieve their privileged places in the religious marketplace by constructing a sacred canopy against modernity (Berger 1967), being stricter than liberal counterparts (Kelley 1972; Iannacconne 1992; Finke and Stark 2005), confronting modern pluralism (Smith 1998), getting in the path of blind luck, or hiding in the trenches of tradition. Rather, our thesis is that religious suppliers thrive in a competitive spiritual marketplace because they are quick, decisive, and flexible in reacting to changing conditions, savvy at packaging and marketing their ministries, and resourceful at offering spiritual rewards that resonate with the existential needs and cultural tastes of the public. Religious suppliers carve out a niche in the spiritual marketplace and distinguish their ministries by offering an array of spiritual goods and services that match the tastes and desires of religious consumers (Stolz 2006).

Chapter 1 provides a historical context for our country's competitive religious marketplace and constructs an archetype for enterprising spiritual leaders we call holy mavericks. Using the pioneering ministry of eighteenth-century revivalist George Whitefield as our starting point, we explore how evangelical innovators enjoy larger shares of the market than other religious suppliers by adapting to changing environments in a multiplicity of contexts.

As one of the newest holy mavericks in America's religious marketplace, Joel Osteen offers salvation and a smile for those who show up, tune in, or log on to Lakewood Church, which at 40,000 weekly attendees is the largest church in the nation. Chapter 2 tells the story of Osteen's rise to prominence and details the dynamics of his multifaceted ministry. Drawing from a career in religious telecasting and media production and a talented ministry team composed of engaging speakers, keen managers, and talented musicians, Joel Osteen excels at practical preaching, offering a welcoming smile and a warm Texas drawl. While he acknowledges the ups and downs of the human condition, Osteen's appeal centers around a message of self-respect and of blessed return on spiritual investment, conditioned most readily by confluences between cognitive psychology and sacred speech. From its home in Houston—in a sports-arena-turned-sacred-space—and through his books, weekly telecasts, archived sermons, podcasts, daily "e-votionals," and monthly ministry events called "An Evening with Joel," Osteen's message of spiritual prosperity and positive thinking appeals to millions worldwide, crossing numerous racial, ethnic, and economic boundaries.

Chapter 3 presents Thomas Dexter Jakes as a metaphor of a new black church. As the pastor of the largest church in Dallas, Texas, a conference organizer who draws tens of thousands to his events, the author of more than a dozen best sellers, including two critically acclaimed novels, and a movie executive who recently signed with Sony Movies to produce nine more films, T. D. Jakes redefines evangelical entrepreneurship. By appropriating a broad range of cultural tools, he tactically blends biblical teachings with psychological theories, folk wisdom, pop culture, and American idealism. His appeal comes from adeptly diagnosing problems overlooked by other evangelicals, including sexual abuse, addiction, and abandonment. Jakes's cultural repertoire for solving practical life problems concerning finances, weight loss, self-esteem, and other issues connects with many contemporary Americans.

Chapter 4 explores how Brian McLaren attracts many followers by challenging evangelicalism. McLaren is a pastor, best-selling author, ministry consultant, and influential leader in a rapidly growing evangelical movement called the emerging church. McLaren engages in progressive dialogues on the global economy, the growing economic divide between the rich and the poor, and the mounting danger of violence from both terrorists and antiterrorists. His writings attract many who criticize and critique evangelicals' partiality with American nationalism and neoconservative politics. By offering a relational and organic model of spiritual community that emphasizes friendship, fosters dialogue, and makes no claim to having a monopoly on truth, McLaren constructs an archetype for a new kind of evangelicalism that addresses the alienation, isolation, and rampant individualism of our society.

Chapter 5 explains how Paula White strategically integrates her message and ministry into mainstream American religious culture and crafts a model of the emotionally healthy Christian who is honest about her shortcomings. She is a best-selling author, noted conference speaker, life coach, and television personality. Her message infuses an emphasis on God's transforming power with the raw and honest faith of postmodern confessional culture. As the "Oprah Winfrey" of the evangelical world, White finesses dialogues with celebrity experts about self-actualization and the nitty-gritty, day-to-day realities of life. By integrating religion with American longings for youth, beauty, health, and sexual fulfillment, she offers an empowering and self-therapeutic brand of Christianity that teaches people how to become physically fit, mentally tough, and biblically literate, while trusting in the promises of God for dramatic change in life. White seeks to make Jesus relevant to the pursuits of everyday life and thereby offers a message that resonates with the experiences of millions of Americans.

Whether he is confronting conservatives about their moral tunnel vision, working with rock music star Bono for AIDS relief, ministering to village chiefs in Africa, addressing students and faculty at Harvard University, teaching rabbis principles for leading healthy congregations, discussing the problem of evil on *Larry King Live*, or mentoring business moguls like Rupert Murdock, Rick Warren is on the vanguard of innovative evangelical leadership. Chapter 6 shows how Warren became the pastor of a 25,000-member church in Orange County, California, and one of the most influential Protestant leaders in the world. Warren's simple sermons, often structured around catchy acronyms, address life issues that affect many Americans. He packages evangelicalism in an unconventional, racially generic, and politically inoffensive way and is the force behind a rapidly growing purpose-driven church movement that blurs denominational distinctions and challenges traditional ways of approaching ministry. By mixing religion with the best marketing and business principles of today, along with other elements of contemporary secular culture, Warren makes evangelical ministry attractive to baby boomers and successive generations of Americans.

The bibliographic essay that concludes this book provides an overview of religious economy, a firmly established paradigm among social scientists and historians who study religious behavior, religious institutions, and religious conviction. We provide clarity to this marketplace approach and show why it is an important framework for understanding religious vitality in the United States, particularly in its many contemporary expressions.

To explore their biographical stories and explain our holy mavericks' intriguing ministry appeal, we rely on original qualitative data obtained through interviews with ministry associates and members of their churches and movements, along with participant observation at their churches, conferences, cohorts, and gatherings. We carefully analyze their books and many of their sermons, keynote speeches, media interviews, websites, blogs, and newsletters. We also benefit from a generous amount of secondary data through scholarly books and articles on American religion as well as magazine features, newspaper articles, and television programs on all five subjects. The application of religious economy tempered with insights drawn from various disciplines broadens the analytical scope and helps to illuminate the complexities of America's religious marketplace. We contacted all five ministries and requested interviews with our five subjects. T. D. Jakes rejected our request through an e-mail communication from his spokesperson. Paula White, Rick Warren, and Joel Osteen never replied to any of our requests, but we are not certain they received them. Brian McLaren was the only pastor to accept our interview request; we later rescinded our offer to avoid the appearance of bias toward one of the five pastors under study.

Despite both historical and accessible analysis of evangelicalism's distinguishing marks of a conversion experience, fidelity to the Bible, focus on the person of Jesus Christ, and evangelistic imperative (Bebbington 1989; Balmer 2006a; Balmer 2006b), media often portray evangelicals as a monolithic group of abortion fighting, gay-bashing, patriarchal, politically posturing religious zealots. Snapshots of the general narrative of the Religious Right include the rise of the Moral Majority and Christian Coalition and their powerful collusions with the Republican Party; the storied scandals of 1980s televangelists Jim Bakker and Jimmy Swaggart; the well-known evangelical apocalyptic faith of George W. Bush; Pat Robertson's comments that blamed the terrorist attacks of September 11 on homosexuals, feminists and liberals; revelations from Colorado megachurch minister Ted Haggard about his involvement with illicit drugs and a male prostitute, activities that led to the resignation of the former president of the National Association of Evangelicals; Rod Parsley's call for the eradication of Islam; and John Hagee's repudiation of the pope and Catholicism.

Bolstering perceptions offered in news media, evangelicals also show up on the big screen with movies like *Saved!* (2004), a comedy that examines the intersection between teen faith, life choices, and religious hypocrisy. Coupled with films such as *Jesus Camp* (2006), a critical examination into one evangelical youth camp and how it trains Christian young people to live in a spiritually passionate and militant way in secular society, and *Friends of God* (2007), a documentary produced and filmed by Alexandra Pelosi, daughter of California Democrat Nancy Pelosi, that surveys the variety of religious expression within evangelical circles, it is important to point out that as illuminating as media and movies can be, the complexities and contradictions of religious movements—and evangelicalism in particular—often gets lost in translation. As Stephen Prothero (2007) points out, America is one of the most religious or spiritual nations on the planet and, astonishingly, one of its most religiously illiterate. Whereas Prothero's larger prescription about religious education is not a concern of this book, his observation is germane to perceptions of and knowledge about evangelicalism: the movement is far more elastic, far more complex, and far more contradictory than what popular accounts reveal, and therefore exceedingly interesting, important, and necessary as the subject of critical scholarly inquiry.

Unfortunately, often imbibing caricatures of the movement, many scholars too often neglect the nuances of evangelicalism, failing to explore its various neo-Pentecostal varieties, for example, and why some branches thrive while others decline. This can lead to a singular focus, for instance, on various strains within evangelicalism that prize femininity, patriarchy, or a disturbing theocratic wing that teaches a spiritualized religious and political militancy, those whom Chris Hedges calls "American Fascists" (2007). Although controversial, such topics are clearly worthy of critical scholarly analysis. Without questioning the worthiness or importance of such investigative projects, analysts' grinding focus on narrow, destructive dimensions of evangelicalism may, ironically, unveil a limited understanding of the movement resulting in oversimplified conflations that often obscure more than they reveal (Goldberg 2006; Phillips 2006). *Holy Mavericks* attempts to highlight stories, trends, and teachings that challenge the conventional view and explain where, why, and how some parts of the evangelical movement display vitality because they often overtly avoid (yet subtly address) hot-button political issues like abortion or gay marriage. This angle of analysis neither defends nor seeks to legitimate evangelicalism, but along with Donald Miller (1997), Kimon Howland Sargeant (2000), Vincent Miller (2005), Randall Balmer (2006a; 2006b), and Richard Kyle (2006), encourages specialists to undertake more critical investigations into evangelicalism's complexities, and point sociologists and religious scholars in new directions toward understanding evangelicalism in its nondenominational, contemporary, and popular forms.

In this light it is important to observe, for instance, that evangelical insiders such as Ronald Sider (2005), Jim Wallis (2004, 2008), and Randall Balmer (2006a; 2006b), to name only a few, offer memoirs and craft prophetically toned responses to the sinews of power the Religious Right has in the Republican Party. Moreover, journalists (Gibbs and Duffy 2007; Sullivan 2008), scholars (Blum 2007), spiritual progressives (Dionne 2008; Gushee 2008; Claiborne and Haw 2008), and even politicians and presidential hopefuls like Barack Obama, for example, discuss where and how issues of faith and belief impact party affiliation and political commitment—all in the context of the Democratic Party. Even more telling are the complex pictures of faith commitments among evangelical youth (Sandler 2006) and evangelical leaders (Lindsey 2007), as well as Michael Young's *Bearing Witness against Sin: The Evangelical Birth of the American Social Movement* (2006), a historical study of religiously inspired nineteenth-century evangelical social activists, many of whose convictions Democrats claim today as their own. Other outlets of critical discussion include radio journalists such as Krista Tippett and her award-winning show *Speaking of Faith*. There are many historical chapters to stories of faith-inspired political engagement, and as the work cited here suggests, discussion and analysis of contemporary evangelicalism neither require nor always cluster around tales of cloistered social conservatives, powerful patriarchs, or militant theocrats.

In turn, we hope to expand both the academic and popular perception of evangelicalism by confirming its tremendous diversity and complexity. We recognize that some evangelical leaders perceive the postmodern cultural turn as a threat to their faith, while others see in postmodernism the conduit to a more biblical faith. Some evangelicals ardently defend the status quo, while others offer progressive perspectives about social change. Some evangelicals resist contemporary culture, while others keenly spot new trends and social conventions. Some evangelicals are tongue-talking Pentecostals, some are traditional Southern Baptists, and more and more are tongue-talking Southern Baptists. Since evangelicalism lacks a single privileged voice, its innovators play important roles in validating their own creative constructions through the power of persuasion rather than ecclesiastical fiat. *Holy Mavericks* explores how evangelical superstars come from diverse backgrounds, utilize different styles and ministry perspectives, and appeal to the needs and tastes of large segments of the religious marketplace.

Certainly some Christians will take umbrage at our economic assumptions about religious vitality, rather seeing the popularity of these five evangelical innovators as the result of God's anointing or blessing. Conversely, others might perceive our subjects as religious demagogues, challenge their integrity, or reduce their popularity to nothing more than creative marketing, clever packaging, and crafty delivery. Assessing the role that divine endorsement or conniving salesmanship plays in contemporary religion is outside of our purview. For this reason, we assess neither doctrinal validity nor spiritual integrity, neither messages nor ministries; nor do we spend time deliberating about the extent to which their innovations impede, impair, or enhance the essence of Christianity.

By focusing on their appeal, we neither suggest that spiritual empires are devoid of complexities and controversies nor deny the possibility that our subjects' appetite for the good life invigorates their enthusiasm for spiritual leadership. We leave discussions about their drawbacks, controversies, and conspiracies in the hands of theologians, apologists, spiritual leaders, and countless Internet bloggers who feverishly devote themselves to those tasks. Moreover, when we discuss spiritual vitality, we do so in an economic sense, referring to their ability to draw market share, not in a qualitative sense concerning the spiritual mission of these ministries. Similarly, when we allude to evangelical innovators offering a "good" product, we mean its appeal in the spiritual marketplace, not "good" in the sense of what is best for people, in the same way that economists might evaluate cotton candy, gangsta rap, or horror movies as "good" products regardless of the disputed effect they have on consumers.

To borrow a line from Woody Allen's movie *Small Time Crooks*: "When you've got something that the American public wants, everything else falls into place." These five spiritual innovators have something that the public wants, and they create new archetypes for evangelicalism similar to how jazz greats like Louis Armstrong, singers like Frank Sinatra, or actors like Marlon Brando opened new doors to their art forms that will never close. None of these five preachers could have foreseen the particular way in which they would impact American religion. Like many powerful people from humble origins, they stumbled upon creative opportunities and made good use of fortuitous events. Because they draw millions of followers in a competitive religious economy, these five holy mavericks are barometers of contemporary American culture. Their fascinating stories provide rich insight into the structural and social changes in our complex society. Their vivid stories are windows through which the reader may get a clearer vision of American religion in its changing forms, and their popularity reveals much about the dynamics that inform national identities.

We wrote *Holy Mavericks* with scholars, students, and the curious in mind. Religious scholars and students who wish to understand more fully the theoretical scaffolding that informs *Holy Mavericks* should consult the bibliographic essay, while readers less inclined to muddle through theory should begin with chapter 1. While chapters 2 through 6 constitute a coherent narrative and establish connections and parallels between the holy mavericks, readers may also choose to tackle chapters in the order of their choice as case studies of evangelical innovators.

1

Evangelical Innovators

The orthodox Jewish faith, as it is followed in the Old Ghetto
towns of Russia or Austria, has still to learn the art of trimming its
sails to suit new winds. It is exactly the same as it was a thousand
years ago. It does not attempt to adapt itself to modern conditions
as the Christian church is continually doing.

—Abraham Cahan

Abraham Cahan's classic novel *The Rise of David Levinsky* illustrates that some religions have been more successful than others at
changing with the times. Cahan's loosely autobiographical narrative depicts a Russian Jew adjusting to a new American setting at the turn of the
twentieth century. In the epigraph that opens this chapter, the protagonist
contemplates how difficult it is for Orthodox Jews to retain distinctive elements of their faith and tradition while attempting to fit in with American
society (Cahan 1917: 110). Cahan's contrast of traditional Judaism to the
flexible Christianity he observed in his new American environs alludes to
an essential theme of our economic perspective on religious vitality: those
religious suppliers who can bend to new winds will more than likely enjoy a larger following than those who remain fixed to the past.

Since the First Amendment provided for the separation of church and
state (as did Thomas Jefferson's letter to a group of Baptists that included
the "separation" clause), American religious firms have had to compete
for "clients," and the "invisible hand" of the marketplace has been as intol-
erant of ineffective religious suppliers as it is of their commercial counterparts (Finke and Stark 2005). The unregulated American religious landscape that emerged in the nineteenth century (whose roots channel back
to the eighteenth) more or less provided a level playing field for ministers
to compete for congregants, and those innovative suppliers who were able

to adjust to the changing needs and tastes were more competitive than those who could not. Throughout our nation's history, spiritual leaders transformed and refashioned religion to address changing environments. According to Wade Clark Roof: "American religion has long been known for its dynamism and fluidity, its responsiveness to grassroots opinions and sentiments, its creative capacity in relation to the cultural environment. It takes on colors drawn from its surroundings, its boundaries always shifting and porous" (1999: 4).

The impressionability of American religion became more dramatic with the emergence of an evangelical style of Christianity. Like nimble jazz impresarios, many evangelical leaders adapted to the unique tastes of their environments. Christianity has thrived in the United States primarily because energetic and inventive evangelicals have crafted persuasive redefinitions of their faith for every generation. Sociologist Alan Wolfe observes:

> Evangelicals have long found ways to reconcile their version of Christianity with the materialistic, consumption-driven American culture, whether reflected in the ostentatious lifestyles of the televangelists, the success-oriented preaching of Robert Schuller, or the explicitly procapitalist prosperity theology of Kenneth Hagin Ministries. (2003: 32)

The pragmatic approach to the American marketplace that evangelicals adopt offers clients what works, stokes curiosity about what is new and fresh, and displays resourcefulness and creativity to adjust messages and ministries to address changing times.

Although it has antecedents in European pietism, many perceive evangelicalism as having been "born in the United States, baptized in its market economy, and married to its national destiny" (Hambrick-Stowe 1996: xiv). Veering away from the more sacramental and institutional faith of Catholics and Anglicans, evangelicalism exhibited a style of Christianity that emphasized personal conversion and commitment to Christ rather than ecclesiastical authority and liturgical worship (xiv). Its illusive parameters led one religion scholar to call evangelicalism the wax nose of American Protestantism (Hart 2004). With no single authoritative creed or confession binding them, evangelicals are a diverse array of Protestant Christians coordinated by a strong support for biblical authority, Christian mission, identifiable conversion, and devotion to Jesus (Bebbington 1989; Smith 1998). Evangelical preachers blossomed in the competitive deregulated religious marketplace of the nineteenth century and continue to dominate American Protestantism, taking many shapes and forms (Noll 2003; Balmer 1999).

American religion from the start was not always packaged in an evangelical style, nor has it always been an open marketplace of ideas for inventive spiritual leaders to compete for members. Moravians, Anabaptists, Quakers, and Puritans set up shop in the New World to free themselves from the shackles of the European religious establishment, but ironically, colonial religion quickly emerged as an allotment of established or official churches throughout the regions of North America. Established churches enjoyed state backing and tax support from all residents regardless of religious affiliation. The Puritan or Congregational church became the established church of the New England colonies with the exception of Rhode Island, which enjoyed religious freedom. The Church of England or the Anglican Church reigned in most of the mid-Atlantic and southern colonies, which nevertheless enjoyed more religious toleration than their New England counterparts.

Recent scholarship demonstrates that religion of the early colonial period played a smaller role in people's lives than previously considered (Butler 1990; Finke and Stark 2005; Noll 1992, 2003; Warner 2005). Less than a majority of colonists in the seventeenth century were members or regular attendees of churches. This low participation did not derive from colonial antipathy against spiritual nourishment; rather, most leaders of established churches failed to bend with the times and capture the imaginations of their hearers. From an economic perspective, religious suppliers of the early colonial period failed to offer an appealing product to potential customers, as Finke and Stark point out:

> What is most noticeable about religion in the colonial era is how poorly the denominations were doing. . . . these firms had failed to make any serious dent in the market. Whatever their religious needs, preferences, or concerns, the vast majority of Americans had not been reached by an organizational faith. (2005: 30)

Of all colonial regions, New England provided the most closed religious environment and punished those who introduced new ways of perceiving and practicing their faith. The Congregationalists prevented competition from enterprising religious leaders who may have offered the early colonists a more appealing brand of Christianity. Seventeenth-century

Puritans often jailed, harassed, or even hanged people for accusations of witchcraft or what they perceived to be religious heresy. The New England authorities administered public whippings and banishment to mid-Atlantic Quakers who traveled to Massachusetts to preach new messages, and on rare occasions they hanged return offenders (Noll 1992). Church authorities also regulated their own pastors. For example, when Puritan pastor Roger Williams's teachings diverted from the "New England Way," the religious establishment exiled him to Rhode Island. Generally, church life became inorganic, and the Puritans used fear, intimidation, and persecution to ward off competition. But the eighteenth century ushered in a trend toward religious pluralism and evangelical revivalism. No one played a more prominent role in the expansion of an evangelical style of preaching than a theatrical English itinerant named George Whitefield.

As America's first religious celebrity and superstar, Whitefield introduced a stimulating brand of Christianity that captured the New World's attention like never before and set the template for successive revivalists. Born and raised in England, Whitefield made six trips back and forth across the Atlantic to hold preaching tours throughout the colonies between the 1740s and 1760s, many of them taking place during a time of spiritual renewal called the Great Awakening. Sometimes thousands traveled far distances to hear Whitefield preach electrifying sermons. Historian and Whitefield biographer Harry Stout explains:

> In the course of his extemporaneous, open-air preaching to mass audiences, he transformed the traditional sermon into something different: a dramatic event capable of competing for public attention outside the arena of the churches—in fact, in the marketplace. Whitefield showed that preaching could be both edifying and entertaining. (1991: xvi)

Varying his pitch and voice and preaching without notes, Whitefield borrowed from the theater techniques acquired as a youth to produce dramatic sermons, in contrast to the dreary, monotonous manuscripts that clerics read to their parishioners in churches throughout the colonies (Butler, Wacker, and Balmer 2003). His message connected with people from all colonial regions and denominations; consequently, his preaching tours became the first authentically American cultural events. Whitefield's unprecedented popularity showed that religion could be packaged and presented in a way that appealed to the masses. His innovative use of print media to generate buzz about forthcoming tours set the paradigm for successive generations of revivalists to market themselves as spiritual commodities (Lambert 1994). "In market terms," Lambert argues:

> promoters shaped the "supply" of religion—how it was packaged and delivered—but lay people determined "demand." To understand the "great awakening," one must consider the interaction between revival producers and consumers. Evangelists engineered revival crusades, reported them as authentic works of God, and publicized them to distant audiences. Lay men and women accepted or rejected revivalists' claims, supported them with attendance and donations, and decided what awakening meant in their individual lives and communities. (1999: 13)

Whitefield also managed an active publishing schedule through a long-term collaboration with Benjamin Franklin and his printing firm in Philadelphia (Lambert 1993; Noll 2003). Whitefield's tours sparked many new churches, and other itinerants modeled his methodologies of preaching and worship to emphasize personal conversion and the pragmatic benefits of the Christian faith.

Many eighteenth-century clergy transformed and responded to the imaginations of their listeners, drawing from conceptual categories of the day and adopting market language of the emerging consumer context in order to make spiritual pronouncements and offer religious advice. British North America was an integral part of an expanding Atlantic economy, and ministers operated as some of the most important religious suppliers for the day's spiritual consumers, both challenged and shaped by itinerancy and migration (Hall 1994, 2002). And in the context of the eighteenth century's Great Awakening, the confluence of consumer demand, individual religious conversion known as the "New Birth," and increasing permeability of traditional societal and cultural boundaries presented a dizzying array of choices. "To survive," writes Boyd Stanley Schlenther, "all churches were forced to engage in a competitive scramble for souls. Free trade in commerce, and faith, was the new world order" (1998: 149).

Whitefield's practical spirituality and entertaining message also generated dissent. His distaste for traditionalism and heavy doctrine sparked leaders from his own Anglican denomination to chastise his preaching. Like many revivalists in successive generations, Whitefield's greatest detractors were part of the religious establishment rather than the secular media. The dramatic denouncements of Whitefield by rationalist ministers like Boston's Charles Chauncy, a cleric who occupied one of the city's most prominent pulpits, inversely attests to the Grand Itinerant's popularity. Notwithstanding his problems with church leadership, Whitefield was the first pop icon to bridge the cultural and religious gulfs separating colonial identities. Harry Stout calls him the Anglo Calvinist with an American soul, adding, "Whitefield and America were both brash and experimental voices outside the mainstream that saw in one another the shape of a new religious and political future" (1991: 255). Whitefield's iconoclastic brand of Christianity set the standard for successive evangelical innovators who would capture the American imagination by offering practical sermons and books to the populace.

In addition to his studies of George Whitefield and the Great Awakening, Lambert, drawing explicitly from Finke and Stark, also identifies vigorous religious competition in eighteenth-century Virginia, even styling it a "de facto free marketplace of religion" (2003b: 4). In contrast to Whitefield, Anglican itinerant Charles Woodmason did not succeed in the earliest days of America's religious marketplace, Lambert argues, as he complained that the sermons of revivalist preachers in the Carolinas proved more attractive than the Anglican liturgy. Woodmason was just one of many Anglican clergypersons competing for souls in eighteenth-century Virginia and Maryland. Church leaders founded the missionary agency called the Society for the Propagation of the Gospel in Foreign Parts in 1701 as a way to solidify market share, something the organization found increasingly difficult (Laing 1995; Schlenther 1998).

Before the Revolutionary War, the Congregationalists, Anglicans, and Presbyterians were the colonial religious powers engaging the majority of American church members. Less than two decades after Whitefield preached his last sermon, the colonies secured emancipation from England through the Revolutionary War. Years into this newfound freedom, the First Amendment to the Constitution distinguished the United States from all other Western nations by prohibiting a state church, resulting in an unregulated religious marketplace. This allowed burgeoning evangelicalism more space to revitalize American Protestantism with more expressive forms of worship and preaching (Olds 1994).

Baptist and Methodist upstarts benefited from this new unregulated economy and drew market share from mainliners who were less in touch with the needs and tastes of the masses, as Robert Wuthnow discusses:

> Methodists used lay ministers and circuit riders to multiply the number of clergy; Baptists relied heavily on "farmer preachers" for the same

purpose. Unlike the better-trained clergy of the eastern seaboard denominations, these preachers earned much of their own livelihood, preached in the simple language of the people, and minimized social division between clergy and laity. (1988: 21)

Methodist membership began to grow so fast that by 1830, its numbers were twice as high as they had been only ten years earlier (Hatch 1989), and by 1850 Methodists and Baptists replaced Congregationalists and Episcopalians as the largest denominations in the United States because they adapted many of Whitefield's methods. Historian Mark Noll points out:

[Evangelicalism] represented a shift in religiosity away from the inherited established churches toward spiritual communities constructed by believers themselves. It featured a form of conversion as much focused on personal experience, as much convinced of the plasticity of human nature and as much preoccupied with claims of certainty as any manifestation of the Enlightenment. And because spirituality was adjusted to an opening world of commerce, communication and empire, that spirituality effectively resolved the psychological dilemmas created by this opening world. (2003: 154)

Religious pluralism offered laity more options, forcing preachers to be more responsive and efficient (Stark and Finke 2000). Hence the period after the deregulation of religion did more to Christianize American society than anything before or since (Hatch 1989; Carwardine 1996).

Religious institutions and denominations arise out of particular cultural moments and garner strength when their leaders become preservers of their traditions and customs. But as religious institutions grow stronger and older, they have a tendency to get stuck in their ways and lag behind the broader culture. Mainstream status may inadvertently set up religious institutions for future decline, a point argued in recent literature by sociologists of religion (Finke and Stark 2005; Lee 2005; Warner 2005). For example, the very same Methodist movement that morphed into the largest denomination in the 1800s lost market share at the close of the century and began to decline by 1960. Its downward spiral coincided with the denomination building large edifices and learning institutions, trading in circuit riders for seminary-trained clergy, and losing touch with common people. Conversely, the Pentecostal movement began as a small upstart in

1906, and not long after, new denominations like the Assemblies of God and the Church of God in Christ became the fastest growing in American Protestantism (Butler, Wacker, and Balmer 2003). The growth of Pentecostal denominations subsided in America toward the close of the twentieth century as independent megachurches began to draw some of their market share (Lee 2005), although this is not fully the case in the global South (Jenkins 2002, 2006). Religious firms are often less successful in offering an appealing product when they reach mainstream status and become fixed in their traditions.

While historians and sociologists of religion take notice of the potential drawbacks of established or mainline churches, even while others continue to grow and thrive (Bass 2006; Percy and Markham 2006; Ellingson 2007), they have been slow to explore mechanisms explaining how competition sparks vitality in a religious economy. *Holy Mavericks* delineates how change often comes through innovators who bridge or collapse the distance between religion and culture by offering a more relevant and appealing message than their institutional counterparts. An unregulated economy allows these innovators to compete in the marketplace of ideas and draw market share from suppliers who fail to change with the times. We see this trend throughout American religious history. Mainline churches become complacent and lag behind cultural changes, and then innovators emerge to fill the gaps where American Protestantism falls short and reconnect religion with emerging cultural tastes. Competing religious suppliers try to imitate their success, which leads to changes in church culture and results in winners and losers in the religious economy. Religious leaders can either yield to the bend of the market or take notice as their churches die (Moore 1994).

Evangelical innovators have enjoyed cherished places in the religious economy by adjusting to each generation. This is not to suggest that Catholics, Jews, liberal Protestants, and inventive leaders of various sects have not affected American religion in salient ways. We do not deny that John Humphrey Noyes, Ellen White, Joseph Smith, Fulton Sheen, Father Divine, and various other nonevangelical innovators have displayed charisma, ingenuity, decisiveness, flexibility, and creative leadership that Whitefield and other evangelicals used to secure large market shares. But a preponderance of scholarly research confirms that spiritual leaders who identify themselves as evangelicals enjoyed (and enjoy) the lion's share of the American religious market. Whether we refer to preachers in the Cane Ridge Revival and the Second Great Awakening of the nineteenth century, or to leaders of the Pentecostal/Charismatic revolution of the mid–twentieth century, innovation is a rich evangelical legacy always available for spiritual communities to address changing needs and tastes.

Evangelical innovators capitalize on untapped niches and new popular trends, utilizing a broad range of cultural tools at their disposal to offer appealing ministries and messages to their contemporaries. George Whitefield utilized the best marketing techniques in colonial America by forging strategic alliances with media innovators like Benjamin Franklin. Richard Allen became the founding bishop of the first black denomination by addressing the burgeoning dissent against segregationist practices in the Methodist Church. Among nineteenth-century revivalists, Charles Finney had an uncanny ability to push the emotional buttons of his audience, and D. L. Moody ran his ministry with marketing principles and organizational strategies reflecting the best commercial standards of his day. A few decades later, Billy Sunday used a professional baseball career as a ticket to celebrity, translating athletic prowess and robust masculinity into energetic and uproarious preaching crusades (Bendroth 2004).

Around the turn of the twentieth century, the confluence of urbanization, mass markets, and the rise of celebrity, along with a keen sense of business expertise, generated more evangelical innovation. Bruce Barton's best-selling novels matched Christianity with the changing times by depicting the human side of Jesus Christ as corporate leader of a vast organization and the best dinner guest in town. Aimee Semple McPherson built one of the largest churches during the 1920s and 1930s with dramatic presentations in her worship services that rivaled the theatrics of Hollywood productions, as well as entertaining radio programs. Carrie Nation fueled fiery rhetoric with impassioned activism in support of Prohibition and profited handily from the creative use of promotional items to market her message (Ribuffo 1981; Sutton 2007; Carver 1999).

By the 1970s, "selling God" with mass appeal solidified the place of televangelism in American culture (Moore 1994), as evangelicals dashed to the airwaves after a new Federal Communications Commission decision facilitated their entry (Finke 1997). Borrowing his format from entertaining television hosts like Merv Griffin and Johnny Carson, Oral Roberts aired prime-time television specials using celebrity guests and talented singers to draw millions of viewers (Lee 2005). Robert Schuller and the late Rex Humbard drew large television audiences by adopting formats from the entertainment media, and Jim and the late Tammy Bakker built a television empire in the 1980s with millions of viewers by offering upbeat and entertaining programs (Grem 2008). Jimmy Swaggart developed a worldwide television ministry by offering passionate sermons striking emotional chords of his listeners. Countless megachurches today broadcast services on national television and skillfully market and run their ministries with modern management techniques. Evangelical innovators adapt to new problems and concerns and build cutting-edge ministries with effective use of media and remarkable organizational and business proficiency (Twitchell 2007; Einstein 2007).

Another characteristic of many evangelical innovators is that they construct narratives that link national sentiments with spiritual integrity and are quite adroit at finding nuances within biblical precedents to address needs and preferences of Americans. During a time when the Midwest cultural mystique was the ideological embodiment of American identity, D. L. Moody presented the gospel through homespun stories and exultation of middle-American values, and Billy Sunday combined the ethics of rural and small-town late nineteenth-century Iowa with Christian conduct (Martin 2002). Billy Graham offered passionate denunciations of communism and endorsed national chauvinism and free-market democracy during the most fearful years in the Cold War. While Martin Luther King Jr. was more countercultural than most innovators, he challenged prevailing social norms and called for social justice by evoking Old Testament prophetic injunctions combined with deeply held principles of American democracy and freedom. Years later, the late Jerry Falwell, Pat Robertson, and John Hagee drew millions of Christians to their conservative political agendas as harbingers of old-time American values. Many preachers who capture the American imagination offer biblical prescriptions and passionate exhortations that affirm American identity; they are especially keen at convincing people to perceive worshiping God and country as one and the same.

Evangelical innovators exhibit pragmatic shrewdness and skill at touching the modern-day ills at the heart of many Americans' social and spiritual struggles. During the 1960s, Chuck Smith turned Calvary Chapel from a small group of members meeting in a mobile home park into one of the most influential churches in the nation by modifying his ministries to reach ex-hippies and Southern California youth culture. Bill Bright's Campus Crusade for Christ became an interdenominational force equipping young Christians with creative evangelistic tools to reach a sight-and-sound generation (Turner 2008). John Wimber forged his Vineyard Christian Fellowship into a fast-growing movement in the 1980s by disparaging outdated Protestant traditions and blending Charismatic theology with elements from contemporary culture. More recently, John Richard Bryant revitalized his waning African Methodist Episcopal denomination with a confluence of "Spirit-filled" worship and cultural consciousness that would eventually become a mainstay in thriving black mainline churches nationwide. Luis Palau forged a popular new genre of revivalism called "festival evangelicalism" by blending elements of Latino culture with entertaining sermons and spirited music. Bill Hybels's seeker-sensitive church model attracts thousands of new converts each year by offering worship services with contemporary music, theatrical presentations, and friendly environments devoid of religious imagery. Juanita Bynum's candid discussions on sex and self-respect have influenced many preachers to be more transparent about their shortcomings. Evangelical innovators are versatile enough to revitalize old visions to draw people into a simpler faith or forgo centuries of tradition if it becomes a stumbling block to addressing the current needs and tastes of their following.

Writing about nineteenth-century trends, historian Nathan Hatch suggests that evangelical movements empowered the masses by adjusting to their deepest drives rather than imposing on them strict doctrinal tenets:

> Increasingly assertive common people wanted their leaders unpretentious, their doctrines self-evident and down-to-earth, their music lively and singable, and their churches in local hands. . . . The rise of evangelical Christianity in the early republic is, in some measure, a story of the success of common people in shaping the culture after their own priorities rather than the priorities outlined by gentlemen such as the framers of the constitution. (1989: 9)

People who capture the American imagination and efficiently refashion American Protestantism rarely come from genteel origins. They often come from the populace and emerge after years of toil under the radar of the religious hierarchy. In the nineteenth century, blue-collar Methodist circuit riders like Francis Asbury and Peter Cartwright spoke the language of the commoners and offered a rugged brand of Christianity with which the Episcopal, Congregational, and Presbyterian lettered preachers could not compete (Hatch 1989). Later that same century, a humble housewife named Phoebe Palmer became a best-selling author and editor of a successful monthly magazine by offering a simple but passionate message of sanctification. In the early twentieth century a poor preacher named William J. Seymour introduced Pentecostalism to the nation with his three-year Azusa Street Revival in a converted horse stable in Los Angeles, California. Billy Graham began his ministry by preaching to alcoholics and prostitutes on street corners in front of saloons (Pollock 1985). Country preachers like Oral Roberts and Kenneth Hagin changed Pentecostalism from an ascetic faith to one that preaches prosperity for all believers. Countless examples illustrate how American Protestantism has been molded and refashioned by innovators of a populist orientation (Hatch 1989). Their humble origins equip them with intangible personal assets to understand and address the needs and tastes of the masses.

Enterprising evangelicals who capture the public's attention are often self-taught. Preachers of the past like D. L. Moody, Billy Sunday, Aimee Semple McPherson, and more recently Benny Hinn and Creflo Dollar embody the kind of social gifts and intuitive ability to tap into other people's feelings and emotions not taught in seminary. Conversely, our nation's leading theological institutions typically produce safe and reliable transmitters of doctrine and managers of traditions, rather than dynamic leaders. Sociologist Tony Campolo points out:

> Hierarchal denominations such as the United Methodist Church and the Episcopal Church will somehow find pulpits for those who go through the ecclesiastically prescribed hoops. The net result is that mainline denominations have far too many churches being pastored by preachers who can deliver properly structured homilies but lack the ability to stir people to action or elicit intense commitment. On the other hand, the independent churches that characterize evangelicalism have pastors whose primary credential is the ability to draw and hold crowds of people. (2004: 17)

Evangelical innovators offer simpler, more effective communication that is in stark contrast to the doctrinal diatribes lettered clergy offer every Sunday. Innovators will sacrifice theoretical precision for dynamic leadership that provides pragmatic solutions to specific problems. They are quick on the draw to forgo years of church tradition if they perceive it is stifling their ability to meet the needs of the laity.

Evangelical innovators have an intuitive ability to scratch where people are itching and use personal struggles as bridges to connect them with the pain and turmoil facing many of their contemporaries. They design worship services in ways that attract new members, assess the right music style to feature, and acclimatize believers to a faith that addresses their own needs first (Wolfe 2003; Kyle 2006). Holy mavericks are a fascination to the general public but a thorn in the flesh of gatekeepers of church traditions who chide innovators for casting wide nets and polluting the gospel with "watered-down" versions of Christianity. Hence one aspect that distinguishes popular evangelical spiritual leaders is their ability to elicit both intense loyalty and venomous contempt from clerical peers and congregants.

Evangelicalism is part of a rich heritage in American Protestantism garnering great success in our competitive religious economy. We make no attempt to offer an exhaustive composite of such a complex multivariate movement like evangelicalism, even in its most popular forms. Nor do we attempt to gloss over profound differences in doctrine and methods that have separated popular evangelical innovators historically and today. We recognize that George Whitefield and Francis Asbury had contrasting approaches, in the same way that twentieth-century revivalists like Billy Graham and Arturo Skinner engaged divergent contexts with dissimilar messages. Similarly, a prosperity preacher like Kenneth Copeland eschews denominational affiliation while a Methodist like John Richard Bryant revitalizes his traditional denomination. And conservative preachers like Tony Evans and John McArthur might adamantly reject any commonalities with faith healers like Kathryn Kuhlman and Benny Hinn. Hence, there are enormous divergences that have characterized evangelical innovators throughout American history. But along with the differences lies one common thread interwoven through the fabric of many spiritual capitalists: they address the existential needs and cultural tastes of their contemporaries. Put more simply, they offer Americans more bang for their buck.

Whether it is the music industry or the evangelical world, superstars do not instantaneously surface as finished products; they emerge as ongoing constructions. The diverse ways holy mavericks construct evangelical archetypes borrow from their personal biographies and the contiguous cultural formations of our postindustrial sight-and-sound generation. Paula White, T. D. Jakes, Rick Warren, Joel Osteen, and Brian McLaren did not suddenly appear out of nowhere; certain life experiences and structural changes equipped them with cultural tool kits to transform their spiritual gifts into saleable commodities. White and Jakes draw homiletics from a black church preaching aesthetic, whereas Warren employs an upbeat motivational speaking style. Osteen feeds Americans' taste for consumption, while McLaren taps into some Americans' commitment to dissent from the status quo. Evangelical innovators navigate their ministries in contrasting ways and formulate unique strategies of action to adjust to their environments, yet there are many common denominators that speak to their vast appeal to contemporary Americans.

Evangelical innovators capitalize on trends and new discoveries brewing in society, but appropriations of such innovations serve as tipping points of change for which these mavericks often receive credit as architects. Put another way, evangelical innovators make their mark by surfing spiritual waves already in motion before their ascent, but with scope and reach unimaginable before they captured the imagination of the public. So, on the one hand we are sensitive to the many ways their creative thinking evolved through personal struggles and years of dedication to their craft. But on the other hand, we reveal how historical moments and opportunity structures shape their messages and marketability and help to bring their individual initiatives to fruition. Holy mavericks possess social, cultural, and spiritual dexterity.

2

The Smiling Preacher
Joel Osteen and the Happy Church

Choose to be happy. Choose to keep a good attitude. Remember, happiness is a choice you have to make. And even when you don't understand it, know that God is at work in you and He's working through you. Make up your mind that from today forward, you are going to bloom where you are planted and enjoy every single day of your life.

—Joel Osteen

On Saturday, October 15, 2006, the Society for the Performing Arts hosted the Houston debut of José Porcel and his flamenco dance troupe from Seville, Spain. The audience responded to the opening showcase with calm and decorum appropriate for Jones Hall, Houston's premier venue for artistic events. But as the concert continued, the passion and technique of the flamenco dance genre gradually provoked more enthusiasm from the audience. By the show's end, the two-hour explosion of vibrant colors, tantalizing rhythms, and sensual choreography transformed an audience of well-dressed urban sophisticates into a rowdy mass of patrons screaming for more. The raucous ovation lasted thirty minutes, during which time Porcel gave ten encores.

Whereas Porcel and his dancers enthralled a thousand Houstonians one Saturday evening, a smiling preacher named Joel Osteen captivates 40,000 worshipers every week at Lakewood Church. Like an evocative flamenco performance, each Lakewood service is a dramatic event with frenetic energy, lively music, and passionate songs, capped by mesmerizing preaching. And like great dancers, Osteen has an uncanny ability to connect with his audience. As one Lakewood member told us, "His words are calming, his voice is soft, his motions slow and smooth; Pastor Joel is hypnotic."

It is hard to believe that just over a decade ago, Joel Osteen was running the media department for his father, John Osteen, Lakewood's founder and longtime senior pastor. In 1999, John's untimely death meant that Joel, a college dropout with no formal theological training, would be the new pastor of the 8,000-member congregation. For years he had operated behind the scenes, but now he would be the new face of Lakewood Church. Some questioned his experience and doubted his abilities, while others scoffed at his lack of ministerial credentials. Yet, the path was clear and the vision large: he would enter the pulpit his father inhabited for almost four decades and step into the shoes of a seasoned veteran, a minister with deep roots, wide connections, and a thriving church. Few thought he was up to the task, and some thought the church would fall apart. With big shoes to fill, and still mourning the death of his father, Joel delivered his inaugural sermon to a packed sanctuary at Lakewood Church in October 1999. The air ripe with anticipation, Lakewood Church welcomed the young pastor; Joel and the church would never be the same.

Rather than falling apart as some predicted, Lakewood Church more than quadrupled its membership and became the largest congregation in the nation, while its new leader emerged as one of America's most popular preachers. Joel Osteen's television ministry draws millions of weekly viewers, his first book in 2004 became an instant best seller, his second secured an eight-figure book deal from a publisher, and his preaching tours sell out arenas in cities nationwide. A January 2005 feature in the *Washington Post* deemed Joel Osteen as "the new face of Christianity" and called him "the smiling preacher" (Romano 2005).

With Texas charm, an ethic of good manners, and biblical wisdom predicated on positive thinking, Osteen's rise to popularity is a remarkable achievement. Osteen is not the first and certainly not the last minister to skillfully use the cultural language of his day to influence and impact those with ears to hear. Yet carefully crafted messages along with media acumen make the Houston pastor a rising star in the evangelical world. Osteen's story, like those of other evangelical innovators, reveals much about the interplay between religion, media, capitalism, and consumer habits in American culture. His attractive evangelical message, indebted to changes brewed in mid-twentieth-century evangelical thought, emanates from the triumph of cognitive psychology in American culture and from the rise of neo-Pentecostal expressions of faith.

Pastor Joel Osteen. Photo courtesy of Associated Press.

Christianity emerged in a prescientific age almost 2,000 years before psychology became a formal scientific discipline. The emergence of psychology around the turn of the twentieth century as a major resource for understanding human behavior left religious leaders an uneasy decision about how they should respond. On the one hand, leading purveyors like Sigmund Freud offended clerics by diagnosing religious belief as childishness to overcome. On the other hand, some clerics understood how a systematic exploration of the human mind could help their congregants. Unsurprisingly, Fundamentalist Christians of the ilk involved with the Scopes Monkey Trial of 1925, and many since, adamantly rejected psychology on all fronts. However, other evangelicals, more willing to engage society than Fundamentalists, approached psychology with varying degrees of acceptance and reconfiguration.

One of the first spiritual leaders to explicitly marry religion with psychology was not an evangelical pastor but a rabbi named Joshua Loth Liebman. In his book *Peace of Mind* (1946), Liebman proposed that psychological advances could help religions adjust to changing human needs:

> Religion, at its best, is the announcer of the supreme ideals by which men must live and through which our finite species finds its ultimate significance. Yet honesty compels us to admit that religion needs help if it is to make these ideals incarnate in human life. Psychology can become one of the real allies in that magnificent religious task. (1946: 13)

Liebman illustrated how Freud's psychodynamic theories on human drives could provide religions with intriguing possibilities for leading people toward healthier lives. Attractive to both Christians and Jews, Liebman's proposals addressed the needs and tastes of the postwar American public (Heinze 1996).

In 1952, Norman Vincent Peale, a Dutch Reformed pastor in New York City, published one of the most influential spiritual books of the twentieth century, *The Power of Positive Thinking*. Peale's practical use of cognitive psychology offered midcentury Americans more personal agency than Freud's deterministic psychoanalysis by teaching members how to control their own fates with their own thoughts (George 1993). Years later, another Dutch Reformed pastor named Robert Schuller also fashioned a fusion of psychology and evangelicalism attractive to the public. After majoring in psychology in college and receiving theological training in seminary, Schuller devoted the rest of his career to incorporating both

Joel Osteen and wife, Victoria, at Lakewood before the church relocated to
the Compact Center. Photo courtesy of Associated Press.

disciplines for his message of personal transformation. Schuller wrote
more than thirty books and, before his recent retirement, had a long-running television ministry offering spiritual instruction on self-actualization
and psychological teachings on healthy and happy living (Voskuil 1983).

The sociologist and cultural critic Philip Rieff (1966) predicted the triumph of the therapeutic in American culture. Rieff's prophecy has come
to pass in the burgeoning "age of Oprah," where psychotherapy and self-
help language pepper America's vocabulary. Motivational speakers like
Tony Robbins, radio personalities like Dr. Laura Schlessinger, and talk
show hosts like Dr. Phil transform complex psychological theories into
million-dollar commodities. By adding psychology to their spiritual
tool kits, evangelical innovators keep pace with the changing American
landscape. Most evangelical seminaries incorporate pastoral counseling
courses in their degree plans, and many evangelical churches utilize professional counselors on staff who are conversant with the latest developments in psychotherapy. Evangelical psychologists like Larry Crabb and
James Dobson thus emerged as celebrities in the church and in popular

culture. It is not uncommon to hear prominent evangelicals warn their congregants to avoid "toxic people," a phrase rooted in psychotherapy.

Consequently, when Joel Osteen assumed Lakewood's pulpit in 1999, Norman Vincent Peale, Robert Schuller, and other evangelical innovators had prepared the groundwork for the convergence of psychological insight with biblical truths. But Osteen's charm, upbeat personality, and messages about a redefined self resonate with the American public in ways that exceed his predecessors. Though drawing striking similarities with their emphasis on positive thinking, self-actualization, and friendly etiquette, Osteen's focus on the Holy Spirit's transforming power distinguishes his appeal from that of many other evangelicals. Hence, in addition to using cognitive psychology, Osteen's distinctive appeal also has roots in the Pentecostal fervor of his father's ministry.

Lakewood Church began in 1959 under the leadership of evangelist, author, missionary, and speaker John Osteen. John Osteen's ministerial career began shortly after his 1939 conversion in Fort Worth, Texas. After preaching in venues such as schools and nursing homes, Osteen received ordination from the Southern Baptist Convention in 1942. Following preaching appointments in California and Arizona, Osteen moved to Houston in the 1950s to pastor Hibbard Memorial Baptist Church. Shortly after the move, John Osteen had a spiritual experience during a prayer retreat in Houston, in which he began to speak in what he perceived as different languages. Osteen interpreted this spiritual experience as what Pentecostal evangelicals call the Baptism of the Holy Spirit; an act of God's grace provides converts with new spiritual power. Osteen's experience and new embrace of Pentecostal teachings did not sit well with his congregants and officials in his Southern Baptist denomination, so he left Hibbard Memorial to start a new church called Lakewood, in a converted feed store (Balmer 2004; Strang 2002; Lawson 1988; Martin 2005; Young 2007).

As John Osteen began to preach more messages in the 1960s concerning the baptism in the Holy Spirit, he began to receive encouragement from popular prosperity Pentecostal ministers like Oklahoma-based preachers Kenneth Hagin and Oral Roberts. With his growing emphasis on God's spiritual power to supernaturally transform the believer's life and bring peace and prosperity, Osteen's ministry took a more redemptive tone, offering hope in the midst of hurt, and healing in the midst of pain. John and his wife, Dodie, also learned much from missionary trips to Mexico, India, and the Philippines. The church enjoyed consistent growth, and by the 1980s, Osteen began to broadcast sermons on local Houston networks and a few national stations. In time, the church raised enough money to build a new worship space that accommodated around 8,000 people, and Osteen's ministry friends Oral Roberts and Kenneth Hagin christened the new building in April 1987. After two more architectural additions in the early 1990s, Lakewood stood poised to transition successfully into the twenty-first century as a popular megachurch (Lawson 1988).

John Osteen wrote several books throughout those years reflecting his Pentecostal emphasis on God's supernatural or transforming power in the life of Spirit-filled believers. His book *The Bible Way to Spiritual Power* (1968) illustrates what it means for Christians to receive God's power and love through the baptism in the Holy Spirit. *You Can Change Your Destiny*, published a decade later, outlined Osteen's prescriptions for a re-routed life, punctuated by miracles, deliverance, positive confession, and identifiable increases in spiritual boldness. This book argues that whether it is a sick child, depression, or spiritual affliction, change comes through believing in biblical promises and enacting the visible faith present in so many of its narratives. Interestingly, more than twenty years before Christian writer Bruce Wilkinson used an obscure Old Testament figure in *The Prayer of Jabez* (2000) to craft a prayerful formula to ensure divine blessing, Osteen championed Jabez as someone who overcame an attitude of defeat and spirit of shame to live a life of spiritual victory.

There are significant parallels and common themes throughout John Osteen's work. First, there is an undeniable sense of the immediacy of God's action in the world, whether it is speaking in tongues, physical healing, or material provision. Tied to this immediacy is a requisite fervency of faith, determined by the right amount of Bible study, depth of belief, and ability to put thoughts and desires into action by speaking change into existence. Additionally, there is a persistent critique of denominationalism and what Osteen saw as the trappings of church tradition. Though it appears John Osteen drew most forcefully on this latter theme in the 1960s, it remained a major fixture of his ministry in successive decades.

Joel Osteen grew up in this Pentecostal nondenominational church with an iconoclastic pastor and father emphasizing the transforming power of God. "Growing up in a pastor's home as I did, I was privileged to meet and talk with a wide variety of 'world-changers,'" Joel Osteen recalls in his most recent book (2007: xi). The Osteen family prayed for sick people to be healed and called forth God's power to deliver people from spiritual oppression. John and Dodie taught their children to believe and confess biblical promises of personal peace, physical wholeness, and financial prosperity for believers. The family believes Dodie's victorious bout with cancer and Lisa Osteen's (Joel's sister) narrow escape from death after a pipe bomb exploded in her lap as she opened the church's mail demonstrate the abiding presence of God's transforming power. Today, Joel, Lisa, and Dodie often encourage members to believe that God will transform their trials and situations. Hence, when Joel took over the helm of leadership at Lakewood, his Pentecostal roots equipped him with an upbeat and empowering message for people to live happy and productive lives.

Drawing strong resemblance with the cognitive psychology motivational speakers and preachers like Norman Vincent Peale and Robert Schuller, Joel Osteen's prescriptions for a happy life also draw from his father's emphasis on biblical authority and God's supernatural power. Joel urges Lakewood members to repeat the following mantra, with raised Bible in hand, at the beginning of all of his sermons:

> This is my Bible. I am what it says I am. I have what it says I have. I can do what it says I can do. Today, I will be taught the Word of God. I boldly confess my mind is alert; my heart is receptive. I will never be the same. I am about to receive the incorruptible, indestructible, ever-living seed of the Word of God. I will never be the same. Never, never, never. I will never be the same. In Jesus' name Amen.

It is more accurate to distinguish Osteen as a Charismatic or neo-Pentecostal preacher because he places less emphasis on speaking in tongues than traditional Pentecostals, and more focus on the power of God's spirit to transform every aspect of the believer's life. Joel Osteen tells members to trust in God's supernatural intervention and yet focuses on personal agency by exhorting members to have positive thoughts and to speak positively in order to shun negativity from all aspects of their lives.

Though intimately acquainted with the sacred mechanics of his father's church, initially Joel Osteen did not envision himself as a preacher. He returned to Houston in 1981 after only one semester as a student at Oral Roberts University, focused on birthing a television ministry for his dad. Happily working behind the scenes, Osteen routinely rebuffed his father's invitations to preach and instead focused all energy toward making John look good. In the midst of his 1999 illnesses, John asked his son to fill in one Sunday; Joel initially refused but later acquiesced. As he recalled:

Daddy's words kept flitting through my mind, and with no other provocation, I began to have an overwhelming desire to preach. I didn't really understand it at the time, but I knew I had to do something. Keep in mind, I had never even prepared a sermon, let alone considered standing up in front of thousands of people to speak. . . . I studied all week and prepared a message, and the next Sunday I spoke at Lakewood Church for the first time. The message was well received by the congregation. (Osteen 2004: 215)

Only a few days after preaching his first sermon, Joel watched his father pass away and then submitted to what he believes is his life's ultimate calling, the senior pastorate of Lakewood Church. His brother Paul, a practicing surgeon in Arkansas, moved back to Houston to join his sister Lisa and brothers-in-law Kevin Comes and Don Iloff, on the pastoral staff and leadership team to help Joel lead Lakewood into a new era.

One of Joel Osteen's first executive decisions as the new pastor was to hire ordained minister and church marketing expert Duncan Dodds. By the late 1990s, Dodds had garnered considerable media experience through his work at Houston's Second Baptist Church, and through the steady flow of clients in his own consulting firm. Combining a pastor's perspective with deep knowledge of America's spiritual marketplace, Osteen knew Dodds would be a critical factor in Lakewood's future (Young 2007).

Another key decision early in Osteen's ministerial career was to hire contemporary Christian music star Cindy Cruse-Ratcliffe, part of the Cruse dynasty of contemporary Christian music fame, as the church's minister of music. Cruse-Ratcliffe's musical and recording experience proved a key ingredient to Lakewood's success, just as the contemporary upgrade of the music and songs became an important part of Lakewood's attractiveness (Young 2007).

Osteen also hired a popular and well-connected African American musician named Israel Houghton to further infuse Lakewood's appeal with deep musical talent, a powerful voice, and considerable experience in the Christian music business. Houghton not only sells many CDs and DVDs through the Integrity Gospel label but also headlines ministry events both at home and abroad, such as the National Inspirational Youth Convention in Orlando, Florida, in 2006, or a major worship gathering in Cape Town, South Africa, in 2005, aimed at cultural and physical healing through music. Houghton's appeal comes from his multiracial background, from his keen inclusive focus to draw energy from various racial, cultural,

Members of the Lakewood Church along with first-time visitors worship on
July 16, 2005, at the grand opening of the new facility in Houston.
Photo courtesy of Associated Press.

generational, and denominational boundaries, and from his immersion in
the Christian music scene. Fellow Lakewood music leader Cindy Cruse-
Ratcliff calls Houghton "a super talent, and as far as what is happening in
the gospel field, he is on the forefront, on the cutting edge" (Vara 2007:
F4). As Cruse-Ratcliff's observations suggest, Houghton's efforts do not go
unrecognized; he has a 2007 Grammy (and four other Grammy nomina-
tions) to his credit, along with Dove, Stellar, and Soul Train awards (F4).
Embodying the postmodern penchant to traverse conventional boundaries, Houghton leads a prominent multiracial and award-winning musical
outfit called New Breed, whose philosophy, according to the CD jacket for
Alive in South Africa, reflects "a purpose driven worship movement car-
rying the sound of the Kingdom through the anointing of God, to lead all
people seeking to glorify God through worship and anointed music."

Cruse-Ratcliffe and Houghton, along with choir director Dakri Brown,
help Lakewood's ten-piece orchestra and large choir generate the energy
of a rock concert. They blend an array of contemporary gospel music
styles to create a worship experience that appeals to the tastes of its diverse audience (Martin 2005).

Early in Joel's tenure, the leadership quickly realized that Lakewood would eventually grow out of its 8,000-seat congregation, then situated in a working-class neighborhood east of Houston's 610 Loop. When the Compaq Center became available in 2001, Osteen jumped at the chance to acquire a location near the heart of metropolitan Houston's business district. In addition to its economic setting, the location possesses senti-mental value, since Joel and his wife, Victoria, had had their first date at the Compaq Center (called the Summit at the time), watching a Houston Rockets basketball game. Lakewood endured almost two years of litiga-tion to secure a $12 million deal with the city council to lease Houston's Compaq Center for thirty years. Lakewood also agreed to fund the $90 million needed for renovations, and the congregation moved into the new space in July 2005. Lakewood's inaugural service in the Compaq Cen-ter was a prime event, with Texas governor Rick Perry, Congresswoman Sheila Jackson Lee, and other prominent politicians and celebrities in at-tendance. During the service, Governor Perry offered a short testimony to God's role in his life, and Osteen returned the favor when he voiced a prayer during Perry's inaugural ceremony in January 2007.

Joel Osteen and his wife celebrate the grand opening of the new home for the Lakewood Church, formerly the Compaq Center, July 16, 2005, in Houston. Photo courtesy of Associated Press.

During the ceremony, Paul Osteen narrated a history of the church suffused with biblical symbolism. Using a story from the Old Testament book of Joshua, Paul reminded listeners that the children of Israel once made a historical passage into the promised land, just as Yahweh provided dry ground on which to pass through the Jordan River. But before the Israelites completed the journey, Paul pointed out that Joshua received a command to gather rocks from the dry bed of the Jordan River and assemble them as a physical reminder of provision, protection, and blessing so that subsequent generations might remember such miraculous moments. Assembling various "stones" of Lakewood's past, the grandchildren of John and Dodie Osteen stood onstage holding various artifacts of the church's history as Paul explained their spiritual significance. Joel Osteen's son Jonathan held the dress shoes of his grandfather as a symbol of someone who not only stepped out in faith but also walked the faith he proclaimed. A chair from Lakewood's original location in a converted feed store reminded the faithful of the congregation's "humble beginnings." A chair from the church's previous campus symbolized the "sawdust trail" that many repentant individuals walked as a testament to newfound faith, spiritual transformation, or physical healing. Another grandchild held an open spread of a church flyer with Joel Osteen standing at the pulpit as a picture to remind people that "God found another man who was willing to leave his comfort zone and find his God-given destiny." An oversized golden key with "December 1, 2003" and the Lakewood logo covering the Compaq Center logo served as a final material reminder of the church's spiritual reality when Houston politicians approved a multi-million-dollar lease of the former sports arena. According to Paul Osteen, and no doubt members and other church leaders, these events served as a testament to supernatural orchestrations on behalf of Lakewood Church.

More than merely a display of religious paraphernalia and church kitsch, Paul Osteen's recitation of Lakewood's history reminded older members and introduced new ones to a congregational identity through an explicit act of collective memory and a stage from which to forecast and proclaim a future. The church clearly has a sense of its history and believes it is living and embracing its destiny. Joel Osteen and his ministry leadership team are singularly focused on charting the church's future course and committed to offering their message to the nation and to the world. He offered this sporty prediction at Lakewood's inaugural service at the former Compaq Center: "For nearly thirty years they've crowned champions in the sports field in this building, but I believe for the next thirty years we can crown people champions in life. We're going to let them know that they are victors and not victims; we're going to let them know they can do all things through Christ." On the surface, Joel Osteen's comments reflect his commitment to deliver a message of hope and salvation to parishioners and listeners. Yet closer analysis suggests that Osteen is very aware of what parishioners expect from Lakewood: the possibility of refashioning one's identity and a sense of spiritual accomplishment in the face of life's disappointments. Moreover, Osteen's remarks indicate the sense in which he believes that a once-secular space built for sporting events and concerts now possesses a sacralized character devoted to spiritual activities. Put another way, Osteen's comments demonstrate a crafty use of symbol, speech, and space.

Osteen transformed a basketball arena into a haven of hope where redemption is possible, where renewal is likely, and where the firm promises a return on consumers' spiritual investment. The renovations expanded the Compaq Center's seating capacity to 16,000, the largest of any church building in the United States. Lakewood currently draws around 40,000 attendees through four weekend services: one Saturday evening, and three Sunday services, the last one in Spanish. Locker rooms where athletes once shared basketball strategies and dirty jokes now operate as sanctified nurseries to care for the young children of worshiping attendees. The megachurch also offers scores of Sunday school classes, a handful of children's services, a Wednesday night service, and several small-group gender-exclusive Bible studies throughout the city.

One of the aspects we find most significant about Lakewood is its racial and ethnic diversity. For each Sunday service the Compact Center jams thousands of people together from many different races and ethnicities, and it is difficult to observe any one group representing anything close to a majority percentage of the membership. Although in media interviews Osteen attributes Lakewood's diversity to God, this notable dimension is a reflection of Houston's multiethnic composition, constitutive of the interracial dynamics of Pentecostalism's history, and a testament to Osteen's ability to craft messages of a meaningful religious self that transcends divisions between race and class.

Lakewood's business approach and state-of-the-art media fit its setting in a thriving corporate space in southwest Houston. Its strategic venue provides a platform for other major events: a choir collaboration with the Houston Symphony, a CD produced by the church's worship team called *The Gift*, Christian rock concerts, and a conference devoted to church leadership and lay ministry, for which ministry leaders came from South Korea, Canada, Taiwan, South Africa, and even Trinidad. Lakewood's design is unique as well. In addition to a massive sanctuary space, with a sprawling stage, a movable and retractable music set, and graded choir loft, the campus has a coffee shop, children's area, nurseries, media center, ice rink, dining and retail plaza, basketball court, and mammoth bookstore. Six former snack bars that surround the outside of the oval arena now serve as "resource centers," fully stocked with text and audio copies of *Your Best Life Now* and *Become a Better You* and CDs of Joel Osteen's sermons. Lines of eager spiritual consumers form in front of these retail spaces after every service, with the faithful eager to return once again to the powerful preaching of their pastor.

The Compaq Center offers a place where parishioners can purchase religious literature in an expansive bookstore that prominently displays pictures of energetic and smiling Joel and Victoria Osteen, and above all encounter a spiritual pulse and vibration that are seemingly larger than life. A pictorial history of Lakewood adorns one part of the church's inner walls. On it rest twenty massive encased frames; eight capture Lakewood Church from its Houston Rockets days to its purchase from the city of Houston, to its opening weekend in July 2005. The remaining twelve cases list thousands of names of people who contributed significant financial gifts to the church, appropriately named the "wall of champions." Religion is literally and figuratively big business at Lakewood; the physical space provides room and creates a context for a multiethnic, multiracial congregation, resembling what Lakewood member Terrence J. Slaughter told us heaven must be like. The massive worship services provide one with a sense of participating in something bigger than oneself, while the more intimate settings of adult education classes or small-group ministries are more conducive to individual experience and preference. Armed with 3,000 volunteers, Lakewood offers various outreach ministries geared toward specific age-groups and needs.

Lakewood's third service on Sunday is one of the nation's largest Spanish services. Though Joel Osteen proposed the ideas that led to its current incarnation, leaders at Lakewood long acknowledged the church's (and Houston's) large and growing Latino population and carefully contemplated how Lakewood might address this rising demand. Houston's current Latino population exceeds 50 percent, and the percentage will continue to increase. Osteen carefully considered his options before hiring Marcos Witt as Lakewood's Spanish service pastor in 2002. Witt, the son of missionaries to Mexico and a graduate of International Bible College in San Antonio, is well known in Latin America, with more than two dozen Spanish music CDs and four Latin Grammy Awards to his credit. Understanding the possibilities with Witt on board, Osteen gave the new Spanish church pastor Lakewood's main stage every Sunday afternoon. The popularity of the Spanish service is a tacit acknowledgment that Protestant evangelical Christianity is becoming increasingly attractive to Latinos of faith. In addition to preaching and singing, Witt published *How to Overcome Fear and Live Your Life to the Fullest* (2007), with a foreword by Joel Osteen. Witt's approach to crafting a better life stems from his own bouts with depression and his conviction that fear is one of the most paralyzing emotions humans experience. Much like his pastoral partner Osteen, Witt believes devotion to God, particularly during trying circumstances, will result in personal change and individual betterment.

Osteen once concluded a sermon by assuring Lakewood's congregants that if they "suit up with God's armor," material blessings would flow. He constructs a vision of happy living that blends well with our consumerist self-indulgent culture and offers a narrative of hope grounded in the discourses of religious and bourgeois American middle-class sensibilities. Osteen's message of redemption reminds his followers that God has a great future for them and that they can leave their past behind. He encourages his listeners to take inventory of interior dispositions, watch what cultural evils they consume, and keep their inner spirits healthy and whole by listening to edifying sermons. His strategic blend of cognitive psychology and prosperity spirituality empowers believers to take charge of their situation and be the architects of change in their own lives. Two themes inform nearly all of Osteen's sermons: the importance of imagining a better, brighter future, and the ability of individuals to speak their future into existence. Positive thinking and positive speaking thus ensure a future charged with hope. Osteen's message of uplift and personal transformation is appealing to his contemporaries because it is profoundly American.

In a sermon series from his early preaching days titled "The Power of Words," Osteen focuses on the transformative importance of religious utterances. Not only does what one says shape human relationships, Osteen contends that words reveal the contours of one's past while they simultaneously shape one's future. Indicative of an understanding of the cognitive power of speech as it relates to religious settings and the Christian life, Osteen remarks:

You are who you are today in large part because of the words that you've been speaking. . . . You've got to begin to see yourselves as the overcomers God made you to be. You've got to see yourselves happy, successful, and fulfilled. And then you've got to give life to that dream by speaking it out. . . . you've got to choose to agree with God, and boldly declare I can do all things; I'm well able to fulfill my destiny. See if you're gonna live in victory, you've got to learn how to speak positive words of faith over your life.

Reflecting the tastes of his audiences, Osteen offered an illustration from the dismal record of Houston Astros pitcher José Lima, who had a losing season because negative words crossed his lips. Had this pitcher possessed a positive outlook and uttered positive thoughts, Osteen suggested, circumstances would have turned out differently. Referencing stories and quotes from his father as he does in many of his sermons, Joel recalled a catchy rhyme uttered by John Osteen: "Great it is to dream the dream, when you stand in youth by the starry stream; but a greater thing is to fight life through, and say at the end the dream is true."

According to Osteen, words have the power to heal and also to hurt, to confirm or condemn, and to uplift or undermine. In *Become a Better You*, Osteen devotes an entire chapter called "Making Your Words Work for You" to suggestions for how people can modify the ways they speak about themselves: "Change the way you speak about yourself and you can change your life. Start each day with saying things such as, 'I am disciplined. I have self-control. I make good decisions. I'm an overcomer. This problem didn't come to stay; it came to pass'" (Osteen 2007: 112). Similarly, in a sermon series titled "Thinking the Right Thoughts," Osteen complements a focus on the power of speech with a close look at the necessity of positive thinking. In one sermon Osteen describes the "enemy" (his description of God's archenemy and the Christian's worst nightmare, Satan), who prowls around waiting to hook the faithful into thinking negative thoughts. To ultimately fulfill what he customarily refers to as "God's best" in one's life, Osteen encourages listeners to fight the enemy's attacks, to "cast down" the negativity the enemy harbors by "thinking God's thoughts." Osteen elaborates further on this theme: "God's thoughts will fill you with faith and hope and victory. God's thoughts will build you up and encourage you. They'll give you the strength you need to just keep on keeping on. God's thoughts will give you that can-do mentality." Just as speech can shape one's destiny, Osteen's focus on positive thinking delivers a message that provides hope for millions of listeners.

Along with a Christianized sense of hope, Osteen offers the tools with which individuals may construct a new religious identity. His upbeat message convinces members that God works mysteriously on their behalf despite what appear to be trying or hopeless circumstances. He urges Christians to believe that God is in control and will transform all trials and tribulations to their personal benefit. Like other holy mavericks, Osteen views faith as a positive outlook in which one believes God is working every day on his or her behalf. In *Your Best Life Now*, Osteen describes this dimension of his philosophy:

> Understand, God is at work in your life whether you can see anything happening externally or not. In fact, one could almost make a case that God often works the most when we see it and feel it the least. You may not see any progress. Your situation may look the same as it did three months or even three years ago, but you must trust that deep inside your · life, God is at work. Beyond that, behind the scenes, He's putting all the pieces together. He's getting everything lined up, and one day, at the appointed time, you will see the culmination of everything that God has been doing. Suddenly, your situation will change for the better. (2004: 197)

Osteen contends that God works for one's good and will ultimately bring about something positive, and that embracing God's cosmic mystery involves trusting in God's provision and protection. Lakewood offers several adult religion education classes that complement Osteen's spiritual teaching and message of encouragement. One class called North Star focuses on maintaining joy in the midst of trials; the teacher encourages listeners to examine motives, remain obedient to God, and trust God in all circumstances, whether battling disease, depression, or financial debt. Like Osteen, the instructor and class members emphasize spiritual hope and encourage attendees to listen to encouraging sermons and surrounded themselves with "positive" people.

Osteen often provides personal examples of God's mysterious activity coordinating divine purposes in human activity, or as he calls it, God's favor. In his best seller *Your Best Life Now*, Osteen relates a story from his media days when he asked his father to work a few more hours per week so that Lakewood's message could cross the airwaves to arrive at numerous global locations. The elder Osteen cited fatigue and was reluctant to take on what could become a prohibitively time-consuming activity.

Joel sulked in disappointment, only to realize after his father's death that God's favor would orchestrate his own vision and implement his own ideas. Soon after taking over for his father, Osteen assessed the need to hit the national airwaves and convinced Lakewood's board to approve a $10 million annual budget for television broadcasting. With greater television exposure, passionate praise and worship, and practical and relevant preaching, Osteen and Lakewood had the formula for great success, and the membership dramatically increased. Osteen cites this as one of many examples of divine favor toward his family and his church.

One example of God's mysterious activities that hit close to home occurred in August 2006, when someone murdered Joel Osteen's great-aunt Johnnie Daniels in her Houston home. Well known to practice the philosophy of divine hospitality the Osteen family preaches and teaches, neighbors and family members told how Daniels would routinely provide money, food, and shelter for those who had hit hard times. In the end, Johnnie Daniels's kindness killed her. In a December 2006 appearance on the talk show *Larry King Live*, the host brought up an array of problems— the horrific disasters Hurricane Katrina wrought, anti-Semitism, and racism, as well as the murder, and asked Osteen how his positive philosophy handled such things. Osteen's thoughts on the ravages of Katrina, borne from a tour of New Orleans, accentuated the positive efforts of those who participate in the energetic rebuilding currently under way; he noted that the response to such events as well as to anti-Semitism and racism should serve to strengthen faith and unite, not to divide or create doubts. Relative to his great-aunt's murder, Osteen and his wife, Victoria, said that life's events, while at times horrifically "sad," sometimes defy explanation; as with Hurricane Katrina, the response to tragedies should bolster one's faith.

Scholars often discuss disasters like Katrina, events like murder, and blights like racism in the context of theodicy as they grapple with the depth of human suffering and the evil acts humans sometimes commit. When justice cries out and when the plight of those stung by poverty is clear for the world to see, for example, encouragement to simply focus on the positive fails to address the structural factors that continue to impale and divide. And while the setting of a talk show provides neither the time nor the forum to flesh out the complexities related to theodicy, the power of positive thinking often melts in the furnaces of human suffering. Choosing to live one's best life now is typically easier said than done.

Osteen also offers a critical tool with which parishioners may construct religious identity: the concept of individual value. Osteen explains that all individuals are unique and part of a larger cosmic order and possess unconditional "value" in the sight of God that increases one's sense of self-worth. His messages provide not only psychological comfort and the tools with which to craft a religious identity but also a palpable sense of participation in cosmic religious activity with earthly relevance and eternal significance. Osteen frequently tells his audience how God's favor helped him with difficult situations, family conflicts, or smaller concerns like finding a parking spot, and that if they trust God, the same favor will accompany all their endeavors.

Osteen does more than massage audiences with proclamations about individual value and personal worth; journals and study guides that accompany *Your Best Life Now* offer ways for individuals to further internalize Osteen's message. The study guide for *Your Best Life Now* marshals quotations and stories from the book and prompts individuals to record their own stories, hopes, desires, and dreams as a way to apply and enact Osteen's message. Osteen challenges readers to embrace the hope of a return on their spiritual investments.

The companion journal for *Your Best Life Now* includes sections from Osteen's book, yet it also offers quotations from famous and notable persons, as well as scripture verses for personal reflection, and plenty of room to record personal reactions and pen spiritual meditations. Osteen believes that in conjunction with *Your Best Life Now*, the journal is "an open door to self-discovery, so step through and begin the journey toward living the life you were born to live" (2005: xi). Reflecting Osteen's commitment to teaching and preaching about individual value while simultaneously providing the tools necessary to cultivate spirituality tailored to personal tastes and desires, the journal's introduction offers further encouragement:

When you write your responses, be as honest as possible. Don't be afraid to freely express your thoughts and feelings. Don't worry about spelling or grammar or sentence structure. Attempt to get your "heart" on paper. Don't try to impress anyone with your answers. No teacher or critic is looking over your shoulder, waiting to correct you if you record the wrong response. In fact, since most of your responses are simply reflections of your own thoughts and feelings, they can't be considered "right" or "wrong." No tests will be given at the end of the book; this is one course you can be sure you will pass with flying colors! (xii)

Like other holy mavericks, Osteen provides several ways for listeners and fans to connect to the essence of his message.

An undeniable part of Osteen's appeal rests in branding himself as "the-boy-next-door" offering messages of encouragement. In interviews and sermons he often argues that for too long churches have discouraged believers by focusing on the depths of human frailty. Osteen instead prefers to focus on human possibility and potential, and he seeks to empower discouraged and defeated individuals. Unlike some evangelicals who continue to preach fire-and-brimstone messages, Osteen never preaches about hell, judgment day, or sin. Similarly, Osteen's biblical exhortations have a pragmatic rather than didactic function: they guide people toward healthy and happy living, rather than moralize about a holy, sinless existence. As in the case of many unlettered evangelical innovators, his simple, pragmatic, and positive message is the force behind his mass appeal. Accordingly, detractors often chide him for compromising the integrity of the gospel by offering simplistic feel-good proclamations or giving people what they want rather than what they need to hear.

Media are a critical variable in the equation of megachurch success and are among the important religious goods offered by Lakewood. Osteen's sermons appear in the top thirty television markets in the United States, including five international networks: Canada, Asia, Europe, Australia, and the Middle East. Lakewood insiders even consult quarterly Nielsen ratings to assess product output (Martin 2005). In addition, the church recently upgraded its media capacity with high definition. Similarly, the advent of the Internet created new possibilities of spiritual production for a much larger market. Lakewood Church sends daily "e-votionals" to subscribers' inboxes, short textual cyber sermons from Joel Osteen called "Today's Word" that link a scriptural text with a positive, meaningful thought for the day.

Osteen is no different than many preachers who make good use of the technological advances of their day, but it is the scope of his reach that separates him from other evangelical innovators. Since its publication in 2004, Osteen's first book, *Your Best Life Now*, appeared at the top of the *New York Times* best-seller list for weeks and sold more than 5 million copies; his latest book, *Become a Better You*, was released as number one on the same list. A large part of Osteen's popularity comes from visibility on television and marketing. His broadcasts inundate viewers with carefully placed pop-up ads four or five times during each sermon to advertise his products and future events before millions each week. Osteen's strategic use of televangelism to market his name and products is commensurate with the practices of evangelical entrepreneurs of the past like Oral Roberts, Pat Robertson, and Billy Graham, while it corresponds to contemporary practices like those of T. D. Jakes, who craftily markets his ministry and products on television.

Your Best Life Now not only secured a prominent spot for Osteen in the hearts and minds of countless Americans but also solidified his status as one of America's key religious innovators. Osteen makes further claim with his second book, *Become a Better You*. This Osteen offering adopts the same seven-step approach to self-help found in *Your Best Life Now*, but it provides tips to enter a realm of even greater personal fulfillment. "But even if you are living your best life now," Osteen writes, "it is important that your do not become stagnant. God always wants to increase us . . . always want to take us deeper into self-discovery and then wants to raise us to a higher level of living" (2007: xiii).

Even as Osteen offers a new variety of ways to improve the self, right thinking and right speech practices proposed in sermons and in *Your Best Life Now*—constitute "action points" provided at the end of each chapter. These action points are three-point and four-point confessions, mental and verbal enhancements and best practices to, as Osteen puts it, become a better person. Action points about thinking healthier thoughts about oneself include deciding each morning to "keep my inner dialogue positive about myself. I will reject any negative thoughts toward myself and others, and I will meditate on thoughts such, 'I am valuable. I am well able to do what God has called me to do'" (131). Osteen suggests this practice for remaining content in whatever circumstances individuals face: "Today I will declare God's favor in my life. I will speak aloud statements such as, 'Thank you, Father, for working in my life. Although I cannot see it yet, I know you are arranging things in my favor. I know the clouds will dissipate, and I will see the favor of God in my life again. I am looking for one touch of God's favor that can turn my circumstances around to my advantage and for his Honor'" (298). Here Osteen models key points in his preaching and writing that reflect an application of market language to spirituality by confessing one's personal value, as well as his two-pronged practice of thinking and speaking a happier life into existence.

The attention surrounding the publication of Osteen's *Become a Better You* further illuminates the methodical strategizing necessary to thrive in America's spiritual marketplace. Starting in the summer of 2007, for example, promotional ads for the book appeared on Osteen's telecasts,

Joel Osteen Ministries events and website, e-votionals, and Lakewood Church's website. Most visibly, however, the week of the book's debut in mid-October 2007, Osteen appeared on *60 Minutes*, *Larry King Live*, *Fox and Friends*, *Neal Cavuto*, and the *Glenn Beck Show*, along with the *CBS Morning Show* and a radio program, the *Alan Colmes Show*. Clearly conscious of the book's impact in national, regional, and local markets, the *Houston Chronicle* published excerpts in five installments, beginning, interestingly enough, the same day Osteen appeared on *60 Minutes*. Not surprisingly, during the first two months of the new book's existence, the ABC, NBC, and CBS affiliates in Houston all ran multiple-segment stories about the book, Lakewood activities, and the impact national notoriety has had on Osteen and his family. In addition, a second Osteen feature article appeared in the November 2007 issue of *Texas Monthly*. It complements William Martin's piece in the August 2005 issue of the same publication by offering an interview format that discusses specifically Osteen's rise to prominence, how he compares to his father, John, the transformation of the Compaq Center, and how a pastor in the spotlight deals with criticism.

Since Osteen achieved national and international attention with *Your Best Life Now*, countless critics—particularly fellow clerics with websites such as Ken Silva's Appraising Ministries—are ever ready to offer criticism and doctrinal clarification about points they feel Osteen ignores or glosses over. And, similar to other holy mavericks, in nearly every interview, journalists ask Osteen to answer his critics. With the release of *Become a Better You*, Osteen responded to his detractors in a way that suggests he is positioning himself to retain one of the top spots in America's religious marketplace. In an October 2007 segment on *60 Minutes*, interviewer Byron Pitts cited Osteen's critics to ask why, as a Christian minister in his new book, he failed to mention God or Jesus in any of his proposals to become a better person. Osteen contended that he is neither a scripture scholar nor a theologian, criticisms Osteen's detractors regularly cite, but a minister equipped to offer people hope and to teach individuals how to become better people, find God's purpose, and live a better, happier life. Similarly, in a *Texas Monthly* interview Osteen says that preaching at Lakewood is "what I was born to do," and that since filling his father's role, he "stepped into my own shoes" at the church (Smith 2007: 110). Focusing on what he feels God called him to do, Osteen implicitly answers critics by continually highlighting his niche in the spiritual marketplace— motivating people to be the best they can be.

Most similar to the marketing methodology Brian McLaren employed with the release of *Everything Must Change*, also in October 2007, Osteen's strategic use of visual and print media to enhance the visibility and viability of his message suggests a tactical approach to gaining the top market share in America's religious marketplace. Osteen, particularly due to work in television and communication, like McLaren and other holy mavericks, keenly understands the power and necessity of crafting niche appeal in competitive religious environments.

In addition to books, podcasts, telecasts, and e-votionals, Osteen takes his message of hope on the road with his "An Evening with Joel" preaching tour, the signature product offered by Joel Osteen Ministries. Multi-city evangelistic events, these nightly gatherings provide a way for Osteen to physically connect with fans and hearers around the country. Most of these gatherings sell out. The inaugural "An Evening with Joel" event took place at Madison Square Garden in 2004. It is notable that Osteen chose such a venue to introduce his specialized ministry to the nation. In 1957, Billy Graham led a four-month long crusade in New York City, one of his most important evangelistic campaigns. The memory of Graham's historic crusade in the annals of American religious history serves Lakewood well. These realities suggest that church leaders possess keen understanding of Lakewood's location in America's religious marketplace, the ability to offer personality in performance, and the crucial creation of a brand name, all considerations necessary to cultivate broad appeal.

Osteen's Madison Square Garden meeting opened, as all "An Evening with Joel" events do, with remarks by Joel and Victoria followed by an energetic music set led by Lakewood's professional worship leaders, Cindy Cruse-Ratcliffe and Israel Houghton. Personalizing the experience, Joel and Victoria shared the story of how they met, and how the family believes that God divinely ordained this unassuming television ministry producer as Lakewood's pastor. Dodie Osteen, as she does at most of Joel's evening events, testified to the miraculous healing from cancer she experienced, and the central role that prayer, confession, and biblical proclamation played in her survival. After citing a litany of Bible verses related to divine healing and restoration, Dodie promised hearers that through deep faith and proper confession they could experience a miracle like her own. The message Osteen delivered took up his staple themes of hope in the midst of hurt, purpose in the midst of uncertainty, and blessing in the midst of bad luck and trying circumstances. "An Evening with Joel" became an almost instant hit, selling out arenas in cities nationwide. Osteen's event in Atlanta turned away 4,000 people for lack of seating in the very same arena that the city's NBA basketball team, the Hawks, struggles to fill each game. Turning away people sparked Osteen's decision to change his preaching tours from open seating to ticketed events at the set rate of $10 per person. Events sell out months in advance, and the demand is strong enough that scalpers and eBay auctioneers sell $10 tickets for as much as $200, thus demonstrating his tremendous appeal.

While the inaugural Madison Square Garden event demonstrates the genius of such a personalized religious product, the "An Evening with Joel" event we observed in central Texas confirms the power of Osteen's appeal. Osteen knew that military personnel and their families would show up at the Bell County Expo Center, located close to Fort Hood, one of America's most important army bases. Standing in lines that weaved around the side of the arena and in between cars in the parking lot, ticket holders expressed great excitement at seeing Osteen in person. Many related that they regularly watched Joel's telecasts, and one Hispanic woman spoke of her attendance at a previous "An Evening with Joel" event in San Antonio, Texas. Inside the arena, the smell of pretzels and popcorn mixed with eager anticipation, the buzz of people, and tables set up with Osteen books, tapes, and CDs for sale, as well as Lakewood and Joel Osteen Ministries T-shirts.

Short videos with images of urban and suburban spaces along with landscape shots with a "Southwest" theme, all centered on texts of Bible verses, grabbed people's attention while they waited for the main program. In addition, advertisements encouraging attendees to financially and prayerfully partner with Joel Osteen Ministries, along with the recorded testimonial of Lakewood member Mark Solz, whose recovery from prison, addiction, and divorce he attributes to Osteen and his church, added to the crowd's anticipation.

As at the Madison Square Garden event, Cindy Cruse-Ratcliffe and her musical attachment led attendees in thirty minutes of praise songs, punctuated by Dodie's healing testimonial, Victoria's short sermon from Jeremiah 29:11 about God's divine purpose for individual lives, and Joel's script about how he met Victoria and went on to become Lakewood's senior pastor. Attending to the tastes of those present, Victoria stated that Lakewood prays regularly for military spouses, and Joel's sister Lisa delivered a special message to the military personnel in attendance. With the crowd on its feet to show respect and with a U.S. flag displayed prominently on the large screen behind the main stage, Cruse-Ratcliffe and

Lakewood's music team followed the military message with "God Bless America." Joel's message quickly followed. He crafted a sermon from Psalm 91:11 and, with military and national defense references discernible, preached that sometimes God sends angels as secret agents to deliver messages and protect the faithful. Above all, much like a nation's military polices its borders, Osteen encouraged hearers to stay faithful and believe in God's ultimate protection.

The central Texas event was not the first time Osteen and his team preached to members of the armed forces. As Houston CBS affiliate KHOU reported in a story by Jeremy Desel, after a chance meeting aboard a commercial flight with Major General David Hicks, head of chaplains in the U.S. Army, Osteen received an invitation to preach at Fort Leavenworth in Kansas. In early 2006 Osteen, along with his brother Paul and other members of Lakewood's ministry team, preached to a packed house. In addition to Joel's positive and upbeat message, full of religious and patriotic fervor, Lakewood's ministry team and musical ensemble sang "God Bless America." Paul Osteen, with a lapel pin of the U.S. flag clearly affixed to his suit jacket, ended the night with a reminder that military personnel are heroes at Lakewood. "With God Almighty on our side," he passionately stated, "and with men and women like you protecting us, that freedom will prevail, and that victory will be ours. From our heart to yours, God bless you, thank you, and God bless America." About this event Major General Hicks remarked that the "spiritual value [of Osteen's message] is just immeasurable"; another army chaplain, Carron Jones, received inspiration to "take that energy, that excitement, and that passion" of Osteen's preaching "to the combat zone." Tapping into the patriotic fervor resident in some quarters of a post–September 11 America, Osteen not only offers something meaningful to men and women in military uniform but creates yet another way to connect with millions attuned to his message.

Joel Osteen specializes in providing what Americans want: the possibility to remake oneself, the ability to find hope in hopeless circumstances, and the fortitude to achieve certainty in the midst of chaos. A major part of his success is an uncanny ability to be winsome, attractive, energetic, and relevant. His boyish charm and friendly demeanor are at the center of his appeal. The "smiling preacher" excels at offering a positive message, one that uplifts the self rather than denigrating the other person. Osteen's focus is not on past regrets but on the future of possibility. It is on the relevance of the here and now, and the material and spiritual return God offers for the right kinds of investment.

Pastors Joel, left, and Victoria Osteen with their son, Jonathan Osteen, thirteen, between them, stand alongside former president Bill Clinton and his daughter, Chelsea Clinton, right, as they attend early services, March 2, 2008, at Lakewood Church. Photo courtesy of Associated Press.

It is the immediacy of Osteen's messages that resonates most closely with the Pentecostal themes of his father's ministry. As outlined earlier in this chapter, his father's preaching and writing focused on the present activities of God, whether healing sickness or disease, or the ability to provide encouraging words in difficult circumstances. God's activities in the human realm, according to John Osteen, depended largely on "confession," cultivating the right thoughts and speaking spiritual desires into material reality. For John Osteen, God's activity in the world provided a potent spiritual energy from which human beings could draw. Yet while both father and son derive much of their appeal from a focus on God's divine presence in the material realm, the younger Osteen crafts his redemptive message in the discourses of cognitive psychology, self-help, and individual betterment. This is not to say that Joel is a secular preacher with a biblical message, or a biblical preacher with a secular message, a distinction for theologians to debate, discuss, and decide. Rather, it is to point out that Joel Osteen is best described as a religious capitalist, an entrepreneurial minister able to draw from his background in Christian media ministry, his knowledge of human experience, and the scores of ministers who preceded him, particularly those whose messages garnered wide appeal.

Part of what makes Joel Osteen's attraction so noteworthy is his ability to mix and match elements drawn deep from the recesses of the American psyche, and craft generative stories that provide a desire for meaning, a quest to belong, and a search for significance (McAdams 2006). He seems keenly aware of where he currently sits in America's religious economy as he offers millions of viewers beacons of hope that correspond to material and spiritual success; the power of positive thinking as a way to relocate one's religious identity; a tangible sense of participation in a large cosmic plan; a sacralized space rich with spiritual possibility; specialized ministry to Houston's Hispanic population; vibrant music that enhances worship experiences; and the traveling displays of "An Evening with Joel" events.

Recently the entertainment company Endless Games produced "Your Best Life Now: The Game," a board game based on Osteen's best seller of the same title. Centered on the seven life principles outlined in Osteen's book, the object of the game is to roll the dice and try to succeed at life. Although church leaders find that the game does not fully "fit the message of the ministry," it is nevertheless remarkable that a board game has appeared based on the broad appeal of a pastor's message (Karkabi 2006). While scholars of American religion continue to debate the significance and influence of popular pastors and ministers, one thing is certain: Joel Osteen will offer salvation and a smile to anyone who shows up, tunes in, or logs on to Lakewood Church.

3

Great Jazz
T. D. Jakes and the New Black Church

I really liked Wynton when I first met him. He's still a nice young man, only confused. I knew he could play the hell out of classical music and had great technical skills on the trumpet, techniques and all of that. But you need more than that to play great jazz music; you need feelings and an understanding of life that you can only get from living, from experience.

—Miles Davis

In his candid autobiography, jazz legend Miles Davis chided heir apparent Wynton Marsalis for playing an "old dead European" genre of music better known as classical. Davis believed that anyone through rigorous practice could master Beethoven's Ninth Symphony, while only special musicians could create in the moment to play jazz. He rendered classical music stagnant, while he saw each melody of jazz as a mélange of talent, ingenuity, and life experience. Davis emphasized that with jazz, one cannot play a song the same way twice—each opportunity involves pairing musical prowess with the demands of the situation to produce something new and lively. Davis believed that jazz enriched the aesthetic life of the twentieth century and came to represent America at its best.

Jazz is a fitting metaphor of the American experience. Like jazz, America emerged without much of a blueprint and had to repeatedly reinvent itself. Like jazz, the American spirit affirms individuality and collaboration, as each person makes his or her own mark while working with others toward a collective goal. Jazz is synonymous with freedom, and freedom is at the core of American identity. Jazz ranks among the most

Bishop T. D. Jakes. Photo courtesy of Associated Press.

fluid forms of expression; America has always been a backdrop of mount-ing mutability. Hence jazz is an echo of American energy; to understand America is to understand jazz.

Jazz is also a fitting metaphor for the black church, which derived from the same struggle, pain, and confusion that produced the musical genre. Instead of political freedom, early African American slaves exerted rhythmic freedom at secret meetings in the swamps to improvise worship beyond the watchful eye of their oppressors. This "invisible institution" inspired early sanctuaries for slaves, with singing, dancing, preaching, crying, and other emotional and spiritual manifestations, evocations inex-tricably linked to their identities as oppressed people.

Like jazz musicians who create fresh and vibrant sounds, early black church leaders drew upon the available cultural and spiritual resources to address the needs of the moment. Their messages and missions addressed the existential absurdity of bondage in a free nation while providing ca-tharsis for thousands of blacks to endure two centuries of slavery. As mas-ters trounced upon the dignity and self-respect of slaves, black preach-ers provided personal affirmation, and their churches became safe havens from subjugation and humiliation. Similarly, the black church stood as a witness against a renewed regime of racial apartheid to help its members cope with second-class citizenship during the Jim Crow era, while it also provided the energy and impetus for the civil rights movement in twentieth-century America.

Imaginative impresarios adapting to changing conditions, leaders of the black church emphasized the power of conversion, biblical authority, and the importance of a Spirit-filled life. These men and women had their fingers on the human condition and adjusted their ministries and messages to meet critical demands. But analogous to how the traditional black church played an important role in helping African Americans make the transition from slave to citizen, a new black church attempts to help contemporary African Americans make a smooth transition into our competitive hypercapitalist society.

The twenty-first century contains a host of superstar black preachers who build megachurches and national ministries that rival entire denominations in power and influence. Armed with well-trained staffs of specialists in finance and community development, many black pastors are both well connected and distinctly entrepreneurial as the first generation of African Americans to directly benefit from the political and economic gains secured during the civil rights movement (Harrison 2005). Leaders of the new black church smoothly adapt to the commercialization, technology, flash, style, and celebrity that characterize our postindustrialist world and creatively provide the type of therapeutic message that resonates in our self-indulgent culture. These trendsetters strive to integrate their members into every facet of secular society and impact their cities with a new style of leadership. Several prominent examples are worth noting.

A. R. Bernard applies the same business acumen that made him a successful banker three decades ago to his responsibilities as pastor of the Christian Cultural Center, the largest African American congregation in New York City. Running his church like a corporation, Bernard receives great media attention for his high-tech ministry and effective work with urban revitalization. Politicians, entertainers, senior executives, athletes, activists, and New York socialites flood the pews every Sunday to hear Bernard expound personal life skills mixed with biblical consciousness. The church's music and worship experience resembles a cool, laid-back jazz concert, and the Sunday sermon is reminiscent of a corporate lecture. After services, members can purchase books and CDs from the large bookstore or socialize and network in the church's café and restaurant. Christian Cultural Center provides many services, including literacy training, substance abuse help, and food pantry programs. Moreover, Bernard presents his leadership philosophies on Ivy League campuses and to the boards of Fortune 500 companies.

Cynthia Hale pastors Ray of Hope Christian Church in Decatur, Georgia, one of the largest churches in her Disciples of Christ denomination. Whether it is through the arts with imaginative programs like "Dance Jubilee," or practical ministries like the marriage counseling group session "Couples Holy Ghost Harambee," Hale has a bold mission to transform her city by "going after the lost at any cost." In an interview, she described her ministry's aim this way:

> If you came to Ray of Hope today, you would know what Ray of Hope is all about because it's everywhere. If you ask any member what's the vision of your church, he would tell you that it's transforming the world. That's our brand, to be a city of hope where persons will impact and transform this present world into the kingdom of God.

Ray of Hope has an athletic ministry that encourages thousands of community residents to participate in various sports and cheerleading, as well as its artistic expression program, which endeavors to instill in members a passion for the various art forms. For her efforts in Atlanta and Decatur, Hale has received various awards and garnered great media attention.

Otis Lockett pastors Evangel Fellowship, a megachurch in Greensboro, North Carolina, which conducts classes on an assortment of topics by trained business professionals. Lockett combines practical teachings with the spiritual vibrancy of Pentecostalism, as he described in an interview:

> I saw the spiritual part of Pentecostalism, you know, the embracing of the Holy Spirit, the gifts of the Spirit, the laying on of hands, the emotionalism that accompanies worship, and I really felt a great need to teach people. One of the basic premises of my life is if it's not practical then it's not spiritual and so I've always tried to do things that were practical, things that were relevant. That's how we've come around to do classes on business ethics, how to start a business, how to get the promotions, classes on marriage; I'm a very need-conscious person.

Like Bernard in New York City, Lockett runs his church using business principles and organizational savvy adapted from large corporations.

Kirbyjon Caldwell accepted the senior pastorate at Windsor Village in Houston, Texas, in 1982 when the church had fewer than thirty members.

Under his leadership Windsor Village morphed into the largest United Methodist Church in the country. The church makes its presence known in Houston with nine separate organizations that constitute the Power Connection. A central part of the Power Connection is the Pyramid Community Development Corporation, home to a multiuse complex, bank, community college, office suites, pharmacy, and conference center. Caldwell and Windsor Village also run several nonprofit organizations and hold empowerment seminars and power lunches attended by business executives of large corporations. Caldwell's influence extends to other places as well. He co-pastored a multiracial church service, held at Minute Maid Park where the Houston Astros play, during Easter 2006 with Ed Young of Houston's Second Baptist Church, for example, and at George W. Bush's request, prayed at inaugural ceremonies in 2001 and 2005. Caldwell's appeal comes from what he terms an "entrepreneurial faith," a worldly-wise devotion to God and fully funded social gospel that seeks ways to engage many facets of American culture, not just participate in praise and worship inside a church building on Sunday. Part of Caldwell's faith package is what he calls "Holistic Salvation," a message that focuses on human possibility and potential (Caldwell 1999; Caldwell and Kallestad 2004).

To a greater extent than ever before, black churches have the skill, flexibility, and resources to adapt to changing conditions. Many utilize extensive mailing lists, display announcements, and dramatizations on large video screens, enhance their facilities with wireless technology, use video infomercials to post announcements, offer lively worship services with contemporary gospel music, operate large Christian bookstores, and run live webcasts and sophisticated websites that allow members to post prayers and donate money. With large memberships, they have the professional infrastructure to launch new business ventures, run hundreds of programs and ministries, and splurge on state-of-the-art equipment.

Not everyone rolls out the red carpet for the new black church. Many prominent leaders criticize megachurches for failing to challenge the structural forces that impede black progress, or for trading in Martin Luther King's progressive activism for a conservative message. In 2006, civil rights activists, including Jesse Jackson and Al Sharpton, met with a hundred other leading black pastors in Dallas for the Samuel Proctor Conference to discuss how prosperity preaching and conservative politics threaten the integrity of the black church's prophetic role in America. The Samuel Proctor Conference convened in New Orleans the following year, drawing even more participants. Some, like Frederick Haynes III, pastor

Former UN ambassador Andrew Young, right, and Rev. T. D. Jakes listen
during the Coretta Scott King funeral ceremony at the New Birth
Missionary Baptist Church in Lithonia, Georgia, February 7, 2006.
Photo courtesy of Associated Press.

of the Friendship West Baptist Church in South Dallas and one of the organizers of the conference, argue that American capitalism contaminates
preaching in the new black church. Notwithstanding such resistance, journalists and religion scholars take note that we are at the dawn of a new
age of African American spirituality, and most agree that the face of this
culture-affirming, industrious new black church is Thomas Dexter Jakes.

T. D. Jakes resembles Booker T. Washington, the most powerful African American leader at the turn of the twentieth century. Both Washington and Jakes transcended humble beginnings, advocated pragmatic approaches to self-actualization, and received criticism from their progressive black contemporaries for failing to fight racism. Both Washington
and Jakes concluded that blacks suffered from the psychological maladies
of oppression, and both sought to help them think in different ways. Most
important, both contributed to the reimagination of what it means to be
black and American: Washington was a postslavery symbol of black excellence; Jakes is a post–civil rights archetype for black innovation.

Jakes is Booker T. Washington reinvented for the twenty-first century. Whereas Washington was primarily an educator, central to Jakes's

multidimensional leadership is his role as pastor of the Potter's House, a 28,000-member church in South Dallas, where he continues to emphasize personal achievement. Detractors often accuse Jakes of ignoring the black church's rich activist legacy. Jakes responded to this allegation in an interview on the Black Entertainment Television show *Meet the Faith* in 2006: "Our issues are evolving, our problems are evolving, and our leadership is evolving. The idea that we are monolithic is antiquated. We are a very diverse community and the idea that we just have one type of problem is antiquated. We have a plethora of problems and we need different types of leadership." Jakes argues that his ministries provide African Americans with the life skills, emotional health, and psychological well-being to be successful. In a sermon series titled "Liberation," Jakes called for a renewing of the mind to conquer the victim mentality that precludes many African Americans from reaching their potential.

Observers of his ministry often classify Jakes alongside prosperity preachers, a popular and controversial group of evangelicals that teaches it is God's desire for all believers to be wealthy. This distinction is not without merit because many of Jakes's earlier sermons and writings embody elements of prosperity discourse. More recently, however, Jakes has been critical of the excesses of prosperity theology. For example, in his recent best seller *Reposition Yourself: Living Life without Limits*, Jakes argues that the term "prosperity" has been hijacked by certain extremists in the faith-based community who teach that faith is only a matter of dollars and cents. In the same book Jakes reproaches prosperity preachers for quoting scriptures that promise great wealth while failing to emphasize "the importance of a practical, pragmatic plan of faith-with-works ethic, education and economic empowerment" (Jakes 2007: 7). Similarly, in a 2006 sermon titled "The Leveling Place," Jakes subtly attacked the belief that Christians with faith should live in financial abundance and argued that "sometimes it takes more faith to be a welfare mother and feed five kids working at Wendy's than it does to live in a mansion where all of your bills are paid." Further in the sermon, Jakes classified this welfare mother's predicament as a temporary situation, which divine intervention could rectify, thus signaling that, like prosperity theology, his brand of personal empowerment promotes the bourgeois conservatism of the new black church. For Jakes, everyone has access to the American dream because faith in Christ levels the playing field and transforms all situations.

The Potter's House's ministries reflect Jakes's conservative vision for black excellence. The church runs an economic development corporation

Mychal Bell, one of the Jena Six, center, listens to activist Rev. Al Sharpton and Bishop Jakes talk at his father's home in Jena, Louisiana, September 27, 2007. Photo courtesy of Associated Press.

that spawns businesses and teaches members accounting and sound business ethics, as well as providing intensive mentoring and training programs for youth, a continuing-education program offering classes on leadership and networking, along with religious education classes and life-skills programs via satellite for 300 prisons nationwide. The Potter's House has hundreds of full-time employees and volunteers to run more than sixty ministries and consequently can meet needs and solve problems that smaller churches lack the infrastructure to confront. After Hurricane Katrina, for instance, the church quickly consigned 2,000 displaced New Orleans residents into homes by utilizing its television equipment and phone centers.

In addition to these ministries, T. D. Jakes Enterprises, the for-profit arm of Jakes's multimedia empire, recently launched the Black Economic Success Training (BEST) group. Jakes assembled a dream team of black superstars, including basketball legend Magic Johnson and intellectual Cornel West to help him lead public mentoring sessions in large arenas across the nation. Jakes believes that his BEST seminars provide the type of liberationist activities African Americans need in the twenty-first century. In an interview, David Yeazell, one of Jakes's former staff members, hailed him as the new voice for African Americans:

Just from observation you've got your Jesse Jackson and others who are from another generation, and the message that they proclaim is a message from another generation, and this generation is listening more to someone like Bishop Jakes because he's much more where people are at, and the last generation's civil rights message does not resonate with this generation in the same way that it used to; the issues are different.

But more than a symbol of the new black church, Jakes is a signpost for postdenominational Protestant America in general. As the pastor of one of the largest churches in the country, conference organizer who draws tens of thousands to his events, television preacher, author of a dozen best sellers, and movie executive who recently signed with Sony Movies to produce nine more films, Jakes redefines evangelical spiritual leadership. His broad-ranging success suggests a kind of realignment in the religious economy where independent churches that adjust their message and methods experience phenomenal growth. Denominational loyalty declines as more Americans explore forms of spirituality they find appealing rather than accepting familial traditions or affiliations (McRoberts 2003; Wuthnow 1988, 2005). Like other evangelical innovators such as Rick Warren, Joel Osteen, and Paula White, Jakes draws many followers by producing live worship experiences, therapeutic and transformative sermons, and spiritual commodities that are more in tune with contemporary sensibilities.

Jakes's vast appeal led *Time* magazine to distinguish him as "America's preacher," suggesting that he may be the next Billy Graham. Graham and Jakes have traveled similar paths. Both made earnest commitments to full-time ministry as teenagers, and both were salesmen before they were preachers. Both had careers that were languishing in obscurity until strategic networking, fortuitous events, and media exposure made them celebrities. Both head ministries with annual budgets in the tens of millions, both are media masters who utilized the technological advances in their era to reach millions, and both received praise from U.S. presidents. President George W. Bush called on Graham to deliver the address for the National Day of Prayer after the terrorist attacks of September 11; the same president called on Jakes to keynote the commemorative ceremony after the next national tragedy, Hurricane Katrina. Though Jakes and Graham share many similarities, there are meaningful divergences.

Jakes appropriates contemporary popular culture in ways that Graham has not. Unlike Jakes, Graham never wrote a best-selling novel or paperbacks on weight loss and financial prosperity and never produced plays and music CDs. Graham produced low-tech movies with an explicit Christian message and agenda; Jakes's first movie, *Woman Thou Art Loosed*, had critically acclaimed actors and ambiguous spiritual undertones for a secular audience. Unlike Graham, Jakes draws from pop culture and adjusts his message to contemporary trends in society. Graham's strong suit is preaching a simple yet compelling message of salvation, while Jakes's forte addresses complex concerns such as sexual abuse and addictive relationships with a blend of scripture, psychology, and folk wisdom. The men are prototypes of evangelical innovation for different eras: Graham for a modern, Cold War period, Jakes for a postmodern, sight-and-sound generation.

Jakes is not postmodern like the late French theorist Jacques Derrida, who basked in relativity, or like the entertainer Madonna, who deconstructs gender norms with risqué displays of sexuality. But Jakes does share many postmodern traits that are commensurate with contemporary trends in American culture. He is conversant with a wide range of elements from contemporary and secular culture, drenches the marketplace with a deluge of images and products, and offers restorative solutions blending the best of psychology and old-fashioned wisdom. Jakes muddles long-established boundaries between the secular and sacred, accentuates personal experience over doctrinal constraints, and supports denominational independence over church hierarchy. Hence, like holy mavericks Brian McLaren and Joel Osteen, Jakes is self-empowering, pluralistic, high-tech, and multidimensional, a model of the new postmodern evangelical preacher.

The triumphs and struggles of his early childhood experiences birthed Jakes's creative ministry. He grew up on Vandalia Hill, a working-class community in Charleston, West Virginia, situated atop a mountain that overlooks the city. Vandalia was a homey kind of town where people addressed each other with playful nicknames. Although Vandalia was racially mixed, blacks and whites lived in separate sections, and Jakes lived in the heart of the black section. Jakes had enterprising parents, Ernest Sr. and Odith, who ran side businesses to help make ends meet. Even as an eight-year-old, Jakes emulated his parents' industriousness, selling vegetables from his mother's garden. Whether he cut the grass for his neighbor Minerva Cole, rose early every morning to deliver newspapers, or sold Avon cosmetics and Amway products throughout high school, Jakes showed early flashes of the doggedness that would later help him become a business mogul.

Jakes's childhood experiences and early years in ministry planted the seeds of the characteristics that would later sprout to distinguish him. His broad appeal and flexible ministry have roots that go back to Vandalia's racially mixed environment and the spiritual freedom in the Jakes household. As a young teenager, watching his father slowly die from renal failure helped bring his compassion for people in pain to fruition. Concomitantly, Jakes left the black Baptist tradition of his youth that emphasized God's grace and human frailty for a Pentecostal experience where Christians thrive in power and holiness; part of his future success would be to utilize both traditions of spiritual fervor and human frailty. The Pentecostal movement introduced new theological presuppositions about the Holy Spirit's role in the life of the believer, as well as strict moral codes and an emphasis on eschewing worldly pleasures. Jakes's teenage conflicts in a pious Pentecostal church helped shape a highly spiritual yet profoundly human message that reverberates with people turned off by traditional religion.

Jakes answered what he perceived as God's call to preach at age seventeen, and his early ministry training took place in an association of churches called Greater Emanuel International Fellowship, an obscure network of small Pentecostal churches composed of relatively unknown preachers. Accordingly, during his early twenties, Jakes spent many years preaching to small churches in coal-mining towns throughout West Virginia and working at a chemical plant. Jakes founded his first church, a storefront in Montgomery, West Virginia, with only ten members, in 1979; shortly after, he met Serita, who would become his wife two years later. The chemical plant closed down in 1982, putting Jakes and his new family in financial distress. Jakes would later relocate his growing church two times while working side jobs and suffering dramatic bouts of poverty before receiving his big break in 1993.

New networks and structural changes prepared the ground for Jakes's ingenuity to flourish. Though his persistence was vital during the years of struggle that preceded his big break, Jakes benefited from a "faith industry" of spiritual power brokers in the Charismatic or neo-Pentecostal world. Neo-Pentecostals' emphasis on the power of the Holy Spirit for healing, prophetic utterances, vibrant worship and music, and prosperity distinguishes many of them from other evangelical Protestants. By the 1980s, Oral Roberts, Jimmy Swaggart, and various other neo-Pentecostal preachers developed international ministries by broadcasting their church services on television. Carlton Pearson, a popular

Democratic presidential candidate Al Gore, right, laughs with Jakes, left, and his
wife, Serita Jakes, during the dedication service for the Potter's House on
October 22, 2000. Photo courtesy of Associated Press.

preacher and singer, provided African American preachers a platform
for national exposure through his annual AZUSA conferences held in
Tulsa, Oklahoma. AZUSA attracted participants from various denominations and displayed the high-tech commercialism that would characterize Jakes's future ministry and entrepreneurial endeavors. In 1992
Jakes visited AZUSA for the first time as an unknown country preacher;
through fortuitous events, he returned a year later as a keynote speaker.
Jakes's masterpiece sermon at AZUSA 93 launched him like a missile.
Pastors from all over the country invited him to preach at their large
churches, and Paul Crouch, the president of Trinity Broadcasting Network (TBN), contacted Jakes about broadcasting his sermons on television. Jakes's dramatic rise represents a new era in which preachers can
become celebrities virtually overnight through television exposure rather
than denominational positioning.

Though key events introduced Jakes to the world in the early 1990s,
shrewd marketing and continued exposure on national television made
him a superstar. Jakes was a quick study after receiving his big break in
1993, swiftly transforming his image from that of a poor coal-mining

preacher to a flashy high-tech spiritual leader. Shortly after his rise in fame and finances, a media blitz of negative publicity concerning Jakes's new opulent lifestyle drove him out of West Virginia to his current location in Dallas. Jakes's conferences quickly began to draw tens of thousands of participants nationwide as he traversed the preaching/lecturing circuit and expanded his influence among politicians and celebrities. Jakes dramatically increased his market share through creative endeavors, including music CDs, theatrical productions, a best-selling novel, and his own line of Hallmark cards, while traveling the country as a motivational speaker. By 2006, Jakes led a 28,000-member church, appearing before millions four times a week on television, drawing more than 100,000 people to his Mega Fest conferences, writing several best-selling books, and producing movies, all while enjoying a first-class lifestyle.

Jakes's rags-to-riches story is a combustible mixture of talent, timing, and tenacity. Armed with the courage and creativity to venture outside the box of traditional Protestantism, Jakes is the small-town preacher who transcended obscurity to achieve a special level of celebrity. Jakes's ability to provide spiritual commodities that resonate with the pluralistic postmodern tastes of his American listeners distinguishes his thriving ministry. Jakes secures a loyal following by preaching sermons that answer many of life's questions, writing books and plays that tackle many of life's problems, and producing songs that soothe many of life's pains. He alternates between his roles as motivational speaker, psychologist, dietitian, financial consultant, entertainer, father figure, and spiritual leader to address many needs.

Entertainers who seize the attention of large crowds understand the importance of performance art. Rap star L.L. Cool J licks his lips and moves his body to push the emotional buttons of thousands of people at his concerts, and the R & B diva Mya knows just the right movements to enthrall her fans. Similarly, Jakes mesmerizes his audiences through the performance art of preaching. "I have never seen Bishop Jakes look down at his notes once," claimed a member of the Potter's House. Jakes raises and lowers his voice, varies his tempo, smiles, dances, or slowly wipes the sweat from his forehead in a manner that creates drama and excitement. Jakes is a master storyteller, creating the feeling that he speaks directly to each person in his audience, rushing back and forth across the stage with verve and passion. Some may call this God's anointing, others may acknowledge it as the preacher's craft; but however one frames it, Jakes radiates the kind of energy that leaves audiences spellbound.

Just as George Whitefield's theatrics left hearers awestruck, Jakes captivates contemporary audiences with poignant dramatizations and visual demonstrations to depict key points in his sermons. For example, during a sermon series on racism, Jakes created a powerful effect by placing people onstage dressed up in chains as antebellum slaves. Similarly, during one of his Manpower conferences, he had Nautilus weight-lifting equipment placed strategically onstage with a man working out to illustrate spiritual growth and development. Another creative tactic Jakes often employs during sermons is to speak in the place of those hurting and longing for relief. At Woman Thou Art Loosed 1999, Jakes offered such a soliloquy with music playing softly in the background to increase its dramatic effect:

> Oh, will you love me. I have some issues. Love me, hold me, if it's just for the night, hold me. If I can't have a man I'll borrow one. If I can't get a man I'll get a woman. I've just got some issues. I was broken when I was a child and I've got some issues. And anybody that will show me some attention, I'll do anything, just hold me. You don't have to love me just act like you love me. Just whisper in my ear—I know you're a liar but just tell me that you love me. Hold me for a little while because I'm leaking issues. Buy something every now and then, make me feel special, just tell me you're going to leave her, you don't have to leave her just tell me that you're thinking about leaving her. Tell me you'd leave her if you could. Tell me that you love me.

As Jakes continued to speak as the characteristic hurting woman, women openly wept in the Georgia Dome, an expression indicating he had struck a chord.

Another aspect of Jakes's appeal involves his use of sensuality. For example, at Woman Thou Art Loosed 2002, Jakes urged his listeners not to obscure biblical references to sensuality:

> The Song of Solomon has been spiritualized often before we take it literally. I think we do an injustice to the text when we spiritualize it before we take it literally—it is a book about love, about intimacy. It sounds sensual because it is, it simply is. It sounds sexual because it is, and if you would take your religious glasses off for a moment and read the Song of Solomon it would make you blush.

Jakes offers tantalizing discussions on love and sensuality that rival Harlequin romance novels. An example is this exhortation in one of his early books for husbands to rekindle the fire in their marriages:

> Have you touched your wife and fondled her, have you toyed with her and played with her, while failing to know her? . . . Roll up your sleeves and reclaim your creativity. Recall the soft songs, light those fragrant candles, take those long walks of longing, and once again murmur passionate words in your mate's ear. (Jakes 1995: 125–26)

Jakes knows that sex sells even in God's kingdom. His CD *Sacred Love Songs*, a compilation of romantic songs with smooth and sexy rhythm tracks for Christian couples, sells tremendously well. Jakes encourages Christians to transfer romantic energy to their worship experience, and he conveys a personal God who desires a passionate love affair with humans. Because many preachers eschew sexual talk, Jakes profits from an untapped market of Christians hungry to explore and appraise sexual energy in a godly context.

Part of Jakes's postmodern appeal involves his penchant for self-reinvention. For example, after years of being chastised for preaching an individualistic gospel, Jakes is beginning to address structural impediments to social problems. In the aforementioned book *Reposition Yourself*, Jakes articulates how structural factors exacerbate the incredible odds most inner-city kids must overcome to be successful, while earlier books tended to focus only on cultural impediments to higher achievement. In recent sermons, writings, and press releases, Jakes links social injustice to poverty and inequality, acknowledges overt and covert racism, and chastises the government for its slow response in helping victims of Hurricanes Katrina and Rita. The fact that Jakes now sprinkles his message of personal empowerment with new liberationist themes displays a more balanced gospel, as well as a pragmatic willingness to adjust his methods and message.

By learning how to exploit new applications from earlier successes, Jakes is versatile enough to extend his market share. A telling example involves MegaFest, his intriguing three-day family vacation event that draws more than a hundred thousand people from different denominations and perspectives to pray and play together. MegaFest includes intense worship services, educational forums, business seminars, and entertainment such as fashion shows and music concerts. In the summer of 2006, Jakes announced his decision to discontinue MegaFest indefinitely. Jakes brought the conference to South Africa and rebranded the event as MegaFest International, drawing people worldwide. The multidimensional component of this event reflects Jakes's ability to blur traditional lines of distinction between the secular and the spiritual.

Similarly, Jakes reinvented a struggling genre by producing black theatrical productions known as gospel plays. In the past, theater critics denounced gospel plays as lowbrow "Chitlin Circuit" shows that lacked depth and reinforced black stereotypes. However, Jakes's gospel plays feature complex characters who wrestle with the existential struggles addressed in his sermons and books. Like African American playwright Tyler Perry, Jakes made millions of dollars for himself by improving a genre that combines complex emotional struggles with subtle Christian themes. Another example involves Jakes's strategic ventures in the music industry. In the spring of 2007 Jakes signed a distribution and marketing deal with a division of Warner Music, an industry powerhouse with unlimited resources. As a result of this new arrangement with Warner Music, Jakes became a major power broker in the gospel music industry.

Jakes has dexterity with touchstones from American culture. He brashly incorporates themes from Hollywood, MTV, or the latest hip-hop video and borrows elements from a number of traditions in interesting and novel ways. In one of his sermons, for instance, Jakes recited a long scripture passage from memory and a few minutes later shouted, "Y'all gonna make me lose my mind, up in here, up in here," a playful reference to the hook of a hit song by rapper DMX. His sermons and books include sprinklings of the individualism of Booker T. Washington, the pop psychology of Dr. Phil and Oprah Winfrey, the self-help expertise of Anthony Robbins and Deepak Chopra, and more recently the prophetic analysis of Cornel West to form a profoundly American and yet highly spiritual message and ministry. In his novel *Cover Girls*, Jakes quotes everyone from writer John Steinbeck to pop singer Mary J. Blige. He demonstrates a broad knowledge of world affairs and preaches like a contemporary Renaissance man.

Another important aspect of Jakes's versatility involves his desire to blur the traditional lines of distinction concerning race. "When I looked all around Reliant Stadium I saw thousands of black, white, Asian, and Hispanic women," recalled Pat Murphy after attending Woman Thou Art Loosed 2003 in Houston. Although Jakes's style and magnetism embody a preaching aesthetic nurtured in the black church, his message is racially

SMITH   SANDERS

Dallas Cowboys players Emmitt Smith, center of left photo, and Deion Sanders, center in right photo, are baptized by Rev. T. D. Jakes, shown on the right in each image, during a ceremony at the Potter's House Church in Dallas, October 19, 1997. Two other Cowboys players, Omar Stoutmire and George Hegamin, were also baptized at the church with Smith and Sanders. Photo courtesy of Associated Press.

neutral. Jakes shows versatility by preaching in diverse contexts, including keynoting rallies for Promise Keepers in the mid-1990s and various other platforms outside the context of the black church. In his last years in West Virginia, Jakes's church peaked with 35 percent white membership, and the Potter's House, though predominantly black, has a small but visible interracial, multiethnic presence. Jakes often makes public statements urging Christians to get out of their racial comfort zones, and his conferences and video sales reflect his growing interracial following.

Another feature behind Jakes's mass appeal involves an ability to address human concerns. "He's not like any other minister that I know because he deals so much with psychology and inner healing," declares John Jacobs, who twice attended Jakes's Manpower conference and purchases his sermon videos. As a frequent guest on television's popular *Dr. Phil Show*, Jakes functions as a life coach combining what he perceives as godly wisdom with insight on the human condition. Whether he delineates the struggles of a single mother raising her family or addresses the frustrations of middle-aged men, Jakes maneuvers a mixture of psychology and scripture to diagnose human crises.

"Bishop Jakes preaches his own struggles and his message is very touchable," asserts George Wilson, a frequent attendee at Manpower. Jakes addresses the emotional disabilities and imperfections that preachers often gloss over, while also emphasizing God's ability to heal and change situations. His childhood struggles with fear and low self-esteem, his father's slow and agonizing death, combined with his toil in abject poverty during early years in ministry generated a soft spot for people who experience deep pain and emotional turmoil. He goes beyond identifying pain to form a teleological appropriation of it, or more simply put, he imputes God's greater purpose to one's hurts and struggles. Jakes argues that pain is a good sign that God is about to generate greatness in a person's life: "If you have been in pain, maybe it is because the baby is coming. The baby is the destiny that God is birthing in your life, and the pain is a sure indication that you are getting close to your delivery. There is no time to faint now, dear lady. Grab the sides of the bed and push!" (Jakes 1998: 75–76). Unlike philosophers Arthur Schopenhauer and Jean-Paul Sartre, who bewailed the absurdity and random afflictions of human suffering, Jakes assures his audience that God has a purpose for all believers and chooses to use pain and struggle to prepare them. Jakes teaches that suffering should not dehumanize and that Christians should link their current pain with God's anointing on their lives.

Along with his appropriation of pain, much like holy maverick Joel Osteen, Jakes creates teleological expectation, or the belief that God's future blessing awaits faithful believers. Jakes tells his listeners that nothing can hold them from a blessed future if they make up their minds and go forward. At Manpower 2002, Jakes urged his male audience to act like men on a specific mission from God:

> Life is asking you a question: What did you come down here to do? Why are you on the planet? You cannot spend the next ten, twenty, thirty years joyriding through life trying to see what happens; looking for the next thrill, the next game, the next opportunity. You have to identify yourself as being a man on a mission. That means, "I'm not a mistake. I'm not an

accident. I'm not just the end result of a man and woman that got together and copulated their way into my existence. I'm not something that
just wandered onto the stage of life"—God has a plan for your existence.

Akin to the way Oral Roberts utilized his popular saying, "Something
good is going to happen to you," Jakes has become famous for his "Get ready,
get ready, get ready" catchphrase that motivates his audience to prepare for
a future with limitless possibilities. Jakes appeals to multitudes of desperate
people longing for a glimmer of hope and offers solace for people in pain.

Jakes has made peace with complexity. He has a penchant for interweav-
ing conflicting theological traditions: one that emphasizes free will and
human agency, and another that focuses on God's control over all events.
On the one hand, Jakes's message of agency exhorts his followers to develop life plans and take control over their destiny. In his best seller *Maximize the Moment*, Jakes places the onus on his readers to take advantage of
every opportunity and to fulfill their potential by practicing good habits
and learning important principles. On the other hand, Jakes often places
success out of the believer's control and into God's hands as part of an in-
controvertible plan and purpose. In his sermon "Potholes on the Road to
Destiny," Jakes argues that God has a blueprint and destiny for everyone;
that "God has from the beginning planned my ending." Such an intriguing
dance between conflicting themes of God's sovereignty and human agency
is useful because Jakes reassures his followers that God orders their steps,
while at the same time urges them to aggressively pursue success.

"I love my pastor because he lets the people know, 'I'm Bishop Jakes
but I go through things too.' He's just all about being real," claims a young
adult female attendee of his church. Another facet of Jakes's message involves his vision of eradicating hypocrisy from the church. Jakes argues
that for too long the church has neglected the human side of Christianity,
that is, vulnerability and imperfection: "When we hide, we turn phony.
We act out a charade. We put on a "face" and participate in our own mas-
querade. Only two things are worse than being phony with other people:
being phony with yourself, and being phony with God" (Jakes 1997: 81).
A recurring theme in many of Jakes's sermons and books is his assertion
that the church should be a safe haven where Christians can be honest
and transparent. Jakes's movie *Woman Thou Art Loosed* dramatized the
common, and yet tragic, practice of covering up serious issues of sexual
abuse with facades of spirituality. Jakes strongly asserts that the church is
guilty of focusing too much on Christian ideals rather than addressing

the realities of contemporary times. Like Paula White's, Jakes's iconoclastic ministry strikes a chord with thousands of Christians alienated by religious hypocrisy or frustrated by the pressure to put on holy masks.

Although some typecast Jakes as a preacher for women, he is quite popular among men as well. "No one in the activist community has been nearly as successful getting men to deal with inner wounds and imperfection as Jakes," claimed Hitaji Aziz, a popular radio personality and activist, in an interview. Aziz recalled one of Jakes's meetings in which hundreds of men came to the altar crying and seeking healing. Religion scholar Rodney Sadler also commented in an interview on Jakes's ability to draw men together:

> I attended one of his conferences a few years back just to see what was going on and was very impressed by the fact that he had gotten black men from across the country to come together and love each other. I spent a good time in Washington, D.C., and I know how African American men usually related in that city but for the time period of Jake's Manpower Conference meetings men were walking around the streets hugging each other where they usually grit on each other so it was a remarkable transformation and I have to give him kudos for being able to make us more self-aware and appreciate ourselves as being made in God's image.

Jakes's best seller *Hemotions: Even Strong Men Struggle* encourages men to discard macho stereotypes, understand their emotions, and control their struggles with power, money, and sex.

Jakes is a realist and a pragmatist. He preaches to those individuals who find themselves in their second or third marriage because he knows that "happily ever after" is found in children's storybooks, not in many homes. He convinces his listeners that they may be broken and wounded, they may be raising their children alone, they may be backed in a corner, but their lives are still meaningful and hopeful. His books provide practical advice concerning the daily vicissitudes of life, including how to work in a hostile environment (Jakes 2005). His compassion for the underdog motivates his national prison ministry, which broadcasts his conferences and church services through interactive satellites to thousands in prisons nationwide. Jakes often prescribes hope for people who experienced sexual and emotional abuse, drug addiction, poverty, and little education. He emphasizes that God gives second chances and new beginnings and that human weaknesses often fertilize God's greatness.

Bishop T. D. Jakes preaches to a crowd gathered at the Georgia Dome in Atlanta
for his four-day MegaFest, June 23, 2004. Jakes drew as many as 200,000 people
to a series of events and concerts at three downtown Atlanta venues.
Photo courtesy of Associated Press.

Jakes identifies with people who are at their lowest moment by ex-
tracting from his personal experience. He frequently alludes to the rough
times of his early years in ministry when he had to dig ditches to feed
his family, and when his wife and kids had to share a hot dog and can of
beans for dinner. Jakes gives hope by conveying that God is ever present,
ready to do new things in people's lives, and that their current struggle is
a platform for God's power. By creating an atmosphere where all people
can feel relevant in God's kingdom, Jakes crafts an appealing message for
people previously neglected in spiritual institutions.

Jakes is the prototype of the new evangelical entrepreneur who generates millions each year through mass-marketing spiritual gifts. A proud proponent of capitalism, he believes his talent and spiritual insights are fair game for commercialization. At any one of his conferences or MegaFest events one sees an army of staff members selling everything from T-shirts to yo-yos, as well as corporate sponsor logos at every juncture. Jakes and many popular pastors are spiritual descendants of frontier preachers, religious innovators in their own right who spoke to the needs and tastes of their times. America's fondness for frontier expansion led to the demise of Puritan asceticism and the rise of an evangelical spirituality that embodies barefaced materialism, idealism, and a strong sense of industry. Hence it is not surprising that innovators like Jakes offer a style of Christianity in line with the principles and values of our free-market society and utilize technology and commercial networks to build large spiritual machines.

Jakes's amazing rise and success are partially attributable to his affinity with today's age of media hype. Jakes quickly learned how to exploit commercial networks and inundate Christians with spiritual images on television, radio broadcasts, the Internet, and Christian magazines to generate his buzz. Like movie stars and athletes, Jakes is the product of a technological age of mass communications that turns celebrities into valuable commodities.

But hype and media exposure were not enough to secure his market share. Jakes adjusted his message and ministry to address the needs and cultural tastes of many Americans. His appeal comes from a message peppered with pop culture and American idealism, and from compassionately addressing problems ignored by other preachers such as sexual abuse, addiction, and abandonment. Whether he uses psychological theories or folk wisdom, Jakes appropriates a broad range of cultural tools at his disposal to fulfill the apostle Paul's mantra of being all things to all men and women. Jakes fights what he perceives as hypocrisy in the church and motivates Christians to be open and honest about their frailties; his message of hope for the underdog resonates with an untapped market of people abandoned by pretentious Protestant churches. Jakes blends a spiritual mission with a profoundly American message of transformation to provide supernatural hope to despondent hearts. His cultural repertoire for solving practical life problems concerning finances, weight loss, self-esteem, and other issues strikes chords with many contemporary Americans. Jakes is America's preacher because he speaks to his generation.

Although Jakes is an international celebrity, his origins, preaching style, and large following all come from the black church, and his message of economic empowerment is carefully calibrated to help African Americans adjust to a competitive postindustrialist world. Hence Jakes is a product of the black church and looms so high by standing on shoulders of powerful African American innovators before him. What jazz great Louis Armstrong accomplished for improvisational music, Jakes does for evangelical ministry by attending to the needs of a new generation and creating cadences that connect with today's audiences. Jakes is a symbol of a new black church that energizes audiences with ecstatic worship, lively music, therapeutic preaching, and hope for economic prosperity. The genius of Jakes and the new black church is an ability to use twenty-first-century style and sophistication to win twenty-first-century souls, and the creativity to blur denominational lines with multidimensional ministries.

Jakes wins unprecedented popularity by offering a relevant message to contemporary Americans. He is business-minded, culture-affirming, and peculiarly American; he has a keen understanding of pop culture, an inexorable drive to produce spiritual commodities for mass consumption, and an ability to offer a vibrant otherworldly worship experience with a this-worldly message and ministry. Jakes keeps an ear to the human condition, and the success of his plays, movie, and family vacation events demonstrates how he creatively adapts to the emerging cultural landscape. His message transcends denominational lines, and his vast appeal is international. Borrowing from Miles Davis's improvisational formulation, we can say that what distinguishes Jakes from other religious suppliers is an ability to play great "jazz."

4

A New Kind of Christian
Brian McLaren and the Emerging Church

The fact is, whatever a new kind of Christian will be, no one is one yet. At this point, we're more like caterpillars cocooning than butterflies in flight. But every transformation has to start somewhere. The sooner the better.

—Brian McLaren

In the late 1940s, Thomas Kuhn, an energetic graduate student in theoretical physics, taught an experimental undergraduate course on the history of science. While preparing for the course, Kuhn studied long-standing scientific theories that newer discoveries later disconfirmed and noticed that many of the leading scientists did not accept the new discoveries but rather feverishly defended the older theories. This research sparked his groundbreaking work, *The Structure of Scientific Revolutions* (1962), in which he demonstrates that scientific advancement does not come from the gradual accumulation of new facts as commonly taught but from political struggles in which new paradigms replaced older ones. Hence Kuhn turned the scientific establishment on its head by suggesting that sociological and political factors influence the kinds of questions scientists pursue and the experiments they conduct.

Kuhn's influential book marked a mid-twentieth-century cultural turn that challenged Enlightenment assumptions concerning the objectivity of reason and science. Scientists were no longer viewed as dispassionate observers of the universe but as subjective practitioners and dogmatic defenders of their theories. Meanwhile, existential philosophers like Jean-Paul Sartre celebrated human freedom to determine one's own fate, and not long after, critical theorists like Jean-François Lyotard and Jacques

Pastor Brian McLaren. Photo courtesy of Associated Press.

Derrida deconstructed grand narratives of modernity, arguing that if science cannot escape the charge of subjectivity, then one should explore how cultural forces that dominate certain epochs or eras influence other areas. Social scientists like Robert Merton and Bruno Latour followed Kuhn's lead and began to deconstruct the sociological underpinnings of scientific experimentation. Put another way, these scientists and philosophers crafted theoretical perspectives to show that human life does not occur in a vacuum; the situatedness of one's cultural context shapes not only what one experiences but also how one understands, interprets, and explains life experiences. Increasingly people began to question the institutional and cultural regimes of modernity, and a far-reaching pattern of changes in art, architecture, aesthetics, literature, science, law, entertainment, and other social spheres exemplified the emergence of a postmodern cultural turn (Lee 2005).

In this new world of uncertainty and complexity, specialists showed that all standards of evaluation are social constructions and therefore candidates for deconstruction. From a postmodern perspective, even a person's identity is not fixed but continuously emerging as she travels like a sojourner through a sea of transforming relationships (Gergen 1991). What is right or wrong, or good or bad, becomes less a matter of truth and more an issue of perspective. This new outlook generated profound new questions for all facets of experience, including faith and religion.

A postmodern perspective explores the various ways subjective interpretations shape religious doctrine and practice. This exploration troubles traditional evangelicals who proclaim the unshakable authority of the Bible and insist on the objectivity of their religious beliefs and practices. Identifying postmodernism as a pervasive threat to the reliability of biblical truth, prominent evangelical preachers like Josh McDowell and John McArthur and theologically conservative scholars like Millard Erickson and Douglas Groothuis offer tireless defenses of the objectivity of Christian truth and experience.

But in past three decades, curious Christian intellectuals, including theologians like Miroslav Volf, Stanly Grenz, and Leonard Sweet and missions scholars such as Leslie Newbigin, Lamin Sanneh, and David Bosch, began to explore what a postmodern perspective might offer for a more biblical faith and practice. Believing they were living on the verge of widespread cultural change, these thought leaders inspired new conversation among evangelicals concerning the intriguing possibilities that a postmodern cultural turn could bring to their faith. This conversation evolved into a spiritual revolution of church practitioners retooling Christianity for an emerging postmodern world. This new evangelical movement took many forms, and by the late 1990s one influential strand began to identify itself as the emerging church. The emerging church quickly gained popularity as a network of young evangelicals devoted to the tasks of exploring how new expressions of church might fit in a complex and pluralistic society.

Like anything postmodern, the emerging church is difficult to define. Some perceive it as a passing fad of Gen X Christians with goatees or soul patches, monastic chanting, homegrown music, and scented candles. Others see it as a bohemian network of house churches, societal misfits, and cosmopolitan metrosexual types. Detractors like Chuck Smith, the founder of Calvary Chapel in Southern California, and New Testament scholar D. A. Carson claim that the emerging church is nothing more than postmodernism masquerading as Christianity. Participants, however, view the emerging church as a nurturing friendship and generative conversation devoted to deconstructing Christian history, doctrine, attitudes, rituals, practices, and politics from the negative effects of modernity in order to construct a faith that addresses the existential needs of the emerging culture. Moreover, there is not one kind of emerging church. Different churches form in different locations, participants come from all walks of life, and pastors and church leaders address the particularities of each context. Emerging churches appeal to those with varied tastes and desires. Emerging church pastor Dan Kimball observes: "Instead of one emerging-church model, there are hundreds and thousand of models of emerging churches. Modernity may have taught us to look for a clean model to imitate. But in today's postmodern context, it's not that simple" (2003: 14).

Yet many offer definitions of the emerging church as a way to capture elements of the movement. Mark Driscoll, the pastor of a popular church in Seattle called Mars Hill, defined the movement this way: "The emerging church is a growing, loosely connected movement of primarily young pastors who are glad to see the end of modernity and are seeking to function as missionaries who bring the gospel of Jesus Christ to emerging and postmodern culture" (2006: 22). Eddie Gibbs and Ryan Bolger, authors of *Emerging Churches: Creating Community in Postmodern Cultures*, seminary professors, and practitioners in the movement, describe the emerging church as a collection of "missional communities arising from within postmodern culture and consisting of followers of Jesus who are seeking to be faithful to their place and time" (2005: 28). Emerging blogger and religious studies professor Scot McKnight imagines the movement as a lake, with four rivers flowing into it. Emerging churches, while all different, according to McKnight, converge to embrace the fluid pronouncements of postmodernism, engage deeply in a variety of spiritual practices, adopt a postevangelical posture critical of rigid conceptions of the place of the Christian gospel in culture, and develop a political consciousness devoted to social enactment of Jesus' message (McKnight 2007).

Walking a middle way between abstract philosophy and pastoral admonition, Drew University professor and emerging church thinker Leonard Sweet has his finger on the cultural pulse of today's religious seekers. In *Postmodern Pilgrims: First Century Passion for the 21st Century Church* (2000), Sweet advocates what he calls an "EPIC" approach to Christian life and practice in a postmodern cultural context, one that is "Experiential, Participatory, Image-driven, [and] Connected" (xxi). With a keen understanding of the tastes and preferences of today's postmodern religious consumers, Sweet contends that in order to have an acknowledged voice Christian churches must study and engage postmodern culture or risk atrophy or irrelevance.

Anthony Smith of Charlotte, North Carolina, is a codirector of what insiders call an Emergent cohort, a meeting of the minds to discuss elements in today's emerging postmodern culture and how these elements inform and challenge traditional religious faith. "One of the values of the emerging church is appreciating the church in all its forms," Smith points out, alluding to the fact that cohorts pop up everywhere, including Internet blogs and chat rooms, urban parking lots, coffee shops, and Ivy League campuses like Princeton University. Episcopalians, Catholics, Pentecostals, Southern Baptists, some with no church background, and others once disgruntled with Christianity participate in cohort conversations. Abstaining from dogmatic proclamations on doctrinal truth, cohort leaders create safe spaces for different opinions and discuss doctrine with an attitude of grace and humility.

The emerging church offers a radical image of the kingdom of God and an organic version of church that especially appeals to those who do not enjoy traditional churches or megachurches. Jennifer Ashley is happy there are like-minded twenty-something evangelicals who do not shy away from culture even as they live out their faith in far-reaching ways. She describes this multifaceted postmodern practice:

> These are churches in skate parks where people are getting on their boards and worshiping God. These are churches in teahouses and nightclubs. There are hip-hop churches where the pastor raps and break dances during the service. There are prayer rooms in pubs, contemplative services in art galleries. (Ashley 2005: xii)

Ashley and thousands of reflective practitioners from various denominations and cultural backgrounds passionately live out their faith according to a whole new organic version of church.

Doug Pagitt's maverick tendencies caused him to be "kicked out of my first church at age 17!" (Pagitt 2005: 67). Years later, his frustration with modern Christianity inspired him to write books and articles portraying the radical message of the kingdom of God. Pagitt also pastors an unconventional church in Minnesota called Solomon's Porch, where there are no suits, ties, and pews but rather comfy couches and people clothed in jeans and loose-fitting attire. Rather than giving monologues like most pastors, Pagitt relies on what he calls "progressional dialogues," open-ended conversations in which members offer their own interpretations of biblical truths intermittently with his sermons. At the beginning of each message,

Pagitt lights a spark, so to speak, and no one knows where the fire is going until it is all burned out:

> I have come to believe there's a kind of dehumanizing effect when week after week competent people aren't allowed to share their ideas and understanding; when week after week one person is set apart from the rest as the only one who is allowed to speak about God; when week after week people willingly, or by some sort of social or spiritual pressure, just sit and take it; when week after week they're taught that the only way to be good learners is to be better listeners. (2005: 76)

In true postmodern fashion, one moment Pagitt exhorts his congregants about "living in the rhythm of God," and ten minutes later a massage therapist discusses spiritual lessons she has learned from her job. Like many emerging church leaders, Pagitt takes a Socratic approach to spiritual leadership in which clergy and laity collaborate in order to learn from each other.

Karen Ward left her comfortable executive position in the Lutheran headquarters in Chicago to lead a new church plant in Seattle called Church of the Apostles, which caters to her new quirky, artistic surroundings. Combining Lutheran and Anglican liturgical traditions with contemporary multimedia and creative arts, Ward leads a postmodern worship experience. As she describes it:

> We are ancient and future. We Bach and rock. We chant and spin. We emo and alt. We write our own church music and incorporate mainstream music as well—everything from Rachel's to U2, Bjork to Moby, Dave Matthews to Coldplay. We have no need to "Christianize" music. God is sovereign, and the whole world is God's, so any music that is good already belongs to God. (Ward 2005: 85)

Holding weekly worship in the Living:room, a popular neighborhood spot that also serves as a net lounge, tea bar, and music joint, Church of the Apostles draws many young seekers who are generally skeptical of organized religion. Ward, an African American Mac geek and film buff, can often be seen in the Living:room in jeans and her cherished baseball cap, sipping her tea, surfing the Internet, and shepherding her flock of local DJs, artists, slam poets, and rockers. Far from seeing culture as lacking spirituality, Ward sees culture as brimming with God's spirituality and

Brian McLaren with Emergent leaders Steve Knight (left) and
Anthony Smith (right). Photo courtesy of Steve Knight.

creativity: "So our thing is not to try to download spirituality into unspiritual people, but to help nurture the spirituality each person has toward God-directed expressions. When new folk come to our community, they become part of an artistic Christ co-op for the postmodern soul" (2005: 84). Ward nurtures a new kind of missional community in her city and is highly active in the emerging church on a national level with writings, conference presentations, blogs, and friendships.

"For many of us, creativity has become an important way of nurturing relationships, experiencing God, exploring and integrating spiritual realities into the messiness of our lives," claims Mark Scandrette, a poet and self-proclaimed rogue lover of Christ who moved to San Francisco to pursue his dream of cultivating an organic form of spiritual community composed of his neighbors and friends (2005: 134). Scandrette calls this experiment ReIMAGINE, a collective friendship exploring different ways to follow Jesus in an emerging world urban landscape. Participants experience camaraderie through sharing life in each other's homes, wrestling with scripture, feasting with the homeless, and enjoying poetry, art, and good conversation. Scandrette sees the emerging church as a multiportal community of all relationships and activities, both local and global, in which he shares "kingdom" vision, values, and practices.

To help members better understand the ethnic complexities involved with urban ministry as well as the visible and hidden dynamics of race

The Emergent Coordinating Group in May 2003 at Conception Abbey, a monastery in Missouri. Seated, from left to right, are Chris Seay, Tim Keel, Holly Rankin, Laci Scott, Ivy Beckwith, and Karen Ward. Standing, from left to right, are Tony Jones, Mark Scandrette, Dieter Zander, Jason Clark, Doug Pagitt, Brian McLaren, and Tim Conder. Photo courtesy of Tim Keel.

that attend evangelical worship, Anthony Smith teaches an eight-week interactive course called "Bridge Building" at Warehouse 242, a Presbyterian church in Charlotte, North Carolina. Classroom lectures and discussions in Smith's "Bridge Building" courses often supplement hands-on work in the community, whether it is helping to build homes for local residents or tutoring students in after-school programs. An African American participant in the emerging church, Smith thoughtfully draws wisdom and insight from diverse strands of American culture featured most readily on his weblog, creatively called "Musings of a Postmodern Negro." After Smith was converted in a storefront Pentecostal church in the early 1990s, his critical and inquisitive mind complemented a deepening faith as he began to read authors such as Brian McLaren, bell hooks, Jacques Derrida, Cornel West, and Stanley Hauerwas, the latter opening the door to the emerging church. A new world opened up as Smith found "an epistemological humility with this particular movement," a deep "notion of friendship," and a desire to "see the *shalom* of God breaking out into the world in God's people" (Jones 2008: 27–28). Pentecostal *and* postmodern, Smith artfully navigates multiple worlds, seeking to live a life of fervent faith and prophetic possibility.

Tony Jones, national coordinator for Emergent Village, a Minnesota police chaplain, and a sought-after speaker, crosses historical, geographical, and denominational borders to offer an eclectic mix of evangelical, Roman Catholic, and Eastern Orthodox practices to enhance spiritual experience and fortify spiritual formation. Jones knows his audience and understands that such a rich compilation of spiritual practices appeals to a wide array of tastes and preferences. "Ultimately," observes Jones, "the application of these or any ancient spiritual practices is up to the individual Christian, because, while some practices hold deep meaning for one person, a different set of practices will appeal to another" (2005: 197).

Other stories from emerging church practitioners provide other frames of reference for the movement. Though she now resides in South Carolina, Holly Rankin Zaher started THREENAILS, a worship community in Pittsburgh that meets in art galleries rather than churches. David Fitch, Northern Seminary professor and author of *The Great Giveaway: Reclaiming the Mission of the Church from Big Business, Parachurch Organizations, Psychotherapy, and Other Modern Maladies* (2005), started Up/Rooted, a regular meeting of pastors, artists, and church leaders in the Chicago area to discuss the church and postmodernism. Donald Miller's provocative book *Blue Like Jazz* (2003) uses humor and candor to delineate his own spiritual pilgrimage and has become a cult classic in emerging church circles. New Zealander Andrew Jones blogs as "TallSkinnyKiwi" and travels extensively throughout the United States and Europe to forge global networks of emerging church leaders. José and Mayra Humphreys developed an urban ministry in New York City that extends the emerging church conversation to Latinos throughout the East Coast. Tim Keel started Jacob's Well, a "missional" community in Kansas City, Missouri, for people averse to attending traditional churches. Chris Seay founded Ecclesia, an emerging congregation in Houston that sees the pastor as storyteller, a fellow spiritual traveler who engages those on the journey with substantive biblical stories articulated through the imagery, metaphor, and the idiom of today's postmodern generation (Seay 2003). These and thousands more reflective practitioners of the emerging church present the Christian gospel in culturally relevant ways that jive well with innovative, free-spirited travelers all over the world.

Many emerging churches operate under an entirely different institutional paradigm than megachurches or traditional churches. Emerging practitioners see the church as "missional" rather than institutional in terms of its calling to live out the gospel within specific cultural contexts (Frost and Hirsch 2003). Because they are birthed in the context of human experience, missional churches often have low overhead costs and do not depend on legions of trained clergy, as Neil Cole, a popular writer in the movement, notes:

> We want to lower the bar of how church is done and raise the bar of what it means to be a disciple. The conventional church has become so complicated and difficult to pull off that only a rare person who is a professional can do it every week. . . . When church is so complicated, its function is taken out of the hands of the common Christian and placed in the hands of a few talented professionals. This results in a passive church whose members come and act more like spectators than empowered agents of God's kingdom. (2005: 26–27)

By emphasizing a missional paradigm, emerging practitioners envision the church as "incarnational," not "attractional," in its ecclesiology. Emerging churches seek to exist and thrive based on the particularities of their contexts:

> By incarnational we mean it does not create sanctified spaces into which unbelievers must come to encounter the gospel. Rather, the missional church disassembles itself and seeps into the cracks and crevices of a society in order to be Christ to those who don't yet know him . . . it will leave its own religious zones and live comfortably with non-church-goers, seeping into the host culture like salt and light. It will be an infiltrating transformational community. (Frost and Hirsch 2003: 12, 43)

Unlike church models concerned with fine-tuning conventional evangelical approaches by employing more effective methods, emerging churches actively reimagine how people do church and how they perceive and understand the kingdom of God and Christian theology. To put it another way, in contrast to seeker-sensitive or purpose-driven church models that ask a tactical question, "How can we present the gospel more effectively in our contemporary culture?" emerging churches ask an existential question, "What should the people of God look like in this culture?" No one provides clearer answers to this provocative question than a soft-spoken pastor and best-selling author from Maryland named Brian McLaren, the man that religion scholar Robert Webber calls the leading voice of the next generation of evangelicals (Webber 2002).

Brian McLaren, a mid-Atlantic pastor, speaker, and activist who recently turned fifty, never intended to become the focal point of a movement of which twenty-something and thirty-something evangelicals make up the largest contingency. He discovered the emerging church in the late 1990s when he began to collaborate with Doug Pagitt and a group of young pastors called the Young Leaders Network (YLN) that questioned traditional assumptions about ministry. Sensing that the evangelistic challenge for the church was a philosophical detachment from the wider culture, YLN made postmodernism its central topic of discussion for three years (Gibbs and Bolger 2005). Pagitt and McLaren transformed this leadership network into the Terra Nova Theological project, which soon after became the loosely structured organization they now call Emergent. Emergent forged a new alliance of evangelical theologians, clerics, and practitioners exploring how to imagine Christianity in a postmodern world. More than a thousand pastors attended the Emergent Convention in 2003, not many fewer than the number attending the National Pastors Convention, the more traditional forum for evangelical leadership (Carson 2005).

The organization Emergent and the emerging church movement are so closely linked that observers often incorrectly treat them as interchangeable. Emergent is the most visible and organized branch of the larger emerging church movement, affiliated mostly with North Americans though interconnected with fellow travelers across the globe (McKnight 2007). Emergent leaders generate writings, theological forums, blogs, and Internet chat rooms and plan conferences and conversations with leading theologians and philosophers that draw thousands of Christians and spiritual seekers from various denominations and theological traditions each year.

Emerging church leaders from across North America met in January 2006 with Jewish church leaders affiliated with S3K, or Synagogue 3000, an emerging movement within American Judaism whose practitioners wish to express ancient faith in a postmodern context. At the historic Los Angeles meeting, attended by Emergent leaders such as Doug Pagitt, Tony Jones, Ryan Bolger, and Brian McLaren, participants discussed commonalities and convergences, along with the ways that each faith community reaches out to spiritual seekers in today's postmodern times.

In February 2006, Emergent organized a three-day theological conversation with theologian Miroslav Volf on the campus of Yale University. Participants from across the nation who represented various denominations packed into Yale Divinity School's Marquand Chapel to hear Volf engage Emergent leaders on theological topics and attend breakout discussion groups addressing questions about social justice, poverty, worship, and the significance of New Monasticism for reshaping church and mission for today's culture. At night, Emergent leaders flooded New Haven taverns to shoot pool, drink beers, and share ministry perspectives. Emergent leaders like Tony Jones, Karen Ward, Andy Crouch, Pagitt, and McLaren proved surprisingly accessible to attendees. Between sessions, Crouch, a writer and former magazine editor, discussed how profoundly theologian N. T. Wright's books had impacted his postmodern pilgrimage. Karen Ward spoke about the role of African Americans in the emerging church, while Pagitt offered his thoughts about how Christians overestimate their place in God's mission in the world.

Leaders met in northern Minnesota for the 2005 Emergent Summit to discuss organizational goals and plan for the future. Those in attendance acknowledged that Emergent needed to respond organizationally to the budding challenges of rapid growth and influence in the widespread emerging church movement. After the summit, they appointed Tony Jones as their national director, which soon after sparked a flood of negative e-mails insisting, "You can't have a director because you can't direct a movement!" as Jones noted in our interview. Emergent quickly changed Jones's title to national coordinator, and his executive efforts provided a much-needed reprieve for McLaren, who by 2006 was receiving countless speaking and consulting solicitations from churches and organizations worldwide.

Compared with other evangelical preachers, "McLaren is better than the average bear, more substantive and courageous," claimed theologian Stanley Hauerwas in an interview. Various television networks, newspapers, and radio broadcasts regularly feature McLaren and other emerging church leaders and participants. Large publishing companies like Zondervan, InterVarsity Press, and Baker Books have scores of works in print that tackle various issues, including the seminal book *An Emergent Manifesto of Hope* (2007), a massive compilation of thoughts and perspectives on the Emergent church edited by Doug Pagitt and Tony Jones. The Society for the Scientific Study of Religion as well as the American Academy of Religion featured panels on the emerging church at recent national meetings;

a small but growing number of scholars are studying the movement, including Davidson College sociologist Gerardo Marti, whose books *A Mosaic of Believers: Diversity and Innovation in a Multiethnic Church* (2005) and *Hollywood Faith: Holiness, Prosperity and Ambition in a Los Angeles Church* (2008) analyze emerging churches in Southern California.

In 2004 the flagship evangelical magazine *Christianity Today* offered a feature story on Emergent, as well as an interview with Brian McLaren, and a year later, *Time* magazine listed him as one of the most influential evangelicals. McLaren is at the helm of a spiritual revolution that seeks to generate a biblical faith that is more suitable for a postmodern world. While most evangelicals disparage anything related to the term, McLaren likens postmodernism to a kind of chemotherapy to weaken the "cancer" of Western colonialism:

My religious friends seem quick to understand the weaknesses and dangers of the pluralist/relativist chemo cocktail (which is usually what they mean by the term postmodernism). One of my sons is a cancer survivor, so I know something about the dangers of chemotherapy. But few of my religious friends seem able to acknowledge the existence, much less dangers, of malignant, modern Western overconfidence—whether in the distant past or in the present. (2007: 145)

Rather than rejecting postmodernism for its excesses, McLaren urges Christians to embrace its moral intentions and form a progressive Christian faith that promotes recognition and repentance of the West's colonial history and arrogance.

McLaren's early struggles put him on a path to offer a message and ministry for people struggling to make sense of their faith in the midst of an increasingly postmodern landscape. He grew up in a conservative evangelical Christian home that emphasized the authority of scripture, considered liberals as outcasts, and frowned on worldly pleasures like social dancing. His family and church introduced him to a faith that focused on Christ's atoning work on the cross. His church and family depicted Jesus as "a nice, quite, gentle, perhaps somewhat fragile guy on whose lap children liked to sit" (McLaren 2006: 33), not the revolutionary prophet later depicted in McLaren's books. In his early teens, McLaren became indignant with what he perceived as hypocrisy in the lives of many Christians. The social and political turmoil of the 1960s brought on by the civil rights movement, the Vietnam War, and the advent of new rock and roll music led the teenager into a period of questioning and rebellion. Participation in the Jesus Movement revitalized his faith as a "thin, raggedy-looking blue-jeaned, guitar-playing, long-haired and bearded young guy without standard credentials" (McLaren 2001: vii). While in his twenties, McLaren completed an undergraduate degree in English at the University of Maryland, married his longtime girlfriend, and participated in an assortment of Protestant settings, including brief stints among Pentecostals, Episcopalians, and Catholics. Though seeds of McLaren's annoyance with modern Christianity took root in the midst of his diverse religious experiences, his graduate studies exposed him to postmodern ideas that fertilized the crisis of faith he experienced in the mid-1990s.

McLaren's graduate studies in literature and language at the University of Maryland sensitized him "to drama and conflict, to syntax and semantics and semiotics, to text and context, to prose and poetry," and gave him a feel for the art and romance of language (McLaren 2004: 157). This occurred during the late 1970s, when postmodern theory was popular in literary criticism and other disciplines, exposing students to a startling new framework of ideas by a number of popular French theorists. McLaren did extensive work on the Catholic novelist Walker Percy, which introduced him to the modern-postmodern transition. He also explored the playful and paradoxical antinarrative method in the novels of Philippe Sollers and Alain Robbe-Grillet. The works of cultural critic Roland Barthes and historian Michel Foucault challenged McLaren's preconceived notions of authorial intent and truth. Philosopher Jacques Derrida's writings revealed the contextual dimension of language and the socially constructed nature of all meaning, presenting the world as a text with all ideas and beliefs subject to multiple interpretations and playful deconstruction. McLaren's studies raised many questions about his own Christian experience and theology for which, at the time, he did not have good answers. He placed those questions on the back burner and balanced his rigorous studies by participating in spiritual leadership.

Newly married, McLaren started a Bible study that attracted University of Maryland graduate students and professors and eventually grew into a house church in 1982. McLaren's church continued to grow after he completed his graduate studies and began teaching English composition at the university. In 1986, the pressing needs of the ministry forced him to quit teaching and function as full-time pastor of the mushrooming church, which met at Eleanor Roosevelt High School in Beltsville. In 1999, Cedar Ridge Community Church purchased its own building in Spencerville, where the congregation currently meets.

During the early 1990s, McLaren became aware of the myriad ways postmodernism affected society outside of the academy. Cedar Ridge began to draw many new attendees not familiar with the type of rationalistic, individualistic, creed-based Christianity typified in many churches. These new attendees grew up outside of the contours of modern Christianity; to McLaren, it seemed as if they came from a different world. The complexity and messiness of life were more apparent to these new attendees as products of an MTV age of mass media that inundated people with a flow of images, ideas, and a tantalizing array of options. Pluralistic out-of-the-box thinking came quite naturally to many of them, and they began to ask hard questions about Christianity. McLaren felt that many of these seekers had questions that were better than his answers, and so he spent a few years in the mid-1990s frustrated and unsure he would stay in the ministry.

In 1994, McLaren, at thirty-eight, was undergoing a spiritual crisis. His old way of thinking and believing—whether the dispensationalism of his childhood, the Calvinism of his adolescence, the "charismaticism" of his early adulthood, or his mature evangelicalism—did not mesh well with the uncertainty and dynamism he began to discover in biblical narratives (McLaren 2001). McLaren grew frustrated with what he perceived as modernity's God: "an uptight God who is about black-and-white easy answers; a conceptual God who is encountered through systems of abstractions, propositions, and terminology; an exclusive God who favors insiders and is biased against outsiders; and a tense God who prefers arrogant and judgmental people" (McLaren 2002: 63–64). McLaren wondered how the religious community could miss the rapidly changing world and eventually concluded either that Christianity itself was defective or that his Western version of it needed recalibration. Having grown aggravated by the way he felt he led others in the faith, and discouraged because he could not find spiritual peers who even seemed to understand his questions, much less suggest answers, he predicted in his journal that in one year he would not be in ministry. His forecast proved wrong when he found out he was not alone; a budding group of reflective practitioners in the emerging church, like Doug Pagitt and Todd Hunter, were wrestling with the same questions.

After McLaren joined the Terra Nova project in the mid-1990s, like-minded evangelicals quickly realized he had much to contribute. This new network of postmodern evangelicals provided McLaren a safe space to challenge traditional aspects of his evangelical faith. His continuous dialogues with other reflective practitioners helped him project a version of God through postmodern lenses. McLaren entered the public conversation with his first book, *Church on the Other Side*, a volume that argues Christians need a new church to match today's postmodern world—not a new Christ but a new Christian, not a new Spirit, but a new spirituality and a new kind of church in every denomination (McLaren 1998). McLaren urged pastors to exchange their rationalistic and constrained sermons for unedited, rough, and lumpy formula-free stories. The book challenges readers to disentangle the modern and individualistic influence over contemporary evangelical versions of Christianity and to construct a postmodern version that embraces humility, healthy skepticism, and thirst for spirituality. He presses for a faith that is more experiential and less dogmatic, less certain and more mysterious.

Two years later McLaren published his magnum opus, *A New Kind of Christian*, a controversial yet critically acclaimed novel that put him on the radar as a leading evangelical. Though all the characters are fictional, their conversations are extrapolations of dialogues and personal crises McLaren experienced during difficult times in ministry. Early in the novel, the protagonist Neil Edward Oliver (Neo), a wise Jamaican high school teacher, diagnoses the source of his friend Daniel's crisis of faith, one that resembles McLaren's real-life battle a decade earlier. For the rest of the book, Neo serves as Daniel's sponsor and McLaren's experiment for reimagining Christianity in a changing world. The dialogues expose the challenges of postmodernism and its relation to Christianity. Daniel's crisis reveals that although a transition to a new kind of Christianity is as unsettling as a refugee leaving the comforts of home, the earliest stages of disillusionment eventually pass, and the weary traveler finds that the new homeland has much to offer, including new ways to look at salvation, the Bible, evangelism, and the spiritual life. Neo enjoys long hikes and cold beers and takes great pleasure deconstructing modern formulas or prescriptions for spirituality. *A New Kind of Christian* became a best seller and won the distinction as *Christianity Today's* book of the year. The book's success inspired McLaren to write two sequels using the same fictional characters.

The second novel of the trilogy, *The Story We Find Ourselves In* (2003), served as McLaren's attempt to deconstruct what he and many emerging church leaders perceive as the modern evangelical approach to the Bible. For most of McLaren's early Christian experience, the Bible was an answer book supplying "exactly the kind of information modern, Western, moderately educated people want from a phone book, encyclopedia, or legal constitution" (McLaren 2004: 159). He admits there are many difficult scriptural passages for onlookers to accept and uses his wily Jamaican protagonist Neo to challenge long-standing interpretations of biblical stories. Neo rejects the popular notion of the Bible as a look-it-up encyclopedia and urges Daniel and other characters to think of it less as a divine answer book and more as a question book that brings people together for conversation about life's most important issues. Neo comments:

> I guess you could say that the Bible is a book that doesn't try to tell you *what* to think. Instead, it tries to teach you *how* to think. It stretches your thinking; it challenges you to think bigger and harder than ever before. It not only records ancient conversations among human beings and God, but it also stimulates new ones, never failing to create a community for essential conversations that enrich all of life. (McLaren: 2003: 82)

The second novel was more controversial for traditional evangelicals than the first because several of the characters reassess time-honored theories of Christ's atonement. During one such discussion one character depicts personal evil as tantamount to a computer virus attaching itself to the software of the human personality, rejecting the traditional belief of evil as the strategic efforts of the devil and his legion of demons. Similarly, Neo advocates a healthy marriage between science and Christianity, which is possibly McLaren's way of deconstructing the anti-intellectual evangelicalism of his youth.

McLaren's third novel, *The Last Word and the Word after That* (2005), raised questions about evangelical Christian teachings about hell and judgment. The book begins with Daniel's daughter Jess, a second-semester freshman at the University of Maryland, returning home to discuss with her dad her troubling realization: "If Christianity is true, then all people I love except for a few will burn in hell forever. But if Christianity is not true, then life doesn't seem to have much meaning or hope. I wish I could find a better option. How do you deal with this?" (McLaren 2005: 5). Jess's crisis brings to the surface complexities that Daniel kept hidden for years concerning the evil of hell in the face of a loving God. Daniel seeks counsel from Neo, who offers an intriguing consideration about divine justice:

> You have to say that God doesn't want people to go to hell, but he's forced to do so against his will by the mechanisms of the court or the

requirements of some higher abstraction called justice or something like that. He's a nice guy caught in a tough fix. He wants to forgive but he has to play by the rules of the court. It's the only way you can save God from seeming like a monster, visiting infinite punishment on poor little finite creatures who have no choice about being born into this high-risk, no-win game called life. Of course, when you solve the hell problem that way, you have the new problem of creating a higher authority than God. You know, the court mechanism or the law to which God is subject or whatever. (McLaren 2005: 40)

Neo chides what he perceives as Christians' wacky way of talking about God: God loves people and has a wonderful plan for their life, though hell awaits those who fail to do or believe the right thing. God is a loving father, but he will treat persons with a cruelty that no human father has ever been guilty of—eternal conscious torture. Following Neo's advice, Daniel embarks on a historical study in which he discovers that hell is not mentioned in the Old Testament and that the notion of heaven and hell seems to have been borrowed from other religions: Mesopotamian, Egyptian, Zoroastrian, and Greek, all in the interim period between the last Old Testament prophets and the coming of Jesus. Daniel also learns that the early church had many conflicting views about hell, including that of church fathers like Origen, who denied its existence. He also discovered that Jesus was turning the Pharisees' use of hell on its head to make a point about what really matters to God: how we live and treat people on earth. Unsurprisingly, Daniel's new findings about hell trouble many evangelicals, who criticize McLaren for challenging long-held doctrines.

McLaren's other writings include a creative book on postmodern evangelism (2002), a postcritical theological treatise used in many seminaries (2004), a meditation titled *The Secret Message of Jesus* (2006), and a sequel about God's kingdom in a globalized world (2007). In a move that not only worked to generate additional interest in *The Secret Message of Jesus* but also appealed to the emerging, postmodern generation, McLaren made available on his website an additional chapter to the book along with a question guide tailored to small-group study.

Titled "The Prayer of the Kingdom," this chapter offers McLaren's social-political meditation on the Lord's Prayer, thoughts designed so readers might internalize the book's message and enact what McLaren believes is Jesus' "revolutionary message" to bring radical transformation to human society. In addition, the study guide offers tips for engaging group study, with questions that prompt readers and participants to articulate how they understand Jesus' message personally, formulate their response to McLaren's interpretation of it, and contemplate how to adopt an inclusive posture of discussion about Jesus' message so as not to alienate outsiders and other varieties of spiritual seekers. As with other evangelical innovators, McLaren effectively packages and markets his message, drawing interested observers to interact with his version of evangelical Christianity. For a generation whose religious nourishment comes also from plugging into cyberspirituality, McLaren provides a host of ways for fans and listeners to internalize his message.

McLaren still serves the congregation at Cedar Ridge Community Church with the mission to welcome people into a dynamic Christian community where they can connect with God and one another, and to help people make a difference in our changing world, while he also consults and speaks widely. Like those of his friend Doug Pagitt, McLaren's sermons are open dialogues in which congregants interject different perspectives on the topic at hand. Recently, he has stepped back from many of his pastoral responsibilities in order to continue his national role in the emerging church. He maintains a hectic schedule as writer, conference speaker, guest lecturer in seminaries and college campuses, and ubiquitous cyberspace provocateur exchanging his ideas on an endless number of websites and blogs.

Sensing the desire for a new way to connect with and appeal to readers and fans, McLaren declined all speaking requests for 2008 to focus on "Everything Must Change 2008," a multicity speaking and workshop tour that adopts the title of one of his books. According to McLaren's website, this traveling revolution "will call people to a deep shift in their thinking about faith, church life, mission, ministry, art, justice, leadership, community, and worship. It will emphasize deep personal transformation integrated with deep organizational transition as well, in the context of the 'Generous Orthodoxy' I write and speak about." Similar to Osteen's "An Evening with Joel" and related to Jakes's tailored conferences and large-scale MegaFest, McLaren finds ways to connect with spiritual consumers by offering the idea of "generous orthodoxy" that permeates his novels and other reflections within a two-day program of speaking and workshops.

For many who perceive evangelicals as judgmental and arrogant dogmatists who are unwilling to listen to others, McLaren is a breath of fresh air. He often describes himself as a quirky and curious guy drawn to innovation; an amateur pastor, hack theologian, and wannabe mystic.

In a recent sermon he identified himself with Balaam's ass—the equine character in the Old Testament (Numbers 22) who spoke prophetic words to his owner—to suggest he too is an unlikely candidate and last resort to lead the ongoing emerging church conversation. But his unconventional route to spiritual leadership and outlier status suit him to lead a controversial movement that deconstructs modern Christianity. McLaren, a literature student who snuck into pastoral ministry accidentally through the back doors of a university English department, is a more likely candidate to confront the seminary establishment than a person who spent years learning Hebrew and Greek and studying biblical hermeneutics, eschatology, soteriology, and other theological tools of modernity.

McLaren and the emerging church's unconventional leadership and postmodern ideas draw their share of detractors. A Christian blogger recently called McLaren "a true son of Lucifer." Conservative biblical scholar D. A. Carson (2005) suggested the movement is dangerous to Christianity because it diverts people from the nonnegotiable tenets of the gospel. The Southern Baptist Convention rescinded its speaking invitation to McLaren because of what it perceived as controversial theological statements in his third novel. The Internet is replete with blogs devoted to chastising his books and the movement, and even fellow emerging church pastor Mark Driscoll (2006) criticized McLaren and other leaders for veering from the pillars of Christian orthodoxy and faith. Adding fuel to the fire, McLaren perturbs many conservative evangelicals when he portrays the kingdom of God as a revolutionary, countercultural movement, or when he frequently quotes Martin Luther King Jr.—not from the sanitized portions of the "I Have a Dream" speech but King's radical statements challenging injustice and oppressive systems. McLaren also ruffles many feathers when he quotes controversial feminist theologians like Sally McFague and Mary Grey, or when he suggests that liberal political figures like Bishop Desmond Tutu, Nelson Mandela, and the late Archbishop Oscar Romero demonstrated a better understanding of the kingdom of God than most contemporary American evangelicals.

McLaren is part of a growing cohort of high-profile evangelicals like Jim Wallis and Tony Campolo who voice concerns about the United States' foreign policy, in particular, the invasion and occupation of Iraq, and do not feel that the public voices of evangelical Christianity speak for them. McLaren raises deep reservations about the alignment of major sectors of Christianity with "red-state republicanism" and dispatches his concern that a kind of modernist, nationalist neofundamentalism tries to claim all Christian territory as sovereign domain. In a 2003 message to his church titled "A Sermon for President Bush," McLaren urged the president to consider the tragic consequences of war:

> In this war, Mr. President, if war must happen, I wonder if you would make history by being the first president to share the death toll of our enemy, not as a score of victory, but as another tragic cost of war? I wonder if you could teach the American people to mourn the death of Iraqi mothers' sons along with our own? I wonder if you could, in this way, deepen our dread and hatred of war, so that if this war happens, it will bring us one war closer to the end of the nightmare, and the beginning of God's dream for us?

McLaren's travels in Latin America made him more attentive to the liberationist interpretation of Christianity that fights oppression and confronts social injustice. He urges evangelical leaders not to let their faith become captive to any political party and to take responsibility for American foreign policy in the ways in which Americans abuse power and colonize nations.

McLaren also offers Christians new ways of thinking and talking about the environment and politics. Unlike many evangelicals who eschew ecological issues, McLaren believes the gospel has much to say about stewardship of the environment. He is a lover of nature who is often waist-deep in the Potomac River casting for bass, or thigh-deep in a marsh enjoying the sounds of wood frogs and watching orioles crossing the riverhead (McLaren and Campolo 2003). His message and accessibility resonate with younger generations because he asks hard questions, refuses to let people get by with shallow answers, and possesses a willingness to challenge the evangelical establishment.

Before McLaren, one would not hear many prominent white evangelical pastors preach on topics like postcolonialism. Right-wing conservatism often defines evangelicals' public political conversations. McLaren acknowledges that white Christians such as himself are finally awakening to Western Christianity's dark side, while African, African American, and Latin American Christians have been articulating postcolonial themes for decades. While entering a postcolonial conversation already in progress, McLaren is strategically situated to articulate how such themes are useful in deconstructing contemporary American evangelicalism:

Here in the United States we see large sectors of the Christian community associated with American hyperconfidence, white privilege, institutional racism, civil religion, neocolonialism, and nationalistic militarism—often fortified by a privatized faith in a privatized nationalistic/tribal god. . . . We find ourselves awakening to a pervasive mindset that feels incapable of self-doubt and is quick to judge "the other," slow to admit its own faults, eager to point out splinters in the eyes of others, but oblivious to the planks in its own. (McLaren 2007: 148)

McLaren once went so far as to suggest that Karl Marx was right about Christianity being an opiate that helps people become comfortable with injustice rather than enraged by it (McLaren and Campolo 2003). In February 2005, when television host Larry King asked his guests what Bush owes evangelicals as the critical mass of support for his second election, in customary contrarian fashion McLaren voiced more concern about what evangelicals owe Bush: to call him to a broader range of moral values that includes making peace, not war, caring for the poor, and being good stewards of the environment.

McLaren desires to lead Christians into what he perceives to be a deeper, thoughtful, and more sincere spirituality. He contends that the version of evangelical Christianity practiced today, with its political creeds, sappy love songs, flashy television preachers, and demonstrative bumper stickers, is embarrassingly individualistic and has little to do with the faith that Jesus and his early followers advocated. He fears that endless singing about celebration may cause the church to lose its vitality and credibility; in turn, he pushes for music and worship to be more honest about the pain, disappointment, doubt, and abandonment that are so much a part of the Christian experience. McLaren believes that if Jesus were physically on earth today he would disassociate himself from Christians, who probably would not recognize him:

If the real Lord Jesus were to knock on our door as Revolutionary King/ Master/Teacher, I think we'd look through the peephole and judge him an imposter, since our "Buddy Jesus" as Savior is already sitting on the couch inside, watching TV with us, thumbs up and grinning, "meeting our needs" very well, thank you very much. Our domesticated, romanticized, spiritualized Jesus has become for us the orthodox Jesus, so an alternative one looks unorthodox, unfamiliar, maybe even dangerous and deserving of . . . what? (2004: 88)

While well-known pastors nationwide urged their congregations to see Mel Gibson's movie *The Passion of the Christ* in 2004, McLaren voiced his frustration with the church's role as a hype machine behind the film. In guest columns, blogs, and interviews, he argued that if pastors really had the mind of Christ, they would urge their congregants to see the movie *Hotel Rwanda*, the story of a hotel manager who saves a thousand Tutsi refugees from genocide. McLaren spent part of the summer of 2004 in Rwanda, where he met Anglican priests who recounted personal stories of the tragedies faced during the genocide a decade earlier. Hence, McLaren could not understand why so many pastors were urging people to see Gibson's film and so few supported *Hotel Rwanda*, which he believed was more thoroughly a Christian film. His concern is that many Christian leaders merely create a faith industry that has lost its prophetic edge:

> Are our churches and broadcasts and books and organizations merely creating religious consumers of religious products and programs? Are we creating a self-isolating, self-serving, self-perpetuating, self-centered sub-culture instead of a world-penetrating, world-serving, world-transform-ing God-centered counter-culture? If so, even if we proudly carry the name evangelical, we're not behaving as friends to the gospel, but rather as its betrayers. (McLaren and Campolo 2003: 11–12)

McLaren builds a diverse following by presenting a multidenomina-tional and less polarizing evangelicalism. Following his cohort meeting at an emerging congregation called Ecclesia in Houston in June 2006, McLaren addressed a regional meeting of Episcopal priests and church leaders, one of many examples that demonstrate his far-reaching appeal and versatility. Unlike modern Christianity, which divides into liberal and conservative theological wings, McLaren urges Christians to appreci-ate the positive aspects of both liberal and conservative theological tra-ditions—liberals for being concerned about racial reconciliation, fighting for women in ministry, the environment, and the poor, and for showing sensitivity to the plight of the Palestinians while questioning our country's unconditional support for Israel; conservatives for being heroic in evange-lism, developing Sunday school curricula and parachurch organizations, and for pioneering Christian radio and television. McLaren advocates systematic theology that is less analytical in structure and more rooted in narrative. In contrast to evangelicals' rigid claims on objective truth, McLaren's advocates a more generous orthodoxy:

A generous orthodoxy, in contrast to the tense, narrow, controlling, or critical orthodoxies of so much of Christian history, doesn't take itself too seriously. It is humble; it doesn't claim too much; it admits it walks with a limp. It doesn't consider orthodoxy the exclusive domain of prose scholars (theologians) alone but, like Chesterton, welcomes the poets, the mystics . . . including the disillusioned and the doubters. And it welcomes the activists, the humanitarians, the brave and courageous and compassionate because their actions speak volumes about God that could never be captured in a text, a sermon, an outline, or even a poem. (2004: 155)

Fighting for a more generous orthodoxy, McLaren contends that conservative Republicans hijack the evangelical community with a myopic focus on two issues, homosexuality and abortion, and he calls for a Christlike compassion that respects their complexity. Unlike many evangelicals, who exert great energy denouncing homosexuality, McLaren believes heterosexual infidelity is a far more serious and pervasive issue for Christians to engage. He refuses to take a specific stance on gay marriage and urges Christians to refrain from judging homosexuals and to instead spend some time developing meaningful relationships with members of this community. In McLaren's third novel, a lesbian encourages a pastor through a difficult time, and at the end of the book the woman and her partner are welcomed attendees at the church.

McLaren believes that a convergence of Christians from various traditions will resuscitate Christianity and bring new hope and life to the world. He calls for a generous orthodoxy that envisions participants in other religions not as enemies but as "beloved neighbors, and whenever possible, dialogue partners and even collaborators" (McLaren 2004: 35). Part of his agenda is to deconstruct late twentieth-century styles of evangelism that he believes deserve disdain and avoidance:

On the street evangelism is equated with pressure—it means selling God as if God were vinyl siding, replacement windows, or a mortgage refinancing service. It means shoving your ideas down someone's throat, threatening him with hell if he does not capitulate to our logic or scripture quoting. When preceded with the word television the word evangelism grows even darker, more sinister—sleazy even. It means rehearsed, mechanical monologues, sales pitches, spiels, unrequested sermons or lectures, crocodile tears, uncomfortable confrontations sometimes made worse by Nutrasweet smiles and over-done eye contact. (McLaren 2002: 12)

Unlike evangelicals who often offer up vigorous defenses for their faith, McLaren urges evangelicals to discard their preoccupation with certainty, proof, and argument and replace it with conversation, intrigue, and quest. He suggests that evangelism in the postmodern world has to be less like an argument and more like a dance where two people are working together (McLaren 2002). Likewise, he argues that the evangelist should never be about winning arguments, nor should she be coercive and pushy, but rather patient and gentle like a midwife.

McLaren contends that a seeker's decision to become a Christian is not simply an issue of being persuaded rationally about the certainty of Christianity but, rather, a profound engagement with the truth, beauty, and goodness that provides the confidence to step away from relative indifference to Christian commitment. He firmly maintains that seekers have much to teach Christians and that they should listen to each other's stories rather than offer propositions or formulas. McLaren sees conversion to Christianity as a journey rather than merely a point of decision. His church has a motto, "Belonging before believing," which encourages seekers to engage in programs and church activities even before they become committed believers. For example, McLaren allowed a young Asian woman to participate in Cedar Ridge's drama ministry and speak to the congregation one Sunday morning even though she was not yet a Christian. Similarly, McLaren engages in meaningful dialogues and friendships with Jews, Muslims, and Buddhists.

McLaren is increasingly frustrated with "the status-quo, male-dominated, power-oriented, cover-up-prone organized Christian religion" that often defines American evangelicalism (McLaren 2006: x) and instead espouses Dorothy, the fictional character from *The Wizard of Oz*, as a model of postmodern leadership. McLaren contends that being young and female, Dorothy flips traditional binaries of power concerning age and gender, and rather than having all the answers, Dorothy is herself a seeker who is lost, vulnerable, and often bewildered—perfect qualities for leadership in our emerging culture. McLaren applied his Dorothy model during a recent trip to Africa by a team of Emergent leaders, as Anthony Smith related in an interview:

Brian said, "When we get over in Africa, we are not going to say anything; we're going to learn, we're going to be quiet. Our African brothers and sisters are going to teach us how to think about our Christian faith." That blew me away! You know as an African American I always get floored when I hear white people talk like that.

Brian McLaren views African landscape during his tour of the continent in 2006.
Photo courtesy of Tim Keel.

McLaren's humble approach to spiritual leadership appeals to many who find distasteful the extravagance and overconfidence exuded by the management styles of powerful evangelicals.

Like postmodern novelists and philosophers, Brian McLaren demonstrates that murkiness, playfulness, and intrigue often stimulate more thought than clarity. He is a gadfly in the tradition of Socrates, asking people hard questions designed to expose the deficits of their deeply held beliefs; an iconoclast in the tradition of Friedrich Nietzsche, lacing writings with overstatement and hyperbole to rouse his audience toward a new way of seeing their world; and a provocateur in the tradition of Jacques Derrida, insisting that all human constructions, including formulations about God and God's mysteries, are subject to deconstruction:

> Deconstruction is not destruction; it is hope. It arises from the belief that sometimes our constructed laws get in the way of unseen justice, our un-deconstructed words get in the way of communication, our institutions get in the way of the purposes for which they were constructed, our formulations get in the way of meaning, our curricula get in the way of learning. In those cases, one must deconstruct laws, words, institutions,

formulations, or curricula in the hope that something better will appear. (2005: xvii)

McLaren's presentation of an edgy, messy, passionate, and playful spirituality and his penchant for debunking sacred cows appeal to many young Christians in an increasingly postmodern landscape.

It is also important to recall that the electronic medium through which McLaren offers his messages appeals to today's younger generation. Prior to the release of *Everything Must Change: Jesus, Global Crises, and a Revolution of Hope* in October 2007, McLaren posted three YouTube segments about his book in June and July of the same year, and by the time of the book's release had retooled his website with a new look, countless more resources, and—due to the new networks formed by his global travels—a section devoted to non–English speakers. Similar to holy maverick Joel Osteen's media blitz the week *Become a Better You* appeared, McLaren often has his audience in mind, and tools messages to inspire and to challenge.

Whether one is rediscovering ancient liturgies, changing music, making services more efficient, or redesigning church architecture, it is not unusual to find occasions where clerics rethink ways to do church. Similarly, in seminaries nationwide, professors like Leonard Sweet rethink

Brian McLaren and Emergent leaders on a bus during their tour of Africa.
Photo courtesy of Tim Keel.

theology and the gospel in profound and radical ways. But rarely does one stumble upon a Protestant movement with people rethinking how to do church while engaging in the highest levels of theological reflection like McLaren and his colleagues. Tony Jones believes both elements are what draw media attention to McLaren and the emerging church, as he explained in an interview:

> What does a publisher care about a professor who's writing radically and rethinking theology if he goes to the most boring church, which is the case for many seminary professors. They're very theologically innovative, but their churches don't reflect that in any sense. Meanwhile, you can only do so many stories on the kind of seeker-sensitive or purpose-driven approaches before realizing that these people are just changing their methods while still functioning like traditional Republican evangelicals who believe in biblical inerrancy and who believe that what really matters is that you go to heaven instead of hell when you die. So when people come across us, they're like, "Wow, nobody's been saying and doing this."

Participants in the emerging church approach theology as a place for innovation and fresh breathings of God (Taylor 2005), challenging the individualized, packaged, and entertainment-driven version of Christianity prevalent in many evangelical congregations. As Anthony Smith put it in an interview, "We are a community that is characterized by empathy and motivated by the love of God to speak to issues of racism, poverty, and injustice."

In a recent attack against McLaren and his movement, a blogger compared Emergent to Al-Qaeda. Although the blogger executed these comparisons pejoratively, it might be helpful to consider how, as an amorphous and highly decentralized movement with ill-defined borders, the emerging church has striking similarities with the organizational structure of Al-Qaeda. Osama bin Laden and his lieutenants play a coordinating function by linking like-minded Muslim fundamentalists in each locality with budding cells. Similarly, McLaren and other leaders promote and enhance the grassroots nature of the emerging church conversation by identifying and assisting a new generation of evangelicals, organizing theological dialogues in various cities, coordinating cohorts, as well as hosting local and regional miniconferences. When bin Laden issues a statement, the terrorist world has open ears; when McLaren writes a new book or posts a message on his website, emerging church practitioners listen. While bin

Laden's symbolic leadership provides inspiration and mission, Al-Qaeda's tentacles spread worldwide through loyal independent cells that do and act in the name of the movement. Similarly, while McLaren has high visibility through writings, conference presentations, and media attention, cohorts of loyal and energetic followers weave the implications of his revolutionary ideas into the fabric of their lives and thus formulate innovative ministries that resonate with many Gen X Americans. Al-Qaeda and the emerging church offer scholars useful prototypes of decentralized postmodern social movements for years to come.

Brian McLaren and the emerging church propose alternatives to the traditional evangelical perspective and worship experience. They depict new ways of following Jesus, new outlooks on mission, new ways of expressing compassion and seeking justice, new formulations of faith communities, new approaches to theology and living biblically, and new styles of worship and service that are more suitable for Gen Xers of an increasingly postmodern society. Their writings and ministries attract many who are uncomfortable with large, impersonal megachurches and people who criticize evangelicals' partiality for American nationalism and neoconservative politics. McLaren and the emerging church give evangelicalism a liberationist facelift by demonstrating what the gospel has to say about the global economy, the growing economic divide between the rich and poor, and the mounting danger of violence from both terrorists and antiterrorists. They illustrate that it is possible to be both evangelical and environment-friendly. They attract a growing number of people from both theologically conservative and liberal denominational backgrounds, as well as seekers outside of the religious establishment. They are living out their faith in unusual places like coffee shops, taverns, bowling alleys, Internet cafés, and other spheres of daily life experience. By offering a relational and organic model of spiritual community that emphasizes friendship, fosters dialogue, and makes no claim to having a monopoly on truth, McLaren and the emerging church construct an archetype for a new kind of evangelicalism that addresses the alienation, isolation, and arrant individualism of a postcapitalist, postindustrial world.

5

Messed-Up Mississippi Girl

Paula White and the Imperfect Church

And to my World Partners. Without you, Paula White Ministries would not be what it is today. Thank you for believing in a
"messed-up Mississippi girl" with a big God and a big dream. Together we are transforming lives, healing hearts and saving souls.
—Paula White

The New Testament mentions that it is healthy for people to
confess their sins to others (James 5:16). Divulging frailties and struggles
to a trusted friend or family member is one thing, but publicly declaring
shortcomings is a riskier endeavor. It is hard to forget televangelist Jimmy
Swaggart's television confession, "I have sinned against God," after his
sexual dalliance with prostitutes in the 1980s. Similarly, in the last year of
a presidency laden with sexual scandals, Bill Clinton chose Willow Creek,
the largest congregation in Illinois, for the site of a public dialogue with
its pastor, Bill Hybels. It was a historic moment in television to broadcast
a standing president confessing his struggles and moral failures.

Hollywood celebrities, athletes, politicians, and business executives often reveal intimate details in "tell-all" books, tabloid magazines, and television interviews. The proliferation of talk shows, reality programs, chat
rooms, Internet blogs and YouTube has transformed the public into voy-
eurs of other people's lives. Few celebrities contribute more to this confessional culture than Oprah Winfrey, who reveals her tragic experiences
with sexual abuse, bouts with toxic romantic relationships, and low self-
esteem, thereby appearing very human to millions of people. Spiritual
leaders know that confession is healthy not only for the soul but also for
the market share. A growing number of leading evangelicals render an

Evangelist and talk show host Paula White.
Photo courtesy of the *Tampa Tribune.*

edgy and raw kind of Christianity, which religion scholar Kathryn Lofton (2006b) calls the perfect muddy authenticity. With humor and candor, a new flock of evangelical innovators attract many people by presenting themselves as vulnerable and by removing elusive holy masks.

Author Anne Lamott, who writes with painful honesty about life's struggles, has become a cult figure among evangelicals. Lamott shares discussions about sex and early encounters with drugs and spares few details about her past abortions and years as a dysfunctional alcoholic. In lighter moments, she discloses her petty resentment against a friend who looks good in spandex bicycle shorts and admits spending a lot of time comparing her butt to everyone else's. In more somber moments, Lamott explains the pain and devastation of watching the slow deaths of her parents and several friends, admitting, "I like having a dead mother much more than having an impossible one" (2005: 47). Lamott carves out an intriguing niche by stripping away all pretension and disclosing insecurities and revealing imperfections.

As a televangelist and best-selling author, Joyce Meyer connects with many people by drawing from her personal testimony to rebuke, encourage, and enlighten. In many of her books and sermons she gives vivid details about growing up with an alcoholic father, suffering verbal, sexual, and physical abuse, and living with a manipulative and exploitive husband in what she describes as a dreadful first marriage. She is also forthright about past foibles, including stealing from her employer, bouts with depression, and difficulty confronting personal troubles. Meyer offers lessons learned from years of suffering to help people overcome the emotional pain of abuse and the circularity of addictive behaviors, in order to find inner peace through the truth of her gospel message.

Paul Morton suffered what he describes as a nervous breakdown in the late 1990s that threatened his leadership of the Full Gospel Baptist Church Fellowship, which at the time was the fastest-growing Baptist movement in the country. Rather than covering up this difficult period, Morton wrote *Why Kingdoms Fall: The Journey from Breakdown to Restoration*, to explicate his dramatic experience. Morton reveals embarrassing details, including his wild mood swings and perplexing paranoia: "According to the doctors, I reached the level of delusional thinking. I was seeing things that were not actually there. I was hearing and perceiving things that no one else was perceiving. I believed that people were out to destroy me, so I acted in mistrust, suspicion, and fear" (1999: 76). Morton now endorses a more transparent church culture where people can address real issues in their lives.

Relatively unknown before 1998, Juanita Bynum has emerged as a popular evangelist by preaching raw messages about struggles with sin and temptation. Her book *No More Sheets: The Truth about Sex*, offers tantalizing details about her struggle to survive on welfare, sexual longings and transgressions, destructive romantic relationships, painful divorce, and attempted suicide, all juxtaposed with a renewed faith and dependence upon God. Demonstrating that sex sells even in Christendom, Bynum presents frank discussions on taboo topics like masturbation and sexual addiction; she discloses her personal struggles in ministry and her battles with current temptations, and also addresses contemporary problems many men and women face that clergy often overlook. In a feature article in the November 2007 issue of *Ebony*, Bynum discloses intimate details concerning her bout with domestic violence and failed marriage.

As part of this growing confessional religious culture, more and more evangelicals write provocative best-selling books admonishing a "naked" spirituality by eradicating holy facades. T. D. Jakes's *Naked and Not Ashamed* attacks what he perceives as self-righteousness and hypocrisy in the church and urges believers to be naked and not ashamed before God. Craig Borlase's book *The Naked Christian* advises believers to strip back bulky layers of religious legalism, be real, choose authenticity, and get "naked." Eric Sandras's *Buck Naked Faith: A Brutally Honest Look at Stunted Christianity*, also challenges Christians to be more transparent about human frailties and reveals intimate details about his own past sins. These works are part of a changing evangelical landscape that advocates a confessional and unprocessed approach to spirituality.

Few spiritual leaders have distinguished themselves with an honest and naked faith more than a self-proclaimed "messed-up Mississippi girl," Paula White, a best-selling author, noted conference speaker, life coach, and television personality. There is a special place in our competitive religious marketplace for a svelte, fiery blonde preacher who can identify with pain and struggle by presenting her life as an open book. Once a master at hiding her own pain, similar to T. D. Jakes, White now urges Christians to take off their masks: "As long as I wear a mask, then I am playing the role of a character. And God is not interested in my role-playing or in yours. He wants to deal with you, the real you! He wants to know the you that struggles with secret issues of the heart. The you behind the fake smile and pretty clothes" (1998: 106–7). In many of her sermons, empowerment seminars, and books she exposes her childhood traumas and teenage flirtations with self-destruction to teach about God's transforming power.

White became a star virtually overnight through her television ministry. She recorded the first broadcast of *Paula White Today* in December 2001, and by 2006 her show appeared on nine television networks, including Trinity Broadcasting Network, Daystar, and Black Entertainment Television. She quickly secured a loyal following by revealing the intimate details of her troubled history and relating her life story of triumph through tenacity. She transferred her past bouts with fear, abandonment, rejection, anger, guilt, and loneliness into motifs for a human message of hope and betterment that garners attention from some unlikely admirers, including pop music superstar Michael Jackson.

A month after he was arrested on child molestation charges in 2003, Jackson summoned Paula White to his ranch in California for spiritual support. It is ironic that these two celebrities would meet at this crucial juncture after traveling such contrasting journeys. Jackson spent some of his youth enjoying fame and privilege; White lived most of her childhood in rustic trailer parks, barely making ends meet. While Jackson generated some of the greatest musical hits of all time, White struggled with depression and teenage pregnancy. Jackson was one of the most recognized people in the world before White preached her first sermon. But eventually the tables turned, and in his darkest hour, Jackson called upon the rising star for spiritual replenishment.

That White comforted a man accused of the same vexing crime that plagued her youth makes her encounter with Jackson even more remarkable. From age six to thirteen, she was the victim of sexual abuse by various perpetrators. But she did not allow her unhappy past to impede her from encouraging the fallen pop icon. Rather than functioning as stumbling blocks, her personal tragedies and struggles serve as stepping-stones to minister to millions of people who faced pain and tragedy.

Michael Jackson is not the only famous person to whom White, a virtual unknown a decade ago, offers spiritual counsel. Business tycoon Donald Trump calls her his personal pastor and wrote the following endorsement that appears on the back cover of White's recent book *You're All That!*: "Paula White is not only a beautiful person both inside and out, she has a significant message to offer anyone who will tune in and pay attention. She has amazing insight and the ability to deliver that message clearly as well as powerfully. Read this and you'll be ready for great success. She is an amazing woman." Trump first discovered White on her television show, and after he contacted her ministry, the two quickly became friends. Trump, who often brings her to Atlantic City for private Bible studies with athletes and celebrities, appeared on her television show for an exclusive interview.

Moreover, various politicians and entertainers seek her out for wisdom and guidance, newspapers and magazines often feature her, and she makes guest appearances on popular television programs like the *Tyra Banks Show* to offer practical advice and counsel. Despite her celebrity status, White undoubtedly has a soft spot for the underdog. In 2006, she accepted offers from the warden and chaplain to broadcast her show at the Coleman Federal Correctional Facility in Florida, one of the nation's largest prisons. She described her troubled past to receptive audiences from the women's division and prayed with many of the female inmates. In her session with the male prisoners, White told them, "I don't care where you've been or what you've done; God is calling you out by your name and out of your shame to the purpose and plan he has for you." Many of the men had tears in their eyes as she told them that greatness is in their futures and that God was fast at work raising them up to be leaders.

White takes pride that Without Walls International Church, the Tampa congregation she co-pastors with her husband, Randy, is full of people with skeletons in their closets. One of these members is former baseball slugger Darryl Strawberry, who credits White with helping him get his life back on track. It is hard to forget the disheartening images of the eight-time All-Star standing trial as a repeated drug offender in the late 1990s. After his release from a Florida prison in 2003, Strawberry began attending Without Walls International with his wife. Its slogan, "The perfect church for people who aren't," has a particular resonance with Strawberry's story and others in the multiethnic, economically diverse membership that now exceeds 20,000.

In an April 2004 feature on her ministry, the *Washington Times* portrayed Paula White as "not your mom's evangelist" and also depicted Without Walls International as not your typical family church. White revels in her church's diversity and often claims that on any given Sunday you may be seated next to a doctor or a former prostitute; a professional athlete or a welfare recipient; a top Florida businessperson or a former Mafia associate; a teacher or a homeless person. The church claims evangelism and restoration as main objectives for its ministries and shattering denominational, racial, and cultural walls that divide Protestants nationwide as one of its primary goals. The church rehabilitates individuals with troubled pasts and then recruits them for leadership positions. During a visit in September 2005, we observed one such leader, a short white woman sporting jeans and a tank top, baring numerous tattoos on her shoulders and chest, stand behind the pulpit during a Sunday night service and exhort the congregation to pay their tithes: "My tithe keeps me from backsliding. My tithe keeps me from shooting up heroin. My tithe keeps me on my feet. I should be dead so I can't afford not to give. If God has brought you from hell the least you owe him is to pay your tithe." She discussed how the church helped her conquer addiction to antidepressants and other drugs and inspired her to answer a prophetic calling on her life. Without Walls International transforms "imperfect people" into leaders, including an ex-stripper who now runs a support network at the church for those trying to leave her former profession.

The lion's share of White's detractors come from the church rather than the secular world. Some Christians often tag her as style over substance, suggesting that her popularity relies on marketing and packaging rather than preaching talent or anointing. Numerous websites and blogs vehemently scorn her theology and criticize her fund-raising tactics. Her gender sparks fierce attacks in cyberspace, ranging from biblical challenges against women preachers to boorish allusions to her sex appeal (a blogger once offered her money to preach topless). But those who perceive White as just another pretty face overlook vital aspects to why she appeals to many Americans. White presents a human spirituality; she provides the tools for recovery and self-actualization for those who feel that mistakes, missed chances, and bad decisions riddle their past and threaten their future. Years of anguish and hardship generated a surprisingly attractive message. In this way, White, like other holy mavericks, taps into that ever-present possibility that is part of American culture: redemption and second chances.

The first five years of her life as an energetic child in Tupelo, Mississippi, lacked the pain and discomfort that characterized subsequent periods. "I was the most fortunate little girl in the world," she recalled in one sermon. Her parents owned a thriving toy and craft store, and Paula and her brother Mark had all their needs and desires met. In her first book she reminisces about her father:

> I still remember Daddy's broad shoulders. His long muscular legs made him seem as tall as a skyscraper. Daddy's hands were big, his smile was handsome, and his eyes were piercing. When I was with him, I felt so safe, so protected. Why? Because I was with Superman, of course. Whatever I needed or wanted, I knew that Superman would give it to me. (P. White 1998: 18)

White was too young and innocent to detect her parents' rocky marriage. When White was only five, her mother departed Memphis with Paula and her brother, Mark, to start a new life. Not long after they left Mississippi, her father appeared at their doorstep and commanded his estranged wife to give him his daughter. Her mother's refusal provoked a violent response, and after seeing his father bash his mother's head against the wall, Mark called the police. Two officers swiftly arrived and took Paula and Mark's father away, promising to keep him in jail until he sobered up. As the officers escorted him out the door, Paula's father promised to kill himself if he could not take his daughter.

Not many days later, Paula's mother held her and Mark in a suffocating embrace after informing them their father had crashed his car into a tree and was pronounced dead on arrival at the hospital. Whether or not car malfunction, intoxication, or inclement weather caused the crash is inconsequential because Paula perceived her father's death as the fulfillment of his vow of suicide—an assessment that would haunt her with guilt and shame. She lived the next fourteen years in a downward spiral of pain and self-destruction.

As a single parent, Paula's mother had to work long, hard hours to support her family. Like many children in single-parent families, Paula and her brother were often cared for by babysitters and friends of the family. In her best-selling book, she describes how caretakers victimized her in damaging ways:

> After my father committed suicide, and my mother struggled to make ends meet, my life became a living hell. From the time I was six years old until I was thirteen years old, I was sexually and physically abused numerous times in horrific ways. Psychiatrists and psychologists told me that, given what happened to me in those early years of my childhood, I should have been institutionalized for the rest of my life—I should never have been able to cope with what happened to me, much less be healed of it. (P. White 2004: 113)

White also claims that her mother's insensitivity exacerbated her poor self-image. She recalls one occasion shortly after her father's death when she sat on the couch with her mother:

> She had probably had one or two drinks too many when she looked at me and said, "God, why did you give me such a beautiful little boy and such an ugly little girl?" From that point on, it didn't matter who told me I was pretty; I knew I was ugly. My mother's thoughtless words were used for many years by the enemy to destroy my self-image. (1998: 98)

Convinced that she was ugly, White explored drastic ways to win the approval of other people and to enhance her physical appearance, which led to bouts with eating disorders such as anorexia and bulimia.

White often states that her quest for love and acceptance caused her to recklessly pursue romantic relationships. She thought physical intimacy would fill the void in her life, but several romantic trysts and sexual encounters left her dissatisfied and empty. One of those encounters resulted in a teenage pregnancy, subsequent marriage, and speedy divorce.

Looking back, she often admits that she was on a self-destructive journey. Her first eighteen years witnessed the death of her father, physical and sexual abuse, bouts with anorexia, bulimia, and depression, a failed marriage, and the hopeless feeling that she was unlovable. An unexpected meeting in the trailer home of an older woman turned her life in another direction.

In all her childhood years, the early part in the South and later years in a Maryland trailer park after her mother remarried, White does not recall ever hearing the gospel message or attending a church service. As a troubled teenager, White had no knee-jerk response to the gospel or ill feelings against religion in general. She was an emotionally scarred divorced young mother who had hit rock bottom. As she sat one day at the kitchenette in a modest trailer home listening to her neighbor's presentation of the gospel message and Christ's love for her, White exclaimed: "Yes, I want real love! Yes, I want my life changed! Yes, I want You, Jesus, as my personal savior" (P. White 1998: 29).

Immediately after her conversion experience, White felt loved for the first time in years and enjoyed the comfort and sense of purpose attained from her new faith. She also believed God placed a special calling on her life. On her television show in July 2005, White recounted the vision she received from God shortly after conversion:

> When I was just eighteen years old and barely saved, the Lord gave me a vision that every time I opened my mouth and declared the Word of the Lord, there was a manifestation of his spirit where people were either healed, delivered, or saved. When I shut my mouth, they fell off into utter darkness and God spoke to me and said I called you to preach the gospel.

But before White would deliver her first sermon, she had to learn how to apply the therapeutic elements of the gospel to her troubled past and deep wounds, a talent that later distinguished her ministry and made her one of the most popular preachers in the country.

White's conversion did not immediately bring emotional, psychological, and spiritual health. In fact, in her early Christian years the Bible did not make much sense to her, and she found many teachings puzzling. Moreover, she had to learn how to trust and establish healthy relationships with people. Still imprisoned by feelings of bitterness and captive to memories of past pain, Paula had to confront resentment against her father, her past abusers, and herself. Conquering her taxing battle with bulimia and anorexia, as well as confronting her self-doubt and insecurities, would come gradually after her conversion experience. Hence, after confessing Jesus as her personal savior, Paula's life was still a mess. As she recalled:

> As a young Christian, no matter how I looked at my life, from every direction I saw a gigantic mess. When I examined my world, the sum total of my life seemed to be brokenness. Unkept promises and shattered dreams had left me in despair. My unwise choices had produced devastating consequences. I had very little to offer God. . . . I realized that I was not a whole or healthy person, that I had made choices that could not be reversed, and now they had produced a "harvest" in my life. (P. White 1998: 76–77)

A vital turning point came in Paula's early Christian experience when she met Randy White, a third-generation preacher in the Church of God denomination, to which Paula affiliated early in her Christian journey. Randy had a promising career as an associate pastor and evangelist in his denomination before his first marriage ended. His traditional denomination did not tolerate divorce, however, and stripped Randy of his associate minister position. Churches that once enjoyed his evangelistic ministry no longer invited him to preach. When he met Paula in 1989, Randy was in the early stages of reviving his career, and Paula was in the early phase of starting a cleaning business to provide for her young son.

Though coming from divergent paths, Randy and Paula had much in common. Both knew what it was like to live in a trailer park, marry young, and suffer the wounds of a difficult divorce. Both probed for biblical answers to their pressing problems and ardently sought to get their lives in order. Their troubled experiences also sparked compassion for hurting people and the desire to offer people hope through a ministry of restoration. The two became friends and dated for several months as they labored together in ministry projects, including serving the poor and homeless of Washington, D.C., ministering to troubled youth, and starting a bus ministry. Less than a year after meeting, Randy proposed during a tour to Israel; Paula gladly accepted.

Randy and Paula married in 1989 and shortly thereafter made the decision to move from Maryland to Tampa, Florida. After reading an advertisement for a youth pastor position, Randy felt God called them to

Tampa, and Paula cautiously conceded. But a more implicit reason behind the risky transplant involved their growing disillusionment with what they now often call denominational religion. Church of God prohibitions against attending movies, dances, and other forms of secular delight, felt Randy and Paula, hampered what God had in store for them. As their church website explained in 2005, they soon abandoned the confines of denominational religion: "Determined to make a difference, together both Randy and Paula rid themselves of denominational restraints and in 1991 with five founding members they launched a ministry of 'Evangelism and Restoration' known as South Tampa Christian Center." A new, independent ministry in Tampa allowed them to carve out a niche with a message of restoration.

After several months in Tampa, they took a trip to Orlando to visit a large church where the popular healing evangelist Benny Hinn preached. This was in 1991, when Hinn regularly drew tens of thousands to healing services in stadiums nationwide. Hinn left them with encouraging words and a $2,500 check to help start a new storefront church called South Tampa Christian Center with three other people. Launching a new church involved tireless effort—from drawing new members, to soliciting donations from local businesses and turning their storefront into a house of worship.

In its initial phase, the church could not generate enough resources to support them, so the couple lived on government cheese and peanut butter during some of the most financially lean days of their lives. While the two struggled financially, South Tampa Christian Center grew rapidly. Randy and Paula converted an old truck into a portable church and conducted inventive outdoor Sunday school lessons in housing projects all over Tampa. From the beginning they sent out evangelistic teams to Tampa's poorest areas, including government housing projects like Oak Park Village and Blythe-Andrews. Their church grew so fast that they had to move out of the storefront in just a few months. By the end of the year South Tampa Christian Center had 700 members, forcing the church to relocate services to an elementary school cafeteria.

Eventually the church took a three-year lease on an old warehouse needing extensive renovations, and faithful members helped clean the building, paint, and construct inside walls in order to get their new building running. The church continued to grow out of its space, eventually requiring two more relocations until it finally secured a building in 1998 that could address the needs of a membership approaching 10,000. Changing the church's name to Without Walls International Church, Randy and Paula drew visits from Myles Munroe, Joyce Meyer, Benny Hinn, and many other popular preachers. By 2006 the membership topped 20,000, and Paula White, at age forty-two, became one of the most recognizable evangelicals in the world.

"People are tired of organized religion!" shouted Paula White to her congregation during one Sunday service, adding that God never intended the church to be a haughty club with padded pews as pedestals conveying superiority. She explained that "the church is not for perfect saints, it's for messed-up people." White believes that most people who attend church are in an emotional intensive care unit; therefore, she works to maintain a friendly environment that addresses the pressing needs of hurting people. She often reminds her members that the church is not a museum for saints but a hospital for people to receive healing. True to her vision, the church has more than 200 active ministries, including drug dependency programs, alcohol rehabilitation, GED tutoring, prison outreach, the X-Strippers Support network, classes to help welfare recipients make a full transition to the workforce, a rolling medical center that treats hundreds of shut-ins, as well as Bible studies for businessmen and professionals and a rock music club for teens. All these ministries reflect the church's mission as a place of healing and restoration. Two weeks after Hurricane Katrina, the church pledged a million-dollar donation to the relief fund for evacuees. Whether raising money every summer for school supplies or distributing toys for Christmas, Without Walls International targets the most disadvantaged areas in Tampa in order to devote energy and resources to help families in need.

Like many fast-growing congregations, Without Walls International utilizes talented singers and musicians to lead energetic praise and worship sessions, often reflecting creative themes. For example, for the "Tropical Island Sunday" worship service, the church was decorated with palm trees and grass huts on the stage while members wore island necklaces and sang and danced to Caribbean music. Similarly, the "Groovy Sunday" service incorporated music and outfits from the 1970s. The church often presents comical skits, one time creatively staging a dancing elderly couple mimicking youth concert dancers during an announcement for an event. As part of a creative strategy to draw new members, Without Walls presents annual concerts that feature secular and gospel music superstars like Brian McKnight, the Winans Family, M. C. Hammer, and MASE, which explains why it is among the largest churches in the nation.

While co-pastoring their budding church, Paula White traveled the nation as an evangelist. White's career soared when T. D. Jakes endorsed her in the late 1990s. Receiving his big break only a few years earlier, Jakes at the time was becoming one of the most popular preachers in the country. White's visibility increased as a regular speaker at Jakes's Woman Thou Art Loosed conferences and God's Leading Lady tours. Preaching at Jakes's conferences introduced White's unique testimony and candid sermons about spiritual and emotional wholeness to thousands of women nationwide. But it was her television show that provided the greatest impetus behind her international renown.

In 2001, Paula discussed with Randy her belief that God called her to start a television ministry. Backed by her husband's full support, White launched her first show in a living room set with a borrowed multicolored sofa and a plain black curtain. She discussed her show's humble beginnings on a recent broadcast:

> We put this rent-to-rent-to-rent-to-own furniture with a single camera, a black backdrop; we had six rotary phones, a computer, and a secretary who could only type twenty-three words a minute. And we launched Paula White media ministry having little idea that God just five years later would touch the world.

White's program became popular because she dealt with real-life issues such as family struggles and self-esteem. In an early broadcast, one of her panelists broke down and cried when asked about her father. The television crew wanted to stop the shoot, but White signaled them to continue recording. On a subsequent broadcast, White reminisced about the incident and explained that she wanted the panelist's pain to be visible to the audience to show that spiritual leaders also suffer with anguish and that everything is not always perfect. Many people value White's ministry for exposing real-life issues and offering candid glimpses of the human condition.

Through her talk show, White became the "Oprah" of the evangelical world by tackling the nitty-gritty, day-to-day realities of life and by finessing dialogues with celebrities and experts concerning various facets of self-actualization. Luminaries such as football star Deion Sanders (whom T. D. Jakes also featured at the Potter's House), management guru John Maxwell, business tycoon Donald Trump, and a bevy of popular evangelical pastors and intellectuals appeared as guest panelists to discuss

Paula White preaches at Carpenter's Home Church in Lakeland, Florida, in 2005.
Photo courtesy of the *Tampa Tribune*.

with Paula their areas of expertise and perspectives on Christian living. Refraining from the churchy format exemplified by many televangelists, White attempts to stay abreast of the times by dealing with popular issues such as finding a spouse or developing an investment portfolio. While television exposure greatly contributed to making hers a household name, she draws more and more loyal fans by offering a relatable message calibrated toward many needs of contemporary Americans.

In sermons and books, White leads people who struggle with a poor self-image to self-acceptance. She often discusses her painful struggle with bulimia and how she found deliverance through reading the Bible. She seeks to prevent countless women from pursuing the impossible ideals of female beauty: flawless face, perfect hair, and a fit body. In a frank and uncompromising manner she tells her listeners to drop the obsession with personal appearance because beauty fades:

> A man might be drawn to that woman who pumps up her breasts and puts on her high heels and struts her stuff. But forty years down the line, she's going to look like her mama. After she has had three babies and done the work of raising them and gravity has taken its toll, those breasts are going to sag and no matter how much toner she uses, she's going to

have wrinkles and stretch marks, and she may be strutting her stuff, but not in four-inch heels. (White 2004: 222)

In a sight-and-sound generation that valorizes thinness and objectifies women, White urges her listeners to reject unrealistic beauty standards and to accept themselves as they are, adding the caveat that they should work out, eat healthful foods, and take care of their bodies.

Though White often challenges contemporary notions of beauty and their residual pressures on women, her success also comes from embodying them. Her television program invites celebrity guests like the best-selling author and wellness expert Jordan Rubin and fitness guru Donna Richardson to discuss diet tips and how to achieve a well-toned look. Her Satisfied Woman Retreat offers the services of beauty consultants who give makeovers and other tips to accentuate women's aesthetic appeal. Since becoming a celebrity preacher, White has reinvented her image with extensive plastic surgery, modish hairstyles, perfectly manicured nails, chic silk suits, fitted dresses, and a leaner size 4 figure, all in contrast to photos and videos from earlier years. She often reveals details about her workout regimen and eating habits that help her stay in shape, and she encourages women to enhance their sex appeal to their husbands. By appearing on television in stylish outfits and form-fitting suits, White constructs a new, trendy prototype for the female televangelist.

White emphasizes a strong sense of proportion, urging people to work hard but warning them not to neglect spending time with their families. In 2006, she launched the 7 Weeks of Wellness campaign to instruct viewers about exercise, choosing supplements, getting enough sleep, emotional health, and how to live a life of prayer and purpose. She encourages viewers to develop healthy relationships and learn new and imaginative ways to have fun. In fall 2005 her Satisfied Woman Retreat drew attendees from across the country to the Omni Orlando Resort for three days of intimate fellowship and fun. The advertisement for the retreat appeared on her television show: "Meet women from all over the world in a casual and relaxing atmosphere. Be prepared to relax, refresh, and renew as we share in this powerful time of fun and fellowship. Reunite with your girlfriends for a giant slumber party, enjoy a high-energy prayer walk, lay poolside and catch some rays." Massage therapists pampered attendees, and programmers offered a slate of fun activities that included dancing, laughing, singing, and worshiping. Mixing of the secular with the sacred is part of White's attraction.

Paula White, a major player in an evangelical world almost entirely dominated by men, represents a nonconfrontational style of postfeminist leadership. Her annual conferences create free spaces for women preachers to exercise their gifts in front of large audiences, and her books and sermons encourage women to self-actualize, aggressively seek change, and draft their own agendas. Her women's retreats and seminars resemble consciousness-raising feminist therapy groups from the 1970s by offering women opportunities to share their feelings and seek healing from internalized self-hatred and damage that brewed during their teenage years. Rather than show new recipes for baking cookies or teach women how to be better homemakers, White's television show invites accomplished businesspersons like Kim Kiyosaki to inspire women to be fiscally smart and financially empowered. Her ministry teaches the next generation of evangelicals that women can be pastors, thought leaders, and business executives, too. White strategically aligns herself with celebrity preachers and often keynotes at churches like Salem Baptist Church in Chicago, where women rarely exercise spiritual gifts from behind the pulpit. Hence, White tactically deconstructs traditional gender norms and reimagines the breadth of talent and reach women can have in the evangelical world.

Racial and ethnic diversity are also salient undercurrents in Paula White's ministry and appeal. She is one of the only white evangelicals to routinely interrogate and attack southern racism. Once active in the inner city of Washington, D.C., during the late 1980s and in postriot Los Angeles in the 1990s, White continues to transcend racial lines with her ministry in Tampa. The Without Walls International membership is a mixture of whites, South Pacific Islanders, Asians, Latinos, and African Americans, and the ministerial staff reflects its diversity. Her television show *Paula White Today* is also a positive model of interracial interaction and often deals with racial and ethnic themes. Among its recurring panel of cohosts are successful African Americans, including television news anchor Secily Wilson and songwriter Javen Campbell, who engage White and other panelists in dialogues about their families and careers. On one show, White discussed with guest panelist Bernice King the pain and tragedy of growing up without her father, Martin Luther King Jr.; more recently, White was a special guest at Radio City Music Hall's "Dream Concert" benefit for the Martin Luther King Foundation along with Stevie Wonder, Aretha Franklin, and Garth Brooks. White has keynoted at Woman Thou Art Loosed conferences and has preached behind the pulpits of prominent black megachurches, including West Angeles Church of God in Christ,

Paula White preaches at Without Walls International Church.
Photo courtesy of the *Tampa Tribune.*

in Los Angeles California. She once broadcast her show on location at a multiethnic Bible study for singles in New York City. At the 2005 Essence Festival, a three-day event that draws more than 300,000 mostly African American tourists to New Orleans annually, White's keynote address drew as many spectators as any other speaker, including T. D. Jakes and Cornel West, a popular African American intellectual.

White offers a conservative bourgeois message with personal empowerment as a central theme. She argues that God's power brings practical change in all aspects of life, including financial success. She contends that it is not the will of God that people should struggle. Aligning one's life with God's values, according to White, sets the stage for tremendous blessings. White often chides what she refers to as the "religious mindset," a point of view that sees wealth as evil. In contrast, she insists that God wants to bless Christians as part of their covenant relationship.

Though she often emphasizes that God is in control, White's empowerment message focuses much attention on human performance. She places the onus on the individual to be successful by adhering to biblically based principles and argues that it is possible for a Christian to have a right heart for God and yet lack the proper mental or psychological perspective. White points this out in her inaugural book: "And with a wrong head, we may very well live in complete defeat and lose ground in the Kingdom of God. This has nothing to do with our hearts or with our worship. Our lives can be destroyed because of ignorance" (1998: 31). White often tells listeners that God gives them everything they need to be successful, but the power to determine victory or defeat is in their hands. She teaches that good intentions are not enough; people must develop the right thinking and apply biblical principles toward every situation to see spiritual, emotional, financial, and physical success. She tells them death and life are in the power of their tongue and that they should be careful to make positive confessions concerning the promises that come with their covenant and God. Like many prosperity preachers, White appeals to the American mentality of success and self-transcendence.

Like the works of a postmodern novelist, White's preaching and writing are more episodic than linear, more evocative than exegetical. She encourages people to have a personal and passionate relationship with God and instructs members to hear the voice of God. Psychiatrists often prescribe years of counseling to individuals with troubled pasts, but White offers her followers an inexpensive route through spirituality and rigorous self-appraisal (White 2007). She presents a healthy and whole mind-set as part of the benefits package that comes with a covenant relationship with God, but she places the activation of God's blessings on the individual through faith and positive confession.

Eschewing commitment to a single denominational perspective, White is a "free agent" who tests and experiments with new ideas and approaches. She is comfortable around everyone, from old-school Pentecostals to high-tech business executives, from conservative evangelicals to Hollywood celebrities and professional athletes. White is the ultimate outlier who cannot be tied down to one tradition, one approach, or one theme. Her intricate journey provided her with the flexibility and interpersonal skill to thrive in varied environments, whether dialoguing with conservative broadcaster Pat Robertson, bringing down the house at the Essence Festival in New Orleans, or preaching to inmates at Riker's Island in New York City. She worked for more than a decade in inner-city parks and project communities, while at the same time ministering to music superstars like Michael Jackson and mentoring businesspersons like Donald Trump and professional athletes like Gary Sheffield. White disturbs stereotypes and established hierarchies of gender in the evangelical world as a smart, blonde, attractive preacher who interviews scholars, preaches fiery sermons, and mingles with powerful politicians.

Moreover, White is an idealized version of the successful and happy contemporary middle-class American and constructs an archetype for the emotionally healthy and psychologically whole evangelical. Learning lessons from her difficult journey and personal transformation, White teaches that spiritual salvation has practical implications on earth. White teaches her followers not only a strong regard for biblical authority but also how to personalize scriptures to make an impact for immediate change. She mixes biblical wisdom with pop psychology and offers a personal God who speaks to Christians and engages all facets of life. She transcends race and teaches people to take inventory of friendships so as to avoid toxic relationships, urging followers to stop looking through the rearview mirror because "yesterday is not your best day, tomorrow is!" Hence White offers a practical and appealing brand of Christianity that speaks to the existential needs and cultural tastes of many contemporary Americans.

White has a similarity with another holy maverick, the Protestant reformer Martin Luther. Both Luther and White spent years feeling unworthy of God's love and inadequate to fulfill their spiritual callings. Resembling the Old Testament patriarch Jacob, Luther and White "wrestled" with God, and their struggles produced feelings of unconditional love and a vibrant message that addresses the vagaries of their ages. Hence Martin Luther and Paula White became reformers by reaching down to the depths of their own personal struggles to fashion a more organic version of Christianity that provides answers to life's pressing questions and healing to life's piercing wounds.

White also shares intriguing similarities with her professed spiritual father, T. D. Jakes. As children, both endured the tragic deaths of their fathers, and both persevered through harsh economic times as young pastors. Both draw from the wellspring of a black church preaching aesthetic, the fire and spirit of neo-Pentecostalism, and the business savvy and marketing genius of a hypercapitalist age. Both exchange legalism and self-righteousness for a raw and transparent spirituality. Both speak the language of twenty-first-century America and thus serve as models of the new postmodern evangelical preacher.

White has an irrefutably powerful presence in pop culture and shares her greatest resemblance with secular talk show host Oprah Winfrey. Like Oprah, Paula was born in Mississippi, suffered through difficult teenage years, had a meteoric rise to success, and continues to discuss past bouts with physical abuse and molestation. Part of their mystique is an air of familiarity and comfort that connects with people of various ethnic backgrounds and spheres of life. Both Oprah and Paula are hip, trendy, postfeminist women with immeasurable influence and symbolic power. Millions of curious onlookers watched Oprah and Paula gain and lose weight and retool their appearance and style. Both run media empires as best-selling authors, public speakers, and television personalities, and both have the savvy and awareness to recognize and maximize new opportunities. Oprah and Paula are iconoclastic and yet profoundly aware that their mainstream status limits just how far they can challenge traditional American ideals. Their incredible drives partially stem from their own fight for peace and self-assurance to win the battles against the demons of their youth.

We can also compare White with contemporary pop icons like Tupac Shakur and Miguel Piñero, deceased poets whose art stemmed from the inner soul of human experience. Shakur's popularity derived from a mysterious ability to extrapolate the emotional upheaval of young African Americans coping to survive in the concrete jungles of inner-city life. Piñero became a Latino icon by channeling a grueling prison stint and fierce life experiences into his craft. Similarly, White turns her life into art to help others overcome the demons of their past. Shakur, Piñero, and White are symbols of America's soft spot for redemption.

White strategically integrates her message and ministry into mainstream American religious culture by constructing an archetype of the emotionally healthy, well-balanced Christian, honest about her shortcomings. White's message infuses an emphasis on God's transforming power with the raw, honest, and gritty faith of our postmodern confessional culture. She offers a self-help brand of Christianity that teaches people how to become physically fit, mentally tough, and biblically literate, while trusting in the promises of God for dramatic change in life. White seeks to make Jesus relevant to the pursuits of everyday life and thereby offers a message that resonates with the experiences of millions of Americans. White's transparency speaks to her vast appeal. A self-proclaimed "messed-up Mississippi girl," she wears her childhood bout with physical and sexual abuse, struggles with eating disorders and depression, teenage pregnancy, and failed first marriage as badges of honor to inspire people yearning for new beginnings.

Paula and Randy White tell their congregation they are going through a divorce in June 2007. Photo courtesy of the *Tampa Tribune.*

Postscript

The year 2007 proved to be a difficult one for Paula White's family and ministry. During a Sunday night service in August, with Paula by his side, Randy proclaimed to Without Walls International Church: "We have a very difficult announcement to make tonight before Tim Storey preaches. And that is that we are going through a divorce. It is the most difficult decision that I have had to make in my entire life and I came to you tonight to first let you know that I take full responsibility for a failed marriage." Paula then added that although this is a closed chapter in their lives, it is not the end of the story for them or their ministries, and that they stand in full support of each other. Neither disclosed the motivating factors behind the divorce. Randy is expected to remain pastor of Without Walls International Church, while Paula navigates Paula White Ministries.

A few months later, the estranged couple generated more national media attention when Senator Charles Grassley, the ranking Republican on the Senate Finance Committee, requested their financial records as part of a probe of six evangelical ministers who enjoy what he perceives as exorbitant wealth. Though these recent developments pose questions about the durability of Paula White's ministry, they have not stopped her momentum as an evangelical superstar. Less than a month after Senator Grassley announced his inquiry into her ministry, White appeared on *Larry King Live* for an exclusive interview to discuss her public divorce, defend her financial integrity, and plug her recently released book, *You're All That*. She continues to appear on her television program that reaches a world audience, crisscross the nation as a public speaker, and pursue philanthropic endeavors, including supporting cancer research and various charities. If Paula White's personal history of turning trials into trophies is predictive, then we should expect a forthcoming book and sermon series delineating an honest reflection on how she landed on both feet.

6

Surfing Spiritual Waves

Rick Warren and the Purpose-Driven Church

Three key responsibilities of every pastor are to discern where God's spirit is moving in our culture and time, prepare your congregation for that movement, and cooperate with it to reach people Jesus died for. I call it "surfing spiritual waves" and it's the reason Saddleback has grown to 23,500 on weekends in twenty-four years.

—Rick Warren

It was an ironic twist of fate that Brian Nichols's and Ashley Smith's paths crossed in March 2005 in an apartment complex in Duluth, Georgia. Smith, a widow and mother fighting addictions to speed, marijuana, Xanax, and methamphetamines, had just moved to her apartment in Duluth earlier that week. Nichols fled there to elude the federal and state authorities. Their courses converged for a dramatic early Saturday morning encounter that would affect the rest of their lives.

Nichols became the target of the largest manhunt in Georgia history only hours before meeting the twenty-six-year-old Ashley Smith. On trial for the rape of his former girlfriend, he overpowered a sheriff's deputy while changing clothes in a holding area. Securing the deputy's gun and keys, Nichols proceeded to the courtroom and killed a court reporter as well as the judge presiding over his rape trial. He left the courthouse and killed his third victim, a police sergeant of the Fulton County Sheriff's Department. Nichols hijacked two cars to divert the police and then slipped away undetected by taking a train to Buckhead, Georgia, where later he found a U.S. Customs agent alone at home. Nichols shot and killed the agent, stole his truck, and headed toward Duluth for his bizarre encounter with Ashley Smith, the next potential murder victim.

Pastor Rick Warren. Photo courtesy of Associated Press.

After purchasing cigarettes from a local convenience store at 2:30 A.M., Smith returned to her apartment. Before Smith could make a move, Nichols approached her at gunpoint, forced his way into her apartment, and threatened to kill her. After Nichols removed his hat, Smith recognized him as the subject of a massive manhunt she had seen reported on television earlier that day. Gripped with fear, Smith attempted to gain Nichols's confidence by discussing her daughter and sharing methamphetamines with him. In a surreal plot twist, Smith requested permission to read, and Nichols acquiesced. Smith retrieved two books that had brought her much peace and instruction, the Bible, and a copy of Rick Warren's best-selling book *The Purpose-Driven Life*. Smith, like millions of Christians nationwide, was a member of a church that participated in Warren's 40 Days of Purpose program by reading a chapter of his book daily and meeting during the week to discuss it with other members. Along with reading the book, Smith watched Warren on videotape once a week in her small-group meetings.

Pleased that Nichols granted her request, she turned to chapter 33 and started to read the first paragraph aloud. Nichols, captivated by Warren's words, requested she repeat the passage about finding one's purpose. The words Smith read caused Nichols to engage in some deep soul-searching. He eventually concluded that his abducted victim was really an angel sent by God. After a series of events, which included Smith cooking him pancakes, Nichols let her leave to see her daughter. Nichols then calmly surrendered to the police after Smith contacted the authorities.

Both Ashley Smith and Rick Warren received a maelstrom of media attention after police captured Nichols. Warren first learned about the Smith-Nichols encounter from *Larry King Live*, while on a ministry trip to Africa. As Warren later related while a guest on King's show:

> I had been in the bush all day. We'd been working with orphans that had been orphaned through the genocide in Rwanda, and also orphaned by AIDS. After a pretty grueling day, we got back to the hotel, and I flipped on the TV and there you were talking about how *The Purpose-Driven Life* had been used by Ashley to convince Brian to turn himself in.

Warren visited Nichols in prison, and his book jumped back to the top of the best-seller list, where it had previously enjoyed a twenty-five-month run. Smith later wrote her own book, *Unlikely Angel*, delineating her night with Nichols and past struggles with drug and alcohol addiction. Warren and Smith appeared together on *Oprah* and discussed how God's purpose for Smith eclipsed the problems that plagued her life.

Rick Warren is the pastor of one of the largest churches in the country. From his early seminary days to the present, he has relished his role as a nonconformist. The scope of Warren's reach in popular culture is unlike that of other spiritual leaders. Not a typical Southern Baptist preacher, Warren puts his sermons on an Internet site that gets more than 400,000 hits a day; while sitting in his pajamas, he presses a button to send *Rick's Toolbox*, his weekly newsletter, to more than 150,000 pastors. His quotations appear on greeting cards and Starbucks cups; he receives personal invitations to U2 concerts from rock music legend Bono; and he also keynoted the 2006 Azusa Street Centennial to commemorate the birth of American Pentecostalism.

Warren's multidimensionality makes him one of the most difficult evangelical innovators to gauge. Not many other preachers are friends with the president of Rwanda, write a monthly column for *Ladies' Home Journal*, and receive a standing ovation after speaking at Harvard University. Not many other conservative pastors possess the flexibility to be pro-life and pro-poor, the ingenuity to lead a preaching seminar for rabbis at the

Rick Warren speaks with at the Global Summit on AIDS and the Church at
Saddleback Church in Lake Forest, California, November 29, 2007.
Photo courtesy of Associated Press.

University of Judaism, or the versatility to work and dine with homosex-
ual activists while maintaining a firm stance against same-sex marriage.
Not many spiritual leaders mentor prominent businesspersons like Rupert
Murdock and Jack Welch, or can claim that after three decades of ministry, they have never been alone in a room with a woman other than their
wife. Few evangelical pastors are friends with both President George W.
Bush and Democratic presidential nominee Barack Obama, a notable participant at Warren's 2006 Global Summit on AIDS at Saddleback Church.
There is even more to the relationship between Warren and Obama: the
presidential hopeful launched a 40 Days of Faith and Family tour while
campaigning in South Carolina in October 2007, an initiative obviously
adapted from Warren's justly popular movement from a few years earlier
(Davenport 2007; Pappu 2007).

The complexity of Warren's personality and ministry transcends many
stereotypes, including race and ethnicity. Warren, a white middle-aged
pastor, heads a church with a large number of Asian Americans, founded
more than twenty Spanish-speaking congregations, and conducted a
citywide 40 Days of Purpose campaign in Philadelphia with 250 black
churches. Of the 4,000 pastors who attended his purpose-driven church
seminar at Saddleback in 2005, 500 were African American, as is his

personal prayer partner for the last twenty-five years. Warren proudly draws from diverse sources: he gained inspiration for his purpose-driven church principles while observing Japanese churches as a short-term missionary; he learned much about small groups from his experience with Korean churches; and he drew insight about support networks for sick· people during his time working with Rwandan churches.

Warren is even more of an exception when it comes to his finances. In an age in which megachurch pastors drive luxury cars and purchase multi-million-dollar mansions, Warren drives the same four-year-old Ford and resides in the same $365,000 home (a modest price in an upscale Southern California real estate market) that his family lived in before *Purpose-Driven Life* generated enormous personal wealth. Moreover, he receives no remuneration from Saddleback and recently donated to the church twenty-five years' worth of his salary. Warren claims to be a "reverse tither"; he lives off of 10 percent of the proceeds from his books and entrepreneurial activities and gives away 90 percent of his income, which according to Forbes magazine exceeded $25 million in 2006 alone. He has also established three foundations, one of which devotes millions to helping people infected with AIDS. After the Purpose Driven Foundation folded in late 2006 due to financial constraints, Warren was able to redirect funds toward ministry in Africa and elsewhere. The profits he generates from selling his sermon transcripts on the Internet fund translation projects that provide teaching materials to pastors around the world in thirty different languages.

Warren's ability to relate to everyday, ordinary people is an important aspect of his appeal. Even though he earned a doctorate from Fuller Theological Seminary and brokers a powerful network of 40,000 churches, his members and associates refer to him simply as Rick. He freely discusses his marital problems in the pulpit and preaches in khaki pants, untucked Hawaiian shirts, and sandals. Warren often passes time between services talking, hugging, signing autographs, and posing for pictures with members and visitors.

Warren's charm comes from appearing as just a normal guy who prefers bear hugs to handshakes. His wife calls him a ham and a goofball, and he often clowns around on the microphone at private luncheons and laughs heartily with staff and members of his church. Warren declined many offers to broadcast his sermons on television and radio as part of his "stealth strategy" to remain under the radar. Despite Warren's quest to remain anonymous, U.S. senators flocked to his side after he delivered the invocation at the gala celebration on the eve of Bush's second presidential

inauguration, thus demonstrating the popularity and appeal of his purpose-driven message. The October 17, 2005, issue of *Fortune* listed Warren
in its "Top 25 People We Envy Most" list; two weeks later, *Fortune* distinguished him as "secular America's favorite preacher." Warren was the only
spiritual leader to make the *Forbes* Top 100 Celebrities list in June 2006.
Listing him at number 60, *Forbes* ranked Warren higher than many popular luminaries, including actors Cameron Diaz and Leonardo DiCaprio,
news personalities Katie Couric and Bill O'Reilly, popular comedians
Dave Chappelle and Larry the Cable Guy, superstar athletes Venus and
Serena Williams, and best-selling author John Grisham. Without a television program, prominent denominational position, or political platform
and agenda, Warren has become one of the most significant and influential evangelical preachers in the world.

Though it received a boost through the media coverage of his connection with Ashley Smith's story, Warren's book *The Purpose-Driven Life* had
already sold millions, spending almost a year at the top of the *New York
Times* best-seller list. By the time the Smith-Warren story broke, President Bush and his wife had read *The Purpose-Driven Life*, as had many
professional athletes, business executives, drug addicts, and prisoners.
Warren honored requests for autographed copies from more than forty
governmental officials worldwide, including Ukraine's president Viktor
Yuschenko and Cuba's longtime leader Fidel Castro. Grieving parents
in Memphis distributed 2,000 copies of *The Purpose-Driven Life* at their
son's funeral, and ironically, a copy of the book sat in Scott Peterson's car
the day he was arrested for the murder of his wife, Lacie. A bipartisan coalition of Florida House and Senate members invited Warren to the state
capital to discuss his book. In a speech at the Pew Forum on Religion and
Public life in May 2005, Warren discussed how his 40 Days of Purpose
program reached various organizations:

> It spread to corporations like Coca-Cola and Ford and Wal-Mart and
> they started doing "40 Days of Purpose." And then it spread to all the
> sports teams. I spoke at the NBA All-Stars this year because all of the
> teams were doing "40 Days of Purpose." LPGA, NASCAR, most of the
> baseball teams—when the Red Sox were winning the World Series, they
> were going through 40 Days of Purpose during the series.

The simultaneous and marketable simplicity and appeal of Warren's prescriptions led some critics to dismiss *The Purpose-Driven Life* as mediocre

and hardly original, suggesting its popularity is the product of consumerism and hype. Some evangelicals contend Warren merely repackages core Christian values; others maintain that New Age values inform Warren's concept of a purpose-driven life (Smith 2004). Still others argue that the psychological principles that shape the philosophy in *The Purpose-Driven Life* are anti-Christian (Sundquist 2004). Similar to the receptions of other holy mavericks such as Joel Osteen and Brian McLaren, much activity on the Internet each year deconstructs Warren's best-selling book and unconventional ministry. Whatever the opinion, it is clear that *The Purpose-Driven Life* reaches vast audiences.

Keeping with a penchant to surf spiritual waves, Warren is in the process of revising *The Purpose-Driven Church*, a church growth manual written primarily for clergy. Drawing from his travels across the globe, attendant to the tastes and preferences of his readers, and capitalizing on the popularity of *The Purpose-Driven Life*, Warren's revisions seek to connect with laypeople. As such, Warren queries what he calls the "everyday Christian" with: "What is my role, and what is God's purpose for me in my local church?" (Morgan 2007).

A large part of Warren's success does reside in his ability to repackage the ABCs of Christianity into catchy and concise prescriptions for healthy living that jive with contemporary Americans. In July 2003, *USA Today* called him the master marketer of a single message: "You are here for God"; even Warren admits in sermons and interviews that there is nothing new in *The Purpose-Driven Life*, which is undeniably evangelical in its theology. The book endorses a literal interpretation of the Bible, for example, and goes so far as to give practical advice for how to avoid the devil's predictable schemes in order to become what he calls a world-class Christian. Warren's book argues that God created humans to become like Christ, and that only through a relationship with Christ can individuals discover their true identity and purpose. *The Purpose-Driven Life* argues that human existence is not accidental; God created individuals for specific purposes, and only through a personal meaningful relationship with God can one find that purpose, by turning not to speculation or the world's wisdom but to God's revelation through the scriptures. The book begins by urging readers to sign a covenant agreement to commit forty days to discovering God's purpose for life. Warren calls it an anti-self-help book that focuses on God. On the surface, it appears to be a book about divine sovereignty, as this passage suggests:

God prescribed every single detail of your body. He deliberately chose your race, the color of your skin, your hair, and every other feature. He custom-made your body just the way he wanted it. He also determined the natural talents you would possess and the uniqueness of your personality. . . . Because God made you for a reason, he also decided when you would be born and how long you would live. He planned the days of your life in advance, choosing the exact time of your birth and death. . . . God left no detail to chance. (2002: 22–23)

Warren contends that God foreknew which two individuals possessed exactly the correct genetic makeup to create the custom "you" that God had in mind; he carefully mixed the DNA cocktail that created you because you were made for a specific ministry. Warren even suggests that God created every animal and plant for a specific purpose. Though God's sovereignty is a resounding theme, the book has much to do with human agency.

The Purpose-Driven Life has a performance-based goal: to provide a forty-day process of personal transformation. Its basic premise contends that God created humans for divine delight and that the purpose-driven life is one totally focused on pleasing God. Living life for the glory of God, Warren advises, requires a change in priorities, scheduling, personal relationships, and just about every other facet of life. According to Warren, these changes reside in the human will, a point that lies in tension with the book's resounding premise that God ordained everything about an individual before birth. Warren teaches readers how to become best friends with a personal God who desires an intimate relationship with creation. Warren expounds on how to make God smile, cultivate community with peers, resist temptation, keep a balanced life, write a personal life-purpose statement, and share one's life message. Hence, like many self-help books, *The Purpose-Driven Life* gives considerable attention to the necessity of human performance.

The book's simple yet radical discussion of purpose resonates with millions of Americans. Many respondents claim that Warren's book made them think, for the first time, about the overall worth and function of all their life activities. He informs readers that their lives have profound meaning, and that knowing their purpose will help them discover God's destiny for their lives. While Warren preaches purpose, he tactically offers a way for individuals to map out their own avenues to a life of meaning.

Rick Warren speaks at the Vine Center at Liberty University in Lynchburg, Virginia, September 26, 2004. Photo courtesy of Associated Press.

In the companion journal to *The Purpose-Driven Life*, Warren reminds readers that while writing the journal he offered divine petitions on their behalf so that they might discover their purpose in life. Space is plentiful in the journal so that readers, guided by Warren's 40 Days of Purpose schedule and methodology, can record their responses to a scripture reference, a thought for the day, and guided questions. The purpose of spiritual journaling, Warrens writes in the journal's introduction, is to record personal spiritual growth and advancement, to establish a record of God's work in individuals as they seek to find their purpose. Modeling encouragement that comes from contemporary experts called life coaches, Warren says:

> I admire you for your interest in this book. It shows you want to know your purpose, and God loves that. You'll learn the big picture—how all the pieces of the puzzle fit together. This perspective on life will reduce your stress, increase your satisfaction, help you make better decisions, and most importantly prepare you for eternity. (2003)

Like other evangelical innovators, Warren discovered a way to reinforce his purpose-driven philosophy through active engagement with his readers. Warren adds a personal touch as he tells readers he prays for them, while he also encourages readers to articulate their own life purpose in their own words and chart personal progress and growth. In these ways Warren effectively responds to the preferences and needs of today's religious seekers.

By 2003 more than 3 million people had participated in Warren's 40 Days of Purpose campaign, committing themselves to reading one chapter a day and participating in an intense program of worship, Bible study, fellowship, and service. *The Purpose-Driven Life* became a world phenomenon, selling more than 25 million copies. The book has also been translated into forty different languages. To celebrate the success of *The Purpose-Driven Life* when it sold 15 million copies by 2004, media tycoon Rupert Murdock threw a party for Warren in the top floor of the Rainbow Room in Manhattan, inviting politicians, entertainers, and prominent New York City socialites. Warren gave a brief talk at this gala and received a standing ovation.

Much like holy mavericks Paula White and T. D. Jakes, Warren transcended humble beginnings to become an influential world leader. He is a self-professed country boy who grew up in Redwood Valley, a rural town of fewer than 500 people in Northern California. He often jokes that his current church membership exceeds the population of his hometown. As a teenager, Warren showed early flashes of evangelistic zeal by starting a Christian club on his high school campus, publishing an underground Christian newsletter, and sponsoring Christian rock concerts. The Southern Baptist Convention's newspaper wrote a story on a revival Warren helped to lead, which put him on his denomination's radar screen.

After graduating from high school, Warren attended California Baptist College in Riverside, California, and word about his ministry activities continued to spread throughout his denomination. Though a talented preaching prodigy, Warren had not considered his current profession until a life-changing event in 1973 put him on the pastoral track. Warren and a friend decided to skip classes and drive almost 400 miles to hear W. A. Criswell, the prominent Southern Baptist pastor of a large church in Dallas, preach at a conference in San Francisco. When Warren met Criswell, the legendary pastor laid his hands upon him and prayed, "Father, I ask that you give this young preacher a double portion of your Spirit. May the church he pastors grow to twice the size of the Dallas church" (Warren 1995: 26). A teary-eyed Warren interpreted Criswell's prayer as God's calling to pastor.

His time at California Baptist College was also special because he became reacquainted with a preacher's daughter named Kay, whom he had met a few years earlier at an evangelism conference. Kay and Rick dated and then married in 1975, the same year the Southern Baptist Convention ordained him. The couple graduated in 1977 and moved to Fort Worth, Texas, so Warren could attend Southwestern Baptist Theological Seminary. An emerging star in his denomination, Warren grew increasingly dissatisfied with the traditional practices of his church culture. Although he was very popular, his growing aversion for the type of classical rhetorical sermons endorsed by the seminary marked him as somewhat controversial. In retrospect, Warren often claims that he did not fit in the traditional Southern Baptist system.

While progressing through his courses in seminary, he began working on *Personal Bible Study Methods*, a book that applied life skills to doctrine-focused Bible study methods. This book would later sell more than 100,000 copies and find an expansive reception nationwide, including Billy Graham's evangelistic ministry. Warren also embarked on another project that reflected his preoccupation with ferreting out principles of healthy churches. He completed an independent study of the 100 largest churches in the country. Although these large churches varied in style and strategies, Warren's findings led him to conclude that healthy churches have to worship, evangelize, minister to the world, foster fellowship, and help Christians grow. These five principles, in turn, later served as the pillars of Warren's purpose-driven church model and would shape his future career as mentor to thousands of pastors worldwide.

When Warren finished seminary in December 1979, he rejected offers for pastoral assignments and eventually settled upon Southern California as the place where he would start his own church. Only a few days after graduating in December, the twenty-five-year-old preacher and his wife, Kay, packed up a U-haul with their old furniture and headed for Saddleback Valley, a fast-growing metropolitan area in Orange County. Warren recollects the early years: "We arrived in Southern California full of hope. We had a new decade before us, a new ministry, a four-month-old baby, and God's promise to bless us. But we also arrived with no money, no church building, and no home" (1995: 36).

Knowing no one in Saddleback Valley, the Warrens understood that their first task was to find a place to live. They met a realtor named Don Dale who found them a condo to rent, with the first month free for the young couple. Grateful for this act of kindness, Warren invited Dale to his church's first official service at his new condo. Warren named his new congregation Saddleback Church after their new environs. Five Southern Baptist churches supported Warren financially, and his former seminary provided fifteen interns to help him during the early stages.

Even back in 1980, Southern California was no stranger to megachurches and had many celebrity evangelical pastors, including Chuck Smith (Calvary Chapel), Robert Schuller (Crystal Cathedral), Fred Price (Crenshaw Christian Center), Charles Blake (West Angeles Church of God in Christ), and the late E. V. Hill (Mount Zion Missionary Baptist Church, Los Angeles). Rather than attracting committed Christians from other churches, Warren's goal was to build Saddleback's membership with new converts. Early on, Warren's ministry philosophy resembled that of Willow Creek Church, which at the time was a fast-growing four-year-old church in Illinois. Willow Creek popularized the "seeker-sensitive" church model, patterning worship services in ways that appeal to non-Christians. Holding services in a movie theater initially, Willow Creek would eventually become one of the largest churches in the nation, and its pastor Bill Hybels, an innovative evangelical entrepreneur (Beuttler 2004; Balmer 2006a; Balmer 2006b).

Like Willow Creek, Saddleback embraced a seeker-sensitive approach from its inception, designing worship services and programs to attract non-Christians and the religiously unaffiliated from Orange County. Before starting Saddleback, Warren accumulated more than ten years of sermons (most of them during seminary), yet the new emphasis on drawing and converting unbelievers prompted him to reevaluate his homiletics, or preaching methodology. Like most seeker-sensitive church pastors, Warren's guiding principle became, "How would this sermon sound to unbelievers?" and he adjusted messages for people unfamiliar with traditional church doctrine or culture. Warren and his team of volunteers spent the first twelve weeks engaging the community with door-to-door visitations in an effort to better understand why Saddleback Valley residents did not attend church. At the same time, Warren and his research team canvassed more than 2,000 homes to discover what would bring Saddleback Valley seekers to church. Warren's findings revealed that many unbelievers avoided church because of boring sermons, an unwelcoming atmosphere, excessive emphasis on money, and lack of adequate child care. Warren constructed all facets of his church with these areas of discontent in mind. Responding to market research remains a hallmark of his ministry.

Like a religious entrepreneur attuned to customer tastes and desires, Warren planned to launch Saddleback's first official service on Easter Sunday and invite non-Christians from the community. To supplement the door-to-door visitation, the church mailed out 15,000 hand-addressed and hand-stamped letters to people in the community. The letter targeted non-Christians, and as a result, Warren received disparaging responses from Christians who chided him for excluding the mention of Jesus or the Bible in the invitation. Yet his approach drew 150 curious spectators to Laguna Hills High School, where Saddleback launched its special Easter service.

Warren worked to build a consistent following, and Saddleback's membership grew to almost 200 by the end of the first year. This growth garnered national attention when the Southern Baptist Convention featured the church in its national publication. During the second year, Warren emphasized the importance of church membership. The Sunday services continued to attract nonbelievers, and small-group meetings and Bible studies during the week helped to train new converts. The third year Warren emphasized spiritual discipline and encouraged members to become more active in the church. For the next ten years Saddleback grew rapidly, utilizing seventy-nine different buildings in thirteen years, including four different high schools, numerous elementary schools, theaters, and professional office buildings until church members erected a high-tech tent with a seating capacity of 2,300. In a recent keynote speech titled "The Myth of the Modern Mega-Church," Warren discussed how members tolerated inconveniences because Saddleback Church met their needs:

> When people's lives are changed you'd have to lock the doors to keep them out, because they want to go where their lives are changed. We put people in a tent for three years where we would freeze in the winter

and it would rain on us all spring and we'd burn up in the summer and the howling winds came through and people would walk about a mile through the mud to get to this tent. I mean everything was inconvenient. And why did they come? Because their lives were getting changed.

After fifteen years of vigorous growth in hot gymnasiums and leaky tents, Saddleback found a permanent home: a 120-acre hilltop designed by theme park experts with various buildings, large parking lots, and Bible story reenactments, including a stream that parts, an allusion to the Old Testament story of Moses and the Red Sea. By 2006 Saddleback boasted close to 25,000 weekly attendees, one of the largest churches in the country.

Rick Warren names three mentors: his father, Billy Graham, and management specialist Peter Drucker. Warren's father modeled manhood, and Graham epitomized spiritual success, but it was Drucker who taught him much about building and running a large ministry. Twenty-five years ago Warren attended a business seminar where he met Drucker, who by then was a well-established author, conference speaker, and management consultant for Fortune 500 corporations nationwide. Warren began a correspondence with Drucker, and the two regularly met and formed a twenty-five-year mentoring relationship. Drucker taught Warren how to apply business principles and management skills to church leadership; to perform only tasks he is good at and to delegate the others; and to be mission-driven and constantly monitor his performance against the backdrop of that mission. The latter point obviously had an impact in Warren's development of a purpose-driven church. In a March 2005 feature in *Fortune* titled "The Best Advice I Ever Got," Warren discusses another important principle he learned from his mentor:

> Peter has taught me that results are always on the outside of your organization, not on the inside. Most people, when they're in a company, or in a church, or in an organization, they think, Oh, we're not doing well, we need to restructure. They make internal changes. But the truth is, all the growth is on the outside from people who are not using your product, not listening to your message, and not using your services.

Thus, the important business principle of matching organizational aims with the needs of potential clients contributed significantly to Saddleback's growth.

Warren believes that he and his team must carefully calibrate every aspect of the church service toward the concerns and interests of its laid-back Southern California target audience. He contends that seeker-sensitive services should consider cultural codes and mores in order to communicate an unchanging gospel message in ways that make sense to non-Christians. For Warren, this means not changing theology but crafting the service's environment and church's culture to remain attractive to outsiders and the unaffiliated. From the way volunteers greet members and visitors, to how church leaders make announcements, to the church's dress code, to the breadth of children's programs, to amenities offered (such as food, clothing, and Bible study materials), and especially to the music and worship style, Saddleback leaders embrace the apostle Paul's ancient dictum to become all things to all people. Saddleback exudes a comfortable Southern California environment where most attendees wear either shorts or jeans with sporty, comfortable blouses and short-sleeve shirts.

Like Disney World, Saddleback is a large and beautifully designed campus that inundates people with options. Seven different worship services take place every weekend, and people can choose from ten different venues depending on their music and worship style preferences (everything from jazz and reggae to punk rock) and then watch a videocast of Warren's sermon. Some members like to sit outside and listen to the service broadcast on one of many outdoor speakers while enjoying the picturesque, mountainous Southern Californian backdrop. Others choose to watch a videocast of the service while sipping iced coffee or munching on a bagel in Saddleback's Terrace Café. This restaurant overlooks the entire campus and sits less than a hundred feet from the Worship Center. Attendees also mingle through an outdoor bookstore stocked with purpose-driven study materials and a variety of Bibles and other books, along with plenty of Warren's trademark preaching attire, a short-sleeve Hawaiian shirt.

Saddleback has friendly greeters and hosts to welcome attendees, preferred parking for visitors, upbeat services that last no longer than seventy minutes, and several mechanisms to receive feedback from members and guests, including welcome cards and surveys. With a penchant for self-assessment, Warren goes so far as to conduct frequent environmental impact reports to gauge the lighting, pictures, and scenery for a welcoming ambience.

Saddleback also offers an entertaining sermon format especially designed for contemporary Americans with short attention spans. Warren's

And I said, "How do you get my sermons? You don't even have water or electricity in this village." He said, "Every weekend I walk an hour and a half to the nearest post office and I download your free sermon and then I preach it. You know, you're the only training I've ever had." And after that I thought to myself I will give the rest of my life for guys like that.

This experience prompted Warren to consider the causes and ponder solutions to some of the bigger problems churches can tackle all over the globe.

In 2005, Warren announced his goal to spark a new Protestant Reformation. But unlike its sixteenth-century counterpart, this reformation is not about creeds, but deeds, an all-out war against poverty, disease, and spiritual emptiness. Warren contends that the twenty-first century is the local church's most exciting period in history. He claims that nearly a thousand churches in Europe participated in his 40 Days of Purpose campaign, 30,000 congregations identify themselves as a purpose-driven church, and more than 400,000 pastors worldwide have attended his seminars, which equip them with intangibles for leading healthy congregations.

Warren is an effective organizer who links his agenda with a global network of churches to attack world problems. As part of the new reformation, Warren presented his global P.E.A.C.E. plan in April 2005 at Saddleback's twenty-fifth-anniversary service. Thirty thousand attended this special service in the Angel Stadium in Anaheim, including Gaddi Vasquez, director of the Peace Corps, who read a special message from President Bush. Warren's P.E.A.C.E. plan is a bold initiative to mobilize 10 million churches, 100 million small groups, and a billion Christians to impact the world by planting churches or partnering with existing ones in every village, equipping local leaders, assisting the poor, caring for the sick, and educating the next generation. The plan assumes that the church is the best institution to eradicate daunting world problems because the United Nations, the business world, and governments are not big enough. Warren launched the P.E.A.C.E. plan at a rally in Kigali, Rwanda's capital city, and a few months later in front of thousands gathered at the country's Amahoro National Stadium. He also announced his desire for a new reformation to a multiracial gathering of 12,000 at the Global Day of Prayer rally in Dallas's Reunion Arena, an event also telecast to 170 cities throughout North America.

Warren is a catalyst in a growing movement of faith-oriented activism among American evangelicals. In 2005 he dispatched an open-letter campaign urging the Bush administration to do more to fight world poverty.

Later that same year, Warren publicly took an AIDS test and then urged the almost 2,000 pastors visiting his conference at Saddleback to get more active in helping people with HIV/AIDS. In 2006, against the advice of evangelical leaders like James Dobson, a conservative radio host, and Richard Land, president of the Southern Baptist Convention, Warren joined the Evangelical Climate Initiative, whose goal is to pressure the government to enact policies to alleviate global warming and other environmental problems. As a global strategist, Warren has addressed the United Nations, the World Economic Reform, the African Union, and the Council on Foreign Relations. In a recent post on his webpage, Warren states that his goal is to take evangelicals back to a time of socially active, muscular Christianity that cared not just about personal salvation but also about social blights, abolishing slavery, and ending child labor.

Warren believes that since there are millions of congregations across the globe, the church possesses the best distribution channels to conquer world problems. His role as a force in a rapidly emerging global faith-based arena prompted one blogger to accuse him of repackaging dominionist theology, in other words, advocating a Christian conquest of world affairs as part of the Second Coming of Christ. Warren, however, sees his role in domestic and global affairs as part of the biblical mandate for pastors to engage society in creative ways. He calls this "surfing spiritual waves," a practice in which spiritual leaders discern where God is moving in one's cultural milieu, and then prepare their churches and themselves to cooperate with the movement.

For example, when Mel Gibson began scouting for prominent ministers to support his controversial movie *The Passion of the Christ*, Warren gladly jumped on board because he saw it as a spiritual wave. Warren planned a two-part sermon series to coincide with the movie's release, booked fifty theaters so Saddleback members could bring their non-Christians friends, and invited hundreds of community leaders from Orange County, including congresspersons, mayors, school superintendents, and four billionaires to a VIP premiere showing. Responding to Brian McLaren's criticism against churches functioning as hype machines for Mel Gibson, Warren defended his support of the movie release in his March 2004 guest column for the *Leadership Journal*, an online magazine for pastors and spiritual leaders:

> Honestly, I can't imagine any pastor being ashamed or reluctant to use a film about the cross. In a culture where visual imagery is the main

language for many, it is the perfect post-modern evangelistic tool. It doesn't preach; it just tells the story in an unsanitized and authentic way, and all of America is discussing it right now. The church should be leading the discussion.

In the same article he claims that "surfing the wave" of Gibson's movie release produced 900 new converts, 600 new small groups, and a considerable increase in Saddleback's average weekly attendance.

Warren does not offer new kinds of theological reflection but rather relocates traditional evangelical doctrine in a more practical and appealing package. His purpose-driven church movement is postmodern because it blurs denominational lines of distinction and challenges traditional ways of approaching ministry. He is a marketing-savvy organizer who established worldwide networks with leaders and churches from numerous ethnic backgrounds. He is quick, decisive, and remarkably bold in taking risks and experimenting with initiatives, constantly reassessing his methods and ministries to conform to the needs of contemporary Americans. Warren thrives because he speaks the language and understands the passions and fears of twenty-first-century Americans and tackles the radical problems of his society.

Whether he chastises conservatives for their moral tunnel vision, works with rock star Bono for AIDS relief, supports village chiefs in Africa or Hurricane Katrina evacuees in Houston, Texas, conducts a campaign with hundreds of black churches in Philadelphia, fields questions from students and professors at Harvard University, teaches rabbis and pastors principles for leading a healthy congregation, discusses the problem of evil on *Larry King Live*, mentors business magnates like Rupert Murdock, feeds the homeless, or ministers to a mass murderer like Brian Nichols, Warren reinvents evangelical leadership. By mixing religion with the best marketing and business principles of his day along with other elements of contemporary and secular culture, he recalibrates an evangelical ministry that is attractive to baby boomers and successive generations of Americans. Like many evangelical innovators, Warren provides spiritual commodities that resonate with the pluralistic tastes of his audience. He preaches simple sermons that answer many contemporary American problems and packages evangelicalism in a therapeutic, unconventional, racially generic, and politically inoffensive way. Warren crafts an entertaining and invigorating evangelical experience that addresses the existential needs and cultural tastes of many Americans.

Epilogue

Organizers claim that the Technology Entertainment Design (TED) event is like no other. Each year, TED invites more than a thousand leaders from various industries to Monterey, California, for "four days of learning, laughter, and inspiration," as stated on its website. Where else could a person connect with a politician like Al Gore, a movie star like Meg Ryan, a rock music icon like Peter Gabriel, and an international motivational speaker like Tony Robbins all in one day? Among the list of actors, politicians, scientists, environmentalists, and corporate executives speaking at the conference in 2006 were Rick Warren and an atheist philosopher named Dan Dennett, who spoke directly after the purpose-driven pastor. During his talk Dennett articulated an aesthetic assessment that many God-fearing evangelicals would not deny: "Today's religions are brilliantly designed." Today's religions depend less on self-sacrifice and blood, and more on self-empowerment, mass marketing, digital technologies, and theatrical performances.

Dennett's assessment points to a larger theme: religious practitioners and spiritual professionals must reimagine religion for each generation. For example, Pope John Paul II redefined the papacy before his death in 2005. He spoke various languages, had his own webpage, wrote best-selling books, produced a CD, and was personal friends with pop cultural icons—in other words, he was the first postmodern pope. He did not wait for the people to come to him; he went to the people, traveling more than any other pope before him, and thereby demonstrated that changes in religious experience embody cultural and technological changes in society.

Like Pope John Paul II, our five subjects have much in common as evangelical innovators who recraft Christianity for their generation. They preach edgy, sexy, iconoclastic sermons that are light on doctrine and heavy on experience, light on fire and brimstone and heavy on therapy and self-empowerment. They mix the secular with the sacred and are undaunted by the personal. They are business-savvy, media-sophisticated, high-tech preachers who not only are acquainted with the sight-and-sound generation but also affable to nonbelievers and the unaffiliated. They are trend-sensitive, socially curious preachers who adjust their methods and messages to the needs and tastes of the masses.

We are a "religiously mad culture," and our religious choices reflect key elements of our national temperament (Bloom 1992: 24). Our marketplace approach to studying religious vitality focuses on the capabilities of entrepreneurial elites to adapt to new tastes and needs. This assumes that religion, like all items for consumption, exists within a complex system of firms and suppliers who expend resources to bring the sacred into conversation with its social environment; winning and losing depends on the effectiveness of making connections with some segment of the public. We have demonstrated that religious suppliers triumph in this highly competitive marketplace when they are quick, decisive, and flexible as they react to changing conditions, remain savvy at packaging and marketing their ministries, and stay resourceful at offering spiritual rewards that resonate with the existential needs and cultural tastes of the public (MacDonald 2005; Carrette and King 2005; Clark 2007).

A noted sociologist once proclaimed that good scholarly analysis produces a deeper understanding of things about which people are already pretty much aware (Becker 1982). Fittingly, our market-based assessments about religion are no surprise to a growing group of church practitioners who already acknowledge the competitive environments in which their ministries exist. Pastoral conferences, church-growth meetings, inventive strategies, and numerous books sprout up every year to instruct spiritual leaders about how to draw more clients and maintain a competitive edge.

Kenneth Ulmer, the senior pastor of Faithful Central Bible Church in Los Angeles, California, secured the services of marketing consultant Gerry Foster to teach classes for the church's pastoral staff and members on how to create a brand identity. Facing declining numbers, the United Church of Canada spent $9 million in 2006 on Emerging Spirit, a media campaign to draw more members. A popular book on church ministry has chapters such as "Enterprising the Audience" and "Show Me the Money," to teach pastors how to conduct culture-sensitive worship services and how to connect their deeds of charity with strategic elements for evangelistic opportunities (Hunter 2004). Another important book, Geoff Surratt, Greg Ligon, and Warren Bird's *Multi-site Church Revolution: Being One Church in Many Locations* (2006), outlines strategies and approaches for churches to replicate and to establish congregations in multiple settings and unique environments. One minister images a cler-gyperson as a "pastorpreneur" and offers a philosophy of clerical leader-ship based on adaptability, resourcefulness, and innovation, variables cru-cial to remain relevant in a competitive religious market (Jackson 2003; Twitchell 2007).

Mark Batterson, a minister in Washington, D.C., is one such practi-tioner to embody several elements of these competitive approaches. His church, the National Community Church near the U.S. Capitol, meets in four locations: a coffeehouse it owns called Ebenezer's, at Ballston Com-mon Mall and Union Station, and in Georgetown. Adopting a multisite approach, Batterson knows the demographics of his church's locations, identifies the competitors in his church's local markets, and understands the preferences of his church's potential consumers.

In addition to publishing *I.D.: The True You* (2004) and *In a Pit with a Lion on a Snowy Day: How to Survive and Thrive When Opportunity Roars* (2006), Batterson understands the value of technology in a com-petitive religious environment: he blogs at Evotional.com, podcasts and webcasts his sermons, and serves as founder and president of Godipod. com. In an interview with the church growth website Church Market-ing Sucks, Batterson argues that the essence of the Christian message de-mands that it

> compete in the middle of the marketplace [because] it is part of our spiri-tual DNA. . . . The greatest message deserves the greatest marketing. Or to put it in other terms, the greatest gift (salvation) deserves to be wrapped in the greatest packaging! That is why we put a ton of energy and re-sources into internal and external marketing at NCC. . . . We really feel called to reach emerging generations in new ways. We have a core value: everything is an experiment. We love trying to do church in new ways.

Some of Batterson's experiments include creating trailers for new ser-mon series, "e-viting" people to church, and shooting preaching videos in which a life story offers a compelling spiritual message, similar to an ap-proach adopted by Grand Rapids, Michigan, pastor, author, and speaker Rob Bell in his NOOMA series. "There are new ways of doing e-vangelism and digital discipleship that we never dreamed of a decade ago," Batterson explains. "I just think there are new ways of doing church that no one has thought of yet! And if we are going to reach emerging generations it is go-ing to require some holy creativity and sanctified imagination."

Consultant, author, speaker, and visionary Phil Cooke specializes in what one might call "holy creativity." Often working with churches, Cooke assists clients in creating a brand, forging an emotional connection with consumers, and sustaining that contact for as long as possible. If perception is everything, there is a science to creating a brand; according to Cooke, conventional wisdom in the marketing community considers the act and art of branding to be a new religion. Effective branding must possess what Cooke calls "tenets" of faith. Building on the work of marketer Patrick Hanlon, Cooke insists that a successful religious (or secular) firm has a founding story, or genesis, and formulates belief, or a "creed." Cooke maintains that religious firms also effectively use images for purposes of product recognition and establish expected routines, or "rituals." Moreover, firms must also address critics, or "nonbelievers," and craft an associated language that employs buzzwords or taglines that initiate immediate identification—all coupled with an effective and inspirational leader who is innovatively connected with the brand. "I speak the language of Christianity, and I also speak the language of media," Cooke writes. "I don't believe there's simply a connection between branding and religion; I believe that religious experience is what the core of branding is all about" (2008: 33). As Cooke suggests, in a spiritual marketplace an effective brand is a key variable in determining winners and losers.

Mark Waltz, a minister at Granger Community Church in Indiana, advises pastors that competition is a prerequisite of church survival:

> Because we live in a consumer environment, there is competition. There are winners and losers. If your church is going to be effective, then you must beat the competition, pure and simple. You must find out who the competition is, what it is doing, and how to win its consumers to your church. You must figure out how to convince potential guests why they should be at your church on Sunday morning. (2005: 17)

Waltz adds that the way for pastors to beat the competition is to construct worship services that make a "Wow!" impression on their guests.

There is much that will make you say "Wow!" at Lakewood Church. Its ten-piece orchestra, large choir, talented worship leaders, and thousands of attendees generate the kind of energy one would feel at a Rolling Stones concert. Joel Osteen's cheerful aura and encouraging message are salutary. Each service is a welcoming environment where no one strains to understand doctrinal terms, no one feels shame because of past sins or imperfections, and everyone basks under the umbrella of peace, prosperity, and fellowship. Osteen's messages and worship services are attractive to twenty-first-century Americans who wish to live happy and prosperous lives.

There is much allure and excitement at Paula White's Satisfied Woman Retreat, where passionate messages on spiritual growth complement pampering sessions with manicures and massages. Successful and trendy women offer practical sessions on parenting, healthful eating, losing weight, and various other dimensions of the human condition, as well as challenging messages designed to enhance spiritual growth. You will laugh, dance, and participate in talent shows and group songs as you develop new friendships with women from all over the country. White promotes an upbeat, empowering, and self-therapeutic brand of evangelicalism that is especially attractive to many Americans.

There is much that is enthralling at Saddleback Church. The expansive campus, manicured landscape, picturesque mountain backdrop, and scenic waterfall will seduce you, along with an array of venues for worship styles, including reggae, hip-hop, and heavy metal. Rick Warren's sermons are carefully packaged practical lessons on how to live a purpose-driven life, and he keeps services compelling with tag-team preaching, dramatizations, and colorful illustrations. You can worship among thousands in the sanctuary or enjoy a Southern California breeze while sipping ice tea from the Terrace Café as you listen to the service broadcast on one of many outdoor speakers. Saddleback offers clown shows for small children, video games and movies for teens, an exciting singles ministry for young adults, and hundreds of small groups and classes to meet various needs and interests. Saddleback Church offers a unique brand of Christianity that is particularly appealing to baby boomers and middle-class families.

There is great enthusiasm and anticipation at a four-day family vacation event in Atlanta called MegaFest, where food, fun, and spiritual fellowship all come in abundance. You will not have to travel far to attend fashion shows, comedy events, celebrity basketball games, and fiery preaching from T. D. Jakes and a bevy of popular preachers, as well as music concerts by leading gospel and secular artists. You can hone your fiscal skills by attending one of the business seminars, or you can shop until you drop at one of the many vendors selling their wares. The electrifying atmosphere of 150,000 people attending various activities and worship services keeps adrenaline pumping for the duration of your vacation.

Jakes offers a creative multidimensional ministry that engages postmodern sensibilities.

Attending a three-day theological conversation with Emergent leader Brian McLaren is an exhilarating event. In the morning you observe a lively discussion with some of the leading theologians in the nation. In the afternoon you participate in breakout sessions that reflect on various aspects of church doctrine, faith, and practice with leaders of the emerging church. At night you shoot pool and drink beers at the local pub while engaging new friends in intense existential conversations and small talk about sports, family, and spirituality. McLaren's meetings appeal to Gen X Christians who seek new ways to live out their faith in a rapidly changing world.

If the preceding paragraphs read like commercials for evangelical innovators, then a visit to their websites reveals remarkable case studies in branding that would impress the faculty of most prominent business schools. Anthropologist and business professor John Sherry offers critical insight into the social locations and cultural meanings of branding. Sherry notes that at its core, branding involves a vigorous interplay between producer and consumer; it attempts to establish a market niche so as to effectively beat the competition, while it must also appeal to the tastes and preferences of the masses. It is clear that today's holy mavericks understand that branding is "a performance, a gathering, an inspiration, . . . a physical and metaphysical presence, an economic and festive fixture that binds stakeholders in a multifaceted relationship. It is the corporeal and noncorporeal webwork of postmodern existence" (2005: 41–42). In this way evangelical innovators have an ear to the culture and possess winsome creativity to effectively display and thoughtfully market their messages.

But while marketing serves its useful purpose, Osteen, White, Warren, Jakes, and McLaren adjust and retool American evangelicalism in appealing ways that attract large segments of the religious market. Each offers a style of Christianity that is dynamic and relevant, changes many lives and meets many needs; an environment that takes varying forms and yet remains simple and satisfying; a message that rests in God's sovereignty while providing intriguing possibilities for human agency; instruction that is pragmatic yet idealistic, self-actualizing and self-therapeutic; a ministry that responds to market forces and yet remains true to core beliefs; and a scope that transcends race, ethnicity, and class. In a nutshell, these innovators offer a brand of evangelical Christianity that is brilliantly designed for contemporary Americans.

Evangelical innovators speak the cultural language of their times to create metaphors, deploy symbols, and make religious utterances at once spiritual, memorable, and marketable. Rather than offering a universal gospel that resonates in all milieus, our subjects offer a timely message for a twenty-first-century Western audience. Osteen, White, and Jakes craft persuasive visions of the happy Christian life that embody middle-class American sensibilities; they reject the Calvinistic Old Testament judgmental portrait of an irascible creator and rebrand God in a manner commensurate with our self-indulgent, therapeutic culture. For Osteen and Warren, God is not a God of wrath focusing on human transgressions; God is a forgiving, loving father who is predisposed toward helping humans to reach their potential and live purpose-driven lives. This bourgeois brand of Christianity might not translate in milieus where people lack the personal agency or institutional structures to transcend their situations. One might wonder how a message of prosperity would sound to an antebellum slave who has no chance to attain wealth, or a contemporary Sudanese Christian struggling to stay alive in the midst of unrest, civil war, and famine. But holy mavericks' blend of spirituality and self-actualization is quite appealing in contemporary capitalist America.

Alexis de Tocqueville, a nineteenth-century French aristocrat who meticulously documents his tour of the United States in *Democracy in America*, marvels at clergy's ability to adjust the Christian message toward Americans' democratic hopes and industrious tastes. Interestingly, French author Bernard-Henri Levy repeats Tocqueville's trip, twenty-first-century style, and registers critical observations about Protestant religion in America after his visit to Chicago megachurch Willowcreek. In *American Vertigo: Traveling America in the Footsteps of Tocqueville*, Levy writes about American religion: "The banks in America look like churches. But here is a church that looks like a bank" (2006: 43). Like his predecessor, Levy understands the economics of religion in America when he notes that Willowcreek uses an array of marketing techniques to attract many followers. The key to draw large segments of the religious market, Levy implies, is "simply to get rid of the distance, the transcendence, and the remoteness of the divine that are at the heart of European theologies," because in many American churches there exists "a God without mystery; a good-guy God, almost human being, a good American someone who loves you one by one, listens to you if you talk to him, answers if you ask him to—God, the friend who has your best interests at heart" (2006: 45).

Popular observations about American religion provide historical observation and contemporary insight into the supply and demand of today's spiritual marketplace. Scholarly attention brings these trends into even clearer focus.

Social scientists and religion scholars can contribute much to our understanding of what it means to be American by exploring how religious innovators popularize new ways of presenting or understanding the gospel and new methods of attracting people. Few spheres of market exchanges reveal more about contemporary preferences, tastes, and needs than a competitive religious economy. Hence, we join with other social scientists, historians, and religious studies scholars to explore the intricacies of religious innovators' vast appeal in order to shed light on the postmodern cultural changes, new media technologies, and hypercapitalist values that characterize our era. Love them or hate them, evangelical innovators capture the American imagination; scholars can no longer ignore their prominent roles in contemporary religion and culture.

Among the theoretical contributions of this book are a serious challenge to the strict church thesis, a long-standing theory in the sociology of religion that explains winners and losers among religious suppliers based on their strictness or leniency, claiming that strict religions thrive, whereas more lenient ones decline. We uncover little that is strict or demanding in our subjects' messages and ministries, and yet four of their churches are among the largest in the country. Their popularity and attractiveness point to a simpler explanation for religious vitality: spiritual suppliers thrive when they are effective at marketing their message and resourceful at addressing the existential needs and cultural tastes of potential clients. Hence note the irony of using the term "mavericks" for spiritual innovators whose appeal comes from conforming to mainstream American culture and constructing archetypes of spirituality appropriate for the needs and tastes of the masses. It is only the religious establishment that perceives them as mavericks; to everyday Americans, innovators are quite pedestrian and relevant.

Discussing with us some of our five subjects, theologian Stanley Hauerwas observed, "The popularity of religiosity in such an unbelievably sentimental form is just a sign of the times or the unraveling of a Christian culture." Similarly, a sociologist recently wrote, "In every aspect of the religious life, American faith has met American culture and American culture has triumphed" (Wolfe 2003: 2). Less tendentiously, we argue that evangelical innovators are seductive because they embody American sensibilities. But if religion must bend to culture to attract people, then one can always ponder, "Where are the real religious prophets? Can there be any in a country whose self-image rests on fast, friendly, and guiltless consumption?" (Moore 1994: 276). In our competitive religious economy, evangelical innovators find themselves in this predicament: on the one hand, their livelihood compels them to satisfy consumer needs and wants; on the other hand, their higher calling commits them to timeless prescriptions for human activity. The requisite rewards of being America's preacher make it very tempting to compromise the latter hand for the former.

Bibliographic Essay
Theory of Religious Economy

Kurt Cobain and his rock band Nirvana exploded onto the music scene in the early 1990s with unprocessed music and deep, dark lyrics that resonated with millions of American contemporaries. Similarly, by appealing to the eclectic tastes and desires of many Americans, Jewish reggae hip-hop artist Matisyahu has the ear of today's alienated, media-savvy, market-saturated individuals. Few financial wizards capture the public's attention like television host and author Suze Orman. With long-running Emmy Award–winning cartoons like *Duck Tales* and *Kim Possible*, and newer shows like *That's So Raven* and *Hannah Montana*, the Disney Channel captivates millions of kids nationwide.

We can provide an endless list of politicians like Barack Obama, entertainers like Sacha Cohen, writers like John Grisham, and wrestlers like Hulk Hogan who capture the public's attention by appealing to a broad range of American tastes and desires. While scholars are quick to assess the intangible skills and talents that help men and women capture commercial markets, they are often reluctant to exercise the same curiosity to explore how spiritual leaders carve out unique niches in the religious marketplace. It is an extraordinary feat for a pastor to draw thousands of weekly attendees or persuade millions to purchase his books or watch her spiritual messages on TV. A preacher needs a special blend of talent and ingenuity to convince thousands of people to cash in their vacation days and travel across the country to attend a worship conference.

Scholars of religion in previous eras were much more willing to reduce the popularity of religious movements to the irrationality of the clients rather than the genius of the suppliers, but a new generation of social scientists recognizes that religion, much like commercial entertainment, depends on innovative leadership to exercise mass appeal. This is not to say that these scholars offer reductionist analyses of religious life and conviction—many of them do not—but rather to point out that the cultural dynamics of today's media-frenzied, capitalist-driven society inform many dimensions of religious life in America. Working within what can be broadly defined as a marketplace approach to American religion, sociologists, historians, and other specialists employ their particular discipline's methodologies to analyze the complexities of spiritual supply and demand within and among America's religious economy.

To more broadly contextualize the theoretical dimensions of *Holy Mavericks*, this bibliographic essay canvasses the scholarly terrain to provide an overview of the marketplace approach to American religion. It begins with a summary of major theorists' formulations of religious economy, followed by analysis of how scholars apply the model.

The theory of religious economy views churches as firms, pastors as marketers and producers, and church members or attendees as consumers whose tastes and preferences shape the goods and services ministers and firms offer. This approach identifies the variables that explain the "supply" of religious firms and can more clearly illuminate the "demand" of religious consumers. Scholars who offer hypotheses and derive conclusions from religious economy conduct analyses based on statistical data, textual evidence, participant observation, and a host of other sources, including electronic media. Among scholars, economists and sociologists pioneered the marketplace approach to the study of religion and religious experience, and later historians, ethnographers, cultural anthropologists, media theorists, and religious studies scholars used religious economy to ask new questions and offer fresh analysis (Ekelund, Hebert, and Tollison 2006; Stein 2002).

Although Max Weber discussed the importance of economic elements in Protestant Christianity in *The Protestant Ethic and the Spirit of Capitalism* (1930) and theorized about religious production and spiritual exchange in some of his other work, the latter half of the twentieth century witnessed the first sustained analysis of religion from an economic perspective. Religious economy as a theoretical tool for analysis of religious behavior and religious experience commenced within the field of sociology in Peter Berger's *Sacred Canopy* (1967). Berger argued that humans construct religion, religious ideas, and religious ideologies to provide an umbrella of psychological protection and comfort from the realities life brings, yet in modern, scientific society a gradual process of secularization would create a kind of religious pluralism and incite considerable competition. Secularization, then, would spell doom (and perhaps eclipse) for firms that fail to compete with alternative ideologies of meaning. In the process, secularization would lead to religion's insignificance and demise, rendering delinquent its plausibility and legitimacy (Berger 1967: 25, 107, 125). Other scholars expanded Berger's conception of the sacred canopy, also called the "sheltered enclave theory" (Smith 1998: 67), to posit that religious firms in America thrive when they construct defenses against what they perceive as menacing forces of modern life. For such religious groups, the threat of secular influence serves to mobilize and unite. Although sociologists such as Steve Bruce continue to champion the triumph of secularization, Berger has since revised and refined his understanding of the secularization thesis (Woodhead 2002).

Whereas Peter Berger and others forecast in the 1960s the decline of religious vitality, in the 1970s sociologist Dean Kelley argued that conservative congregations thrive when they demand strict adherence to faith claims and provide a coherent platform of meaning for members. Unlike traditional mainline congregations that witnessed declining membership during the mid–twentieth century, Kelley surmised that strict churches such as those of the Anabaptist tradition and the Methodists, Mormons, and Jehovah's Witnesses articulate goals, sanction controls, and facilitate communication where demand inspires commitment.

Economists such as Laurence Iannaccone extended and refined Kelley's strict church thesis to claim that the "costs" of membership, affiliation, and devotion increase participation precisely because high adherence weeds out "free riders," congregants who attempt to enjoy the benefits of the firm without equitable investment. In an important article, "Why Strict Churches Are Strong" (1994), Iannaccone noted that whereas the religious marketplace abounds with less demanding options, groups like Mormons and Seventh-Day Adventists place strict measures on members to abstain from worldly delights. Strictness of firms in this sense, according to Iannaccone, increases commitment, results in higher levels of participation, and offers more attractive membership benefits, eliminating those who do not put in the time, effort, and energy to enhance the vitality of the firm. Hence strictness "does more to explain individual rates of religious participation than does any standard individual-level characteristic" (Iannaccone 1992: 1200).

Building upon Iannaccone's work and refining further marketplace analyses of American religion, sociologist Rodney Stark, along with other scholars such as William Sims Bainbridge and Roger Finke, in the 1980s began to champion rational choice theory as a crucial factor to explain why individuals affiliate or associate with religious groups. Along with a host of articles, essays, and the theoretically grounded *Acts of Faith* (Stark and Finke 2000), Finke and Stark's most expansive application of religious economy emerged with *The Churching of America, 1776–2005: Winners and Losers in Our Religious Economy* (2005), a seminal book originally published in 1992 and now in its second edition. The authors marshal a considerable amount of statistical data to explain American religious history in supply-side terms. In this scenario, the most successful religious suppliers, denominations, groups, and the clergy respond to the changing needs of the masses in a given market. Religious monopolies grow stagnant and stale, according to Finke and Stark, and the most successful religious firms adapt to the changing needs of the moment. They write:

> Religious economies are like commercial economies in that they consist of a market made up of a set of current and potential customers and a set of firms seeking to serve that market. The fate of these firms will depend upon (1) aspects of their organizational structure, (2) their sales representatives, (3) their products, and (4) their marketing techniques. Translated into more churchly language, the relative successes of religious bodies (especially when confronted with an unregulated economy) will depend upon their polity and local congregations, their clergy, their religious doctrines, and their evangelization techniques. (2005: 9)

The religious economy Finke and Stark envision reveals a dynamic marketplace, a deregulated environment where the most successful firms innovatively key their messages to the tastes and preferences of the consumers. Similar to Kelley's conclusions, though the argument moves in a slightly different direction, Finke and Stark argue mainline denominations failed to attend to the tastes and desires of the masses. And while competing firms vied for market shares, those who chose to affiliate made a choice to surrender to the demands of the firm even as the most successful firms remained conscious of the tastes and preferences that drove such surrender.

Whereas studies by Berger, Kelley, Iannaccone, and Finke and Stark created new yet related interpretive possibilities for understanding religious history and religious experience in marketplace terms, sociologist R. Stephen Warner's important article "Work in Progress toward a New Paradigm for the Sociological Study of Religion in the United States" (1993) helpfully but critically surveyed the field to articulate a more exacting analytical model for specialists of American religion. Warner's "new paradigm" offers five foundational propositions that acknowledge the vibrancy of religious faith, the meaningful products firms offer, and the conscious choices consumers make: America's disestablishment religious environment; the reality of religious pluralism; elasticity and flexibility in a religiously competitive marketplace; potential for personal and collective empowerment through religious commitment and affiliation; and the thread of individualism that runs through American religious traditions. Whereas the old paradigm focused on the limits of religious competition imagined as a sacred canopy, the new paradigm envisions the possibility and potential within a religiously pluralistic environment (so legislated by the First Amendment in the United States), a context where firms must be responsive to and flexible with consumer demands (Gelen 2002).

Warner's article also points out that use of religious economy to explain and understand religious behavior in America considers the choices made by both producers and consumers to be meaningful, not superfluous, shrewd, or deceptive. Warner in effect argues for nonreductionistic analyses of American religion and calls for careful attention to the multiple contingencies that inform and shape consumer religious demand. Put another way, Warner does not assume that ministers, evangelists, and religious specialists are spiritual charlatans out to make an ecclesiastical buck or maintain religious hegemony over beguiled masses, although that could obviously be the case. Like Finke and Stark's marketplace formulation, Warner's theory of religious economy provides both the concepts and the grammar to effectively explain religious dynamics in a disestablished, pluralistic environment.

The preceding paragraphs highlight the key theoretical formulations of a marketplace approach to religious vitality. From one angle, Peter Berger assumes that competing firms would cancel each other out as he forecast religion's demise in secular society. Yet research effectively challenges the viability of this conclusion, and from other angles, Kelley, Iannaccone, Finke and Stark, and Warner argue that religious vitality stems from the reality that human beings are rational agents who decide life's ultimate questions based on meaningful choices, and that to compete, successful firms in a religious market must attend to the tastes and preferences that shape such decisions to offer meaningful and attractive products in return. From this view pluralism and deregulation actually stoke the fires of competition, whereas for some firms, the sinews of affiliation operate according to strict terms of membership as "free riders" ultimately have to pay a price to join or move on. With the theoretical parameters clearly in view, and as a way to more clearly situate the holy maverick archetype constructed in this book, it is helpful to examine the interpretive insight this approach brings in the fields of sociology, anthropology, ethnography, religious studies, media studies, and history.

Before providing more specific coverage and analysis of America's religious marketplace, it is important to note the model's application to religious trends across the globe. R. Andrew Chesnut (2003, 2005), for instance, applies the theory of religious economy to Latin America's contemporary spiritual landscape in order to assess the ramifications of religious competition and the nature of spiritual production, a contest between Protestant Pentecostalism, charismatic Catholicism, and the various strains of African diaspora religions. Anthony Gill, on the other hand, studies the religious economy of Latin America's Roman Catholic landscape in *Rendering unto Caesar: The Catholic Church and the State in Latin America* (1998), whereas anthropologist Raquel Romberg's *Witchcraft and Welfare: Spiritual Capital and the Business of Religion in Modern Puerto Rico* (2003) examines an "unusual alchemy" between Puerto Rican witchcraft that often works alongside Catholic traditions, displaying a certain pliability and vying for a market share. The application of religious economy in R. Andrew Chesnut's *Competitive Spirits* (2003) and Romberg's *Witchcraft and Welfare* sheds considerable light on the business of religion in the twenty-first century's marketplaces of faith, and the exchanges taking place in Latin America are important to watch.

Not only does religious economy illuminate the spiritual dynamics of Latin America and the Caribbean's spiritual marketplaces; scholars effectively apply the model to places beyond the Western Hemisphere. Sociologist Massimo Introvigne (2005) identifies niche variations (e.g., ultrastrict, strict, moderate-conservative, liberal, ultraliberal) in societies perceived to possess a religious monopoly. Using Turkey to test his theory, Introvigne finds that competition exists most readily in the moderate-conservative niche and argues that religious suppliers in Islamic countries compete for consumers similar to counterparts in non-Islamic societies. Economist Laurence Iannaccone (2006) applies religious economy to Islamic contexts as well but focuses his study on suicide bombers in what he calls "the market for martyrs." In China, as Lang, Chan, and Ragvald (2005) demonstrate, competition among Daoist temples in various provinces reveals consistent religious competition, since temple managers respond to local desires, tastes, and preferences; entrepreneurial religious specialists with secular business experience often offer the most popular goods and the richest returns on consumers' spiritual investment.

Paul Gifford (1998) surveys churches in several African countries—Ghana, Uganda, Zambia, and Cameroon—to explain the significant ways churches participate in social and political affairs, very often influenced by larger market concerns. Gifford's more recent work (2004) focuses on Pentecostal churches primarily in Accra, Ghana, arguing that competition explains their broad appeal and large influence. Gifford's analysis shows that sermons are lively, music is energetic and appeals to the masses, and pastors calculate marketing campaigns to have the largest impact, be it television broadcasts, radio programs, tape and DVD ministries, or publications. Although topics like divine blessing and financial stability surface as common themes in the sermons of preachers and evangelists in Accra, Gifford observes that individuality is the central feature of this Christianity, and so to remain competitive in the marketplace ministers must find their particular niche. About Ghanaian charismatic preachers, Gifford continues:

> Whatever else they are, they are also entertainment and have to compete in a crowded field. The speakers, like their US models, are performers/entertainers, and the repeated screening of their programmes makes them to some degree media personalities and stars—thus, unlike the mainline churches, these churches are often personalized. (2004: 32)

Gifford's research also shows that Pentecostal churches are not the only religious groups competing in Ghana's spiritual marketplace. Similar to Chesnut's identification of the "Pentecostalization" of Roman Catholics and African diaspora religions in Latin America, Gifford observes that Ghanaian mainline religious groups like the Methodists have had to undergo what he terms a "charismatisation" (2004: 38) to compete in the religious marketplace. Gifford reports that the Methodists currently maintain their numbers because, as one practitioner put it, "we are now doing all they [the charismatics] do" (2004: 39).

Although not totally distinct from their counterparts in Ghana, Nigerian Pentecostal preachers compete in their own religious market, promising spiritual and material returns on religious investment. David Oyedepo, one of Nigeria's better-known preachers, ministers at Winner's Chapel and also founded an accredited university. Bimbo Odukoya, along with her cominister and husband, finds a niche in Nigeria's spiritual marketplace with an emphasis on marriage enrichment. The Nigerian spiritual marketplace, which contains a number of celebrity preachers, also witnesses foreign competition with American superstar preachers like Benny Hinn and T. D. Jakes, who visit the country to lead services and network with fellow ministers (Odunfa 2005).

The work of Chesnut, Romberg, Introvigne, Gifford, and others sheds considerable light on the business of faith across the globe, yet the extensive use of economic categories and economic language in the application of religious economy broadens the analytical scope and helps to clarify the complexity of America's religious marketplace. Following the lead of fellow social scientists, both Wade Clark Roof and Robert Wuthnow conceptualize the religious phenomena they study as a religious marketplace. Roof's studies of baby boomer spirituality note key changes in America's religious landscape; he uses the concept of a spiritual marketplace to identify and explain important trends. Roof observes:

> In recent times especially, religious messages and practices have come to be frequently restylized, made to fit a targeted social clientele, often on the basis of market analysis, and carefully monitored to determine if programmatic emphases should be adjusted to meet particular needs. An open, competitive religious economy makes possible an expanded spiritual marketplace which, like any marketplace, must be understood in terms both of "demand" and "supply." In a time of cultural and religious dislocations, new suppliers offer a range of goods and services designed to meet the spiritual concerns; and, in so doing respond to and help to clarify those very concerns. (1999: 78)

Like most proponents of religious economy, Roof contended that religion thrives in a competitive market where it can respond in innovative ways to changing social realities and to people's own recognized, but changing, needs and preferences. Similar to the work of Finke and Stark, Roof demonstrates that imagining the United States as a vast spiritual marketplace offers a way to clearly explain changing trends among baby boomer religious seekers. Suppliers and firms respond to consumer preference and demand. Similarly, Roof also notes the entrepreneurial imperative that exists for religious suppliers to be successful: they must know their audience and reconfigure their messages and ministries in ways that meet felt needs.

Fellow sociologist Robert Wuthnow (1988, 1994), well known for his extensive analysis of trends in America's contemporary religious life, explains that religious experience is the result of exchanges between producers and consumers. Spiritual production, according to Wuthnow, is a two-way street, finding its roots in what he terms the "patron-client mode" (1994: 28). Wuthnow's recent work tackles religious diversity in postmodern America, and the configuration of a spiritual marketplace is part of the story. He identifies the phenomenon of "spiritual shopping" where religious seekers assess, pick, and choose from a vast array of religious options. Spiritual shoppers generally identify themselves not as loyal members of a community or group but as individuals who have become alienated from certain communities or groups and have found it necessary to strike out on their own, searching for the sacred by metaphorically going from place to place (2005: 128).

Owing to the rise of the new cultural history and a rich confluence of interdisciplinary methodologies, other scholars find the formulations of a spiritual marketplace helpful in delineating the role media, space, discourse, and celebrity play in the choices religious consumers make. Sociologist John Walliss and cultural observer Wayne Spencer (2003) draw from Roof's concept of a spiritual supermarket to examine the work of journalist Graham Hancock, an author who popularizes theories about the recovery of lost worlds and ancient religions. Walliss and Spencer identify the commodified nature of Hancock's eclectic literary output and show how his choice to present evidence and let the reader draw conclusions exemplifies the interplay between producer and consumer.

Media studies scholar Mara Einstein (2007) uses marketing theory to study the ways in which secular celebrities couch products in spiritual terms, and religious superstars secularize their discourse. Her analysis shows that both groups' concern for the bottom line results in messages and products that are more affable and responsive to wide consumer demand. Similarly, sociologists R. Danielle Egan and Stephen Papson (2005) consider life coach and celebrity "Dr. Phil" (Phil McGraw) in their discussion of the rich intersection of religion, media, spectacle, and discourse. They uncover the structured nature of his show, where steps to recovery and psychological wholeness conform to a morphology of religious conversion. They argue that television heightens the appeal of Dr. Phil's methodology and further establishes his market niche, where week after week potential consumers observe the power of confession and become convinced by the repetition of testimonies. Dr. Phil is not the only celebrity to capitalize upon religion as commodity. Religious studies scholar Kathryn Lofton (2006a, 2008) and literary scholar Trysh Travis (2007) situate Oprah Winfrey's diverse media offerings in an economy defined by both religion and capitalism, and Stanley Steward (2003) confounds perceptions of Las Vegas as "sin city" to show that religion is an equally profitable game in that town, at least for those who are savvy and able to establish a popular niche.

Whereas the work of Mara Einstein (2007) and others identifies and situates the sacralizing tendencies of secular producers, other scholars describe the deft ways that religious producers employ marketplace methods to meet the tastes and preferences of their audiences, again demonstrating the powerful explanatory appeal of interdisciplinary analysis. Leonard Sweet (1993) offers a broad analysis of these trends; David Nord (1993) focuses on evangelical publishing trends in nineteenth-century America; Quentin Schultze (1990, 1991) provides case studies of leading televangelists of the 1980s whose popularity derived, at least in part, from branding and name recognition. Similarly, Kathryn Lofton (2006b) offers a richly textured examination of late nineteenth-century and early twentieth-century evangelists who actively engaged in self-promotion and thoughtfully considered how messages might impact not only their hearers but also their clerical competitors. Christopher Lynch (1998) points out that Bishop Fulton Sheen, a Roman Catholic priest active in the 1950s, beat innovative Protestants to the television screen through a weekly teaching show, though subsequent televangelists learned quickly from his pioneering programs.

Scholars show that more recent religious figures and religious groups vigorously compete for market shares, much like their spiritual predecessors. Sociologist Mark Shibley leans against the strict church thesis to find that contemporary evangelicals are "world-affirming" (1996a: 72), as churches like Willow Creek in Chicago consciously adapt business and marketing models to target specific groups. "As evangelicals engage the world," Shibley observes, "they are becoming more like the world" (1996a: 78). Using similar methodologies, Campus Crusade for Christ, an evangelical ministry devoted to impacting college students, cornered the university religious market (Turner 2006), and evangelical publishing feeds the phenomenon of spiritual celebrity to transport ideas, ideologies, and practices across the globe (Bartholomew 2006). Religious television aimed at younger audiences also commands its own niche, where media studies scholar Hillary Warren (2005) captures the broad televisual appeal of the cartoon series *Veggie Tales*. Similar to Colleen McDannell's cultural analysis of "material Christianity" (1995), which takes a longer historical look at production and marketing, media studies scholar Heather Hendershot (2004) explains the market appeal of religious suppliers who creatively offer Christian T-shirts, buttons, CDs, DVDs, and a host of other media products to spiritual consumers. R. Marie Griffith's *Born Again Bodies: Flesh and Spirit in American Christianity* (2004) identifies similar trends in another area of religious investigation: evangelical Christian weight-loss culture. Griffith's historically grounded cultural analysis of "fitness merchants" (3) effectively captures the market-based yet spiritually resonant concerns of those whose souls seek to tone born-again bodies. Industries devoted to healing and wholeness, much like fitness culture, have eagerly competed (and compete) for market shares as well (Bowman 1999; Curtis 2006, 2007).

Whereas the theory of religious economy finds a warm welcome among some social scientists, some historians find the marketplace approach problematic. One place to gauge such discontent is to survey the reviews of Finke and Stark's aforementioned seminal text *The Churching of America* by prominent historians of American religion. These reviews provide not only a way to better understand the explanatory power with which disciplinary perspectives operate but also an avenue for interpretive clarification.

George Marsden began his review of *The Churching of America* (1993) with this analogy: "The authors of this volume are to most scholars of American religion what Jerry Falwell and Pat Robertson are to the National Council of Churches" (451–53). This comment set the tone for Marsden's analysis, as he noted the book's "taunting style" and described it as "simplistic," with a "populist message." Similarly, Jon Butler labeled Finke and Stark's work as "unsophisticated, confusing, and thoroughly derivative 'history,'" based on "shallow philosophizing" (1994: 288–89). This led, in Butler's estimation, to a certain "reductionism" that dichotomizes American religious history into camps of "winners" and "losers," an interpretive scheme that he argued largely misses the subtleties of historical circumstance and change over time. Joel Carpenter echoed the sentiments of Marsden and Butler, describing *The Churching of America* as provocative but irritating due to what he saw as a lack of historical and cultural context. Although Carpenter admitted that the sect-to-church syndrome and the market dynamics of religious behavior are critical variables in the large equation of American religion, he nevertheless concluded that "there are so many discreditable things about this book that it will be tempting for the field to dismiss it" (1994: 1448–49). In Edwin Gaustad's estimation, *The Churching of America* contained "a remarkable blend of innocence and arrogance," related to Finke and Stark's claim to use hitherto neglected statistical data on American religion. Gaustad, like Carpenter, roiled at Finke and Stark's "insults" hurled at the supposedly shoddy scholarship of historians, although he reciprocated when he wrote that the authors' knowledge of Puritanism was "on a par with that of H. L. Menken" (Gaustad 1993: 640–42). Importantly, Gaustad credited Finke and Stark with infusing American religious history with a new market-oriented vocabulary. The use of marketplace grammar is the only positive observation in Martin Marty's review of *The Churching of America*. Like other historians, Marty roundly condemned the authors' historical reductionism and "chancy extrapolation" of statistical data (1993: 88–89). Finally, Timothy Weber found Finke and Stark's thesis somewhat problematic, particularly what he deems a selective understanding of the field of American religious history, not to mention the reductionism that results from historicizing statistics to explain why groups win or lose in a religious economy (Weber 1994).

A 1995 forum in *American Studies*, "Why Upstarts Win in America: Religion in the Market Place," provides additional perspective on the reception of Finke and Stark's *Churching of America*. Bryan F. LeBeau largely praises the book, particularly its strong explanation of Methodism's rise and fall in America's religious marketplace. Stephen Stein registers some praise as well, signaling an appreciative tone for the way Finke and Stark push the interpretive envelope. Similarly, Mark Hulsehter finds Finke and Stark's arguments compelling, yet all three reviewers, like Butler, Marsden, Carpenter, Gaustad, Marty, and Weber, criticize sociologists for overlooking the nuances of historical context and attributing historical change simply to statistical variation.

Although most historians who reviewed *The Churching of America* fault its reductionistic analysis and sharp tone, the scale of attention it received actually attests to the interpretive power of the marketplace approach. Left solely to sociologists, these reviewers suggest, religious economy often relies on statistics to the exclusion of historical context. And while some historians clearly disdain the marketplace approach, others appreciate the explanatory power economic categories provide for interpretations of contemporary American religion.

With hindsight, we see great irony in many of the critical reviews of Finke and Stark's work. The criticisms historians launched at *The Churching of America* in the early 1990s overlooked the concurrent marketplace formulations their disciplinary cohort was beginning to adopt. Identification of this irony allows for clearer theoretical articulation and interpretive sophistication. This irony also suggests that historians of American religion must broaden their disciplinary vision (indeed, many have), but also that sociologists of religion must better capture the historical circumstances around which data attest. Allying statistical data with the complexities of historical situatedness is a tall order, to be sure, but collaborative, multidisciplinary scholarship that attends to the social, cultural, economic, and political dimensions of times and places both past and present can render powerful, convincing stories. It is this middle way that *Holy Mavericks* adopts.

In his important historiographical essay "Jack-in-the-Box Faith: The Religion Problem in Modern America History" (2004), Jon Butler uses the glaring lack of attention that history textbooks pay to religion in modern American life as a way to discuss religion's powerful, if complex, presence in contemporary times. He attributes this analytical absence to an implicit embrace of secularization theory, a tacit assumption that the rise of modern science in the nineteenth century coincided with the declining significance of religion and religious practice in Western societies.

Butler documents secularizing trends within American society (e.g., science and education) but also observes the deeply entrenched ways religion informed Americans' relationship to modernity (e.g., electoral politics, Social Gospel). The scandal, according to Butler, of much of the scholarship that analyzes contemporary America is its failure to understand the ways religion so often informs both private and public life. "The surprise of a vital religious force in modern American politics," Butler observes, "leads inevitably to the question of religion, secularization, and modernity." From recent cases of broad ecumenical collaboration across denominational boundaries, to the ways religion intertwined with suburbia, to the enthusiasm conservative evangelicals often display to embrace modern technology, and to the rise of therapeutic religion, Butler concludes that "religion could 'work' in the century of its reputed demise" (Butler 2004: 1373–74).

Interestingly, one of the critical points Butler makes is what Finke and Stark suggest with religious economy: religion thrives *precisely* when it appeals to the tastes and preferences of its "consumers." If it understands the importance of product placement and brand name in a religious economy, then it can capture a market share. Butler registers several notable examples that demonstrate that religion exhibited more continuity than obstruction in modern America's advancing material and consumer culture. Selecting works that detail Christianity's material history in America and commodification of religious holidays, for instance, Butler (2004) shows that the collusion of religion and modernity is both provocative and powerful and makes for fascinating history.

Two points are worth noting here. First, although the scholars Butler cites acknowledge no explicit debt to the marketplace formulation Finke and Stark use, all their work appeared after *The Churching of America*, and each in its own way analyzes the locations of religion in a spiritual marketplace. Second, although Butler roundly criticizes the particular sociological application of religious economy found in the work of Finke and Stark, he pays tribute to a more multilayered, multicontextual approach that seeks to understand spirituality within the dynamics of a religious marketplace. In one way this vindicates the broader approach Finke and Stark offer in *The Churching of America*, while it also demonstrates interpretive appeal when historians work thoughtfully across disciplinary boundaries.

In this context it is important to mention historian Mark Noll's analysis of R. Stephen Warner's work, which, like Finke and Stark's book, identified, articulated, described, and applied the marketplace approach. Noll's 2006 review of *A Church of Our Own* in the *Journal for the Scientific Study of Religion* glowingly praises Warner's articulation of the subtle nuances between religious economy and rational choice theory and offers clear support, contra the previously cited reviews of *The Churching of America*, for the possibilities inherent in the marketplace approach to American religion: "While sociologists will reap greater professional reward from following Warner's give-and-take with his peers on such matters, historians will benefit from having such a clear statement accounting for the dynamism, but also the confusions and complexities, of American religious life" (2006: 462). Noll's admission attests to the promise of using a marketplace approach to explain the vitality of contemporary American religious life.

Other historians of American religion have employed a broadly construed marketplace approach, though very few pay tribute to the trails blazed by Stark, Warner, and their sociological cohort. Put another way, while social scientists birthed the theory of religious economy and led the way in quantifying this dimension of American religion, some historians picked up this explanatory configuration to offer snapshots of religious supply and spiritual demand in America's past.

One important and largely overlooked study that employs a market-place approach to religious life in nineteenth-century America is Terry Bilhartz's *Urban Religion and the Second Great Awakening: Church and Society in Early National Baltimore* (1986). A careful work that details the competitive religious environment in an important southern city, Bilhartz uncovers Methodist revival strategies and even notices the importance of church architecture in promoting spiritual renewal. In Baltimore:

> revival erupted among those who wanted it, and who labored diligently to promote it. It was one strategy for church survival in a competitive and increasingly materialistic era. Rather than seeking for clues from the demand side of the equation, perhaps Baltimore's awakening more simply can be understood as "supply-side religion." (Bilhartz 1986: 99)

Published in 1986—the same year Rodney Stark and Roger Finke began to recontextualize church membership within a religious economy—Bilhartz's book effectively uses market terminology to explain religious change in nineteenth-century Baltimore. "In the decades following disestablishment," Bilhartz wrote: "when the virgin denominational market was unusually fluid, voluntary churches fiercely competed with each other for contributing members. . . . large numbers of Baltimoreans bought into evangelical religion largely because the price was right and the streets were filled with vendors" (1986: 139). The appearance three years later of Randall Balmer's insightful ethnography of American evangelicalism, *Mine Eyes Have Seen the Glory*, offered a similar way to imagine America's religious landscape. From summer youth camps, to black Pentecostal worship, to seminary training, to Christian book publishing, to evangelical televangelism, to crusades and revivals of various kinds, and with the inclusion of chapters on Rick Warren and Thomas Kinkaide in the book's fourth edition published in 2006, Balmer's snippets of popular religion devoid of statistical analysis reveal a "patchwork quilt" of folk evangelicalism, innovative and creative religious expressions that thrived in countless ways, particularly on the heels of disestablishment. According to Balmer, this constitutional reality prompted "a kind of free market of religion" (2006a: 338) in which religious language, television media, and celebrity, among other factors, shaped (and shape) the competitive environment of America's spiritual marketplace.

R. Laurence Moore's *Selling God: American Religion in the Market-place of Culture* (1994) proposes that the secularization thesis historians and social scientists debated back and forth was, in fact, more about the commodification of religion in a competitive marketplace. Moore marshals evidence from antebellum booksellers, early national political and religious leaders, upstart denominations throughout the nineteenth century, religious progressives who championed the Social Gospel, and television preachers like Norman Vincent Peale, Fulton Sheen, and even Jim Bakker to demonstrate that in a variety of contexts purveyors of religion throughout America history found powerful niches in the marketplace of American culture that expressed (and continue to express) themselves in complex, nuanced ways. To put it another way, Moore (2003) effectively explains the multileveled ways that sacred and secular interact in American culture.

Like Moore's, other analyses of American religion to appear in the 1990s and thereafter explored the intersections between American religious and consumer culture. Leigh Schmidt's study of American holidays, *Consumer Rites* (1995), not unlike Dell deChant's *The Sacred Santa: Religious Dimensions of Consumer Culture* (2002), captures the multilayered ways commodification and religion adhere to and repel one another. Stout's *The Divine Dramatist* (1991) and Lambert's *"Pedlar in Divinity"* (1994), studies of eighteenth-century evangelist George Whitefield and the rise of American evangelicalism, place the itinerant's methods and message within the context of a consumer revolution where both producer and client understood production and consumption in market terms. Edith Blumhofer's biography *Aimee Semple McPherson: Everybody's Sister* (1993) tells the story of a remarkable and complex woman, confident and savvy enough to employ early twentieth-century communications technology in the service of the Christian gospel. Through her theatrical preaching and radio broadcasts McPherson grabbed a market share in early twentieth-century evangelicalism (Sutton 2007).

A flurry of studies to appear in the late 1990s, and several early this century, use religious biography to demonstrate that interpretations of American Christianity cannot separate the history of evangelicalism from careful consideration of its role in America's spiritual marketplace. Most of these studies do not credit specifically the work of Finke, Stark, or Warner with interpretive inspiration but offer marketplace configurations of their own. The sacred success and secular notoriety coupled with the religious language and secular methodologies of preachers and celebrities like Dwight Moody (Evensen 1999, 2003), Billy Sunday (Bendroth 2004), Carrie A. Nation (Carver 1999), E. W. Kenyon (Simmons 1997), Joseph A. Booker (Giggie 2003), Bruce Barton (Ribuffio 1981), Norman Vincent Peale (George 1993), Fulton Sheen (Lynch 1998), Charles Fuller (Goff 1999), Pat Robertson and Jerry Falwell (Schultze 1991), Oral Roberts (Harrell 1985, 1993), Bill Bright (Turner 2008), Eddie Long (Walton 2006), Rick Warren (Balmer 2006; El-Faizy 2006; Sheler 2006), Bill Hybels (Beuttler 2004), Joel Osteen (Einstein 2007), and T. D. Jakes (Lee 2005) accurately reflect the power of personal appeal in the history and practice of American religion.

Related studies consider social and cultural locations of religious theme parks, spiritual tourism, and electronic evangelism and their confluences of meaning with American popular culture (Beal 2005; Chidester 2005; Mattingly 2005; Murley 2005; Ketchell 2007). Carolyn Morrow Long (2001) identifies "spiritual merchants" in diverse strains of African-based religious practices in America to explain the contours of exchange between specialists and clients. Even Oprah figures into the stories of American religion, as an individual who engages in what religious studies scholar Kathryn Lofton calls the "spiritual practice of capitalism" (2006a). As a cultural construct, evangelicalism is pliable and situated in the nooks and crannies of American culture. By providing requisite goods and services, producers hope that consumers might more fully invest in the firm by tithing, volunteering, or participating in its array of activities. Such an arrangement does not minimize the reality of religious experience, as the review of previous work shows, but encourages active and energetic participation. Literally and figuratively, consumers buy into the firm and the products it offers.

The success of a religious firm also depends on its religious grammar, particularly on the visual enactment, rhetorical relevance, and spatial significance of the goods it offers. Words highlight context, imbue meaning, display intention, and locate experience, and as such can offer religious practitioners tapestries of identities and provide options from which to construct identity. Words and phrases matter to both producer and consumer, and so any application of religious economy must examine a firm's spiritual terminology and religious language (Witten 1993; Harding 2000; Percy 2000). Similarly, spiritual grammar and sacred space operate in deeply complex fashion; therefore, religious entrepreneurs take great care when constructing sites—both physical and virtual—of production and consumption, since these spaces display *and* inscribe multiple meanings.

Adopting this mode of analysis for the spiritual marketplace renders a megachurch both a sacred site and a consumptive space (Thumma 2006; Thumma and Travis 2007; Kilde 2006), for example, even as it allows for more varied understandings and nuanced analysis of more ordinary religious ideas and expressions (Orsi 2004; Tweed 2006; Bender 2007; Ammerman 2007).

Made possible by key cultural factors like an expanding commercial marketplace in the eighteenth century, legal disestablishment in the nineteenth century, and new media outlets in the twentieth and twenty-first centuries, critical study of America's spiritual marketplace opens a window not only to the complexities and contradictions of American religion but also to the ins and outs of American identity, realities that studies and statistics continue to reflect. For instance, an early 2008 Pew Forum on Religion and Public Life survey on the religious life of Americans indicated a marked increase in the spiritually inclined who defined themselves as "unaffiliated." It is interesting to note that, among other interpretations, prominent journalists found in this rise evidence of a spiritual marketplace. At the collective blog On Faith, hosted by John Meacham and Sally Quinn, author Susan Jacoby, for example, writes about an "American spiritual bazaar," and Chester Gillis maintains that Americans are "seekers and shoppers." "I don't think Americans are just shopping for their beliefs in a trivial sense, trying on creeds like this year's vestment, searching for the latest spiritual fashion," observes *Boston Globe* columnist Ellen Goodman. "About 40 million of us move to another home every year. So too, we drop in and out of church, U-Hauling our beliefs off in search of a better fit" (2008: E3).

Building on the vast interpretive powers of religious economy, *Holy Mavericks* delineates how talented and savvy spiritual suppliers we call innovators recalibrate their messages and ministries toward the existential needs and tastes of more potential clients than their competitors. An unregulated economy allows them to compete in the marketplace of ideas and draw market share from suppliers who fail to change with the times.

Bibliography

Abanes, Richard. 2005. *Rick Warren and the Purpose That Drives Him: An Insider Looks at the Phenomenal Bestseller.* Eugene, OR: Harvest House.

Ammerman, Nancy T. 2007. "Studying Everyday Religion: Challenges for the Future." In *Everyday Religion: Observing Modern Religious Lives*, ed. Nancy T. Ammerman, 219–38. New York: Oxford University Press.

Anderson, Gary M. 1988. "Mr. Smith and the Preachers: The Economics of Religion in the Wealth of Nations." *Journal of Political Economy* 96/5: 1066–88.

Ashley, Jennifer. 2005. "Introduction." In *The Relevant Church: A New Vision for Communities of Faith*, ed. Jennifer Ashley, xi–xiii. Orlando, FL: Relevant Books.

Atkinson, Gordon. 2004. *RealLivePreacher.com*. Grand Rapids, MI: Eerdmans.

Balmer, Randall. 1999. *Blessed Assurance: A History of Evangelicalism in America.* Boston: Beacon.

———, ed. 2004. "John Osteen." In *Encyclopedia of Evangelicalism*, 516. Revised and expanded edition. Waco, TX: Baylor University Press.

———. 2006a. *Mine Eyes Have Seen the Glory: A Journey into the Evangelical Subculture in America.* New York: Oxford University Press.

———. 2006b. *Thy Kingdom Come: How the Religious Right Distorts the Faith and Threatens America: An Evangelical's Lament.* New York: Basic Books.

Bartholomew, Richard. 2006. "Publishing, Celebrity, and the Globalisation of Conservative Protestantism." *Journal of Contemporary Religion* 21/1: 1–13.

Bass, Diana Butler. 2006. *Christianity for the Rest of Us: How the Neighborhood Church Is Transforming the Faith.* San Francisco: Harper.

Batterson, Mark. 2004. *ID: The True You.* Longwood, FL: Xulon Press.

———. 2006. *In a Pit with a Lion on a Snowy Day: How to Survive and Thrive When Opportunity Roars.* Colorado Springs, CO: Multnomah.

Beal, Timothy K. 2005. *Roadside Religion: In Search of the Sacred, the Strange, and the Substance of Faith.* Boston: Beacon.

Bebbington, David. 1989. *Evangelicalism in Modern Britain: A History from the 1730s to the 1980s.* London: Unwin Hyman.

Becker, Howard. 1982. *Art Worlds.* Berkeley: University of California Press.

Bender, Courtney J. 2007. "Touching the Transcendent: Rethinking Religious Experience in the Sociological Study of Religion." In *Everyday Religion: Observing Modern Religious Lives*, ed. Nancy T. Ammerman, 201–18. New York: Oxford University Press.

Bendroth, Margaret. 2004. "Why Women Loved Billy Graham: Urban Revivalism and Popular Entertainment in Early Twentieth Century American Culture." *Religion and American Culture* 14/2: 251–71.

Berger, Peter. 1967. *The Sacred Canopy*. New York: Doubleday.

Beuttler, Fred. 2004. "Revivalism in Suburbia: 'Son City' and the Origins of the Willow Creek Community Church, 1972–1980." In *Embodying the Spirit: New Perspectives on North American Revivalism*, ed. Michael J. McClymond, 168–95. Baltimore: Johns Hopkins University Press.

Bilhartz, Terry D. 1986. *Urban Religion and the Second Great Awakening: Church and Society in Early National Baltimore*. Rutherford, NJ: Farleigh Dickinson University Press.

Bloom, Harold. 1992. *The American Religion: The Emergence of the Post-Christian Nation*. New York: Simon and Schuster.

Blum, Edward J. 2007. "What Barack Obama (and the Democratic Party) Can Learn about Religion from W. E. B. Du Bois." History News Network, July 16.

Blumhofer, Edith. 1993. *Aimee Semple McPherson: Everybody's Sister*. Grand Rapids, MI: Eerdmans.

Borlase, Craig. 2005. *The Naked Christian: Taking Off Religion to Find True Relationship*. Orlando, FL: Relevant Books.

Bowman, Marion. 1999. "Healing in the Spiritual Marketplace: Consumers, Courses, and Credentialism." *Social Compass* 46/2: 181–89.

Butler, Jon. 1990. *Awash in a Sea of Faith: Christianizing the American People*. Cambridge, MA: Harvard University Press.

———. 1994. Review of *The Churching of America, 1776–1990: Winners and Losers in Our Religious Economy*. *American Historical Review* 99/1: 288–89.

———. 2004. "Jack-in-the-Box Faith: The Religion Problem in Modern American History." *Journal of American History* 90/4: 1357–78.

Butler, Jon, Grant Wacker, and Randall Balmer. 2003. *Religion in American Life: A Short History*. New York: Oxford University Press.

Bynum, Juanita. 1998. *No More Sheets: The Truth about Sex*. Lanham, MD: Pneuma Life.

Cahan, Abraham. 1917. *The Rise of David Levinsky*. New York: Harper and Brothers.

Caldwell, Kirbyjon, with Mark Seal. 1999. *The Gospel of Good Success: A Road Map to Spiritual, Emotional, and Financial Wholeness*. New York: Simon and Schuster.

Caldwell, Kirbyjon, and Walt Kallestad, with Paul Sorensen. 2004. *Entrepreneurial Faith: Launching Bold Initiatives to Expand God's Kingdom*. Colorado Springs, CO: WaterBrook Press.

Campolo, Tony. 2004. *Speaking My Mind: The Radical Evangelical Prophet Tackles the Tough Issues Christians Are Afraid to Face*. Nashville, TN: W Publishing.

Carpenter, Joel. 1994. Review of *The Churching of America, 1776–1990: Winners and Losers in Our Religious Economy*. *Journal of American History* 80/4: 1448–49.

Carrette, Jeremy, and Richard King. 2005. *Selling Spirituality: The Silent Takeover of Religion*. New York: Routledge.

Carson, D. A. 2005. *Becoming Conversant with the Emerging Church: Understanding a Movement and Its Implications*. Grand Rapids, MI: Zondervan.

Carver, Francis Grace. 1999. "With Bible in One Hand and Battle-Axe in the Other: Carry A. Nation as Religious Performer and Self-Promoter." *Religion and American Culture* 9/1: 31–65.

Carwardine, Richard. 1996. "Unity Pluralism, and the Spiritual Marketplace: Denominational Competition in the Early American Republic." In *Studies in Church History: Unity and Disunity in the Church*, ed. R. N. Swanson, 297–335. Oxford: Oxford University Press.

Chesnut, R. Andrew. 2003. *Competitive Spirits: Latin America's New Religious Economy*. New York: Oxford University Press.

———. 2005. "Witches, Wailers, and Welfare: The Religious Economy of Funerary Culture and Witchcraft in Latin America." *Latin American Research Review* 40/3: 266–72.

Chidester, David. 2005. *Authentic Fakes: Religion and American Popular Culture*. Berkeley: University of California Press.

Claiborne, Shane, and Chris Haw. 2008. *Jesus for President: Politics for Ordinary Radicals*. Grand Rapids, MI: Zondervan.

Clark, Lynn Schofield, ed. 2007. *Religion, Media, and the Marketplace*. New Brunswick, NJ: Rutgers University Press.

Cole, Neil. 2005. *Organic Church: Growing Faith Where Life Happens*. San Francisco: Jossey-Bass.

Cooke, Phil. 2008. *Branding Faith: Why Some Churches and Nonprofits Impact Culture and Others Don't*. Ventura, CA: Regal.

Curtis, Heather D. 2006. "'Acting Faith': Practices of Religious Healing in Late-Nineteenth-Century Protestantism." In *Practicing Protestants: Histories of Christian Life in America, 1630–1965*, ed. Laurie F. Maffly-Kipp, Leigh E. Schmidt, and Mark Valeri, 137–58. Princeton, NJ: Princeton University Press.

———. 2007. *Faith in the Great Physician: Suffering and Divine Healing in American Culture, 1860–1900*. Baltimore: Johns Hopkins University Press.

Davenport, Jim. 2007. "Faith 'Plays Every Role' in Obama's Life." *Washington Post*, October 7.

deChant, Dell. 2002. *The Sacred Santa: Religious Dimensions of Consumer Culture*. Cleveland: Pilgrim Press.

Dionne, E. J., Jr. 2008. *Souled Out: Reclaiming Faith and Politics after the Religious Right*. Princeton, NJ: Princeton University Press.

Driscoll, Mark. 2006. *Confessions of a Reformission Rev.: Hard Lessons from an Emerging Missional Church.* Grand Rapids, MI: Zondervan.

Egan, R. Danielle, and Stephen D. Papson. 2005. "'You Either Get It or You Don't': Conversion Experiences and *The Dr. Phil Show.*" *Journal of Religion and Popular Culture* 10. www.usask.ca/relst/jrpc/.

Einstein, Mara. 2007. *Brands of Faith: Marketing Religion in a Commercial Age.* New York: Routledge.

Ekelund, Robert B., Robert F. Hebert, and Robert D. Tollison. 2006. *The Marketplace of Christianity.* Cambridge, MA: MIT Press.

El-Faizy, Monique. 2006. *God and Country: How Evangelicals Have Become America's New Mainstream.* New York: Bloomsbury.

Ellingson, Stephen. 2007. *Megachurch and the Mainline: Cultural Innovation, Change, and Conflict in Mainline Protestant Congregations.* Chicago: University of Chicago Press.

Ellwood, Robert S. 1994. *The Sixties Spiritual Awakening: American Religion Moving from Modern to Postmodern.* New Brunswick, NJ: Rutgers University Press.

——. 1997. *The Fifties Spiritual Marketplace: American Religion in a Decade of Conflict.* New Brunswick, NJ: Rutgers University Press.

Evensen, Bruce. 1999. "'It Is a Marvel to Many People': Dwight L. Moody, Mass Media, and the New England Revival of 1877." *New England Quarterly* 72/2: 251–74.

——. 2003. *God's Man for the Gilded Age: D. L. Moody and the Rise of Modern Mass Evangelism.* New York: Oxford University Press.

Finke, Roger. 1997. "The Illusion of Shifting Demand: Supply-Side Interpretations of American Religious History." In *Retelling U.S. Religious History*, ed. Thomas A. Tweed, 108–24. Berkeley: University of California Press.

Finke, Roger, and Rodney Stark. 2005. *The Churching of America, 1776–2005: Winners and Losers in Our Religious Economy.* New Brunswick, NJ: Rutgers University Press.

Fishwick, Marshall. 2002. *Popular Culture in a New Age.* New York: Haworth Press.

Fitch, David. 2005. *The Great Giveaway: Reclaiming the Mission of the Church from Big Business, Parachurch Organizations, Psychotherapy, and Other Modern Maladies.* Grand Rapids, MI: Baker Books.

Freston, Paul. 2001. *Evangelicals and Politics in Asia, Africa, and Latin America.* Cambridge: Cambridge University Press.

Frost, Michael, and Alan Hirsch. 2003. *The Shaping of Things to Come: Innovation and Mission for the 21st Century Church.* Peabody, MA: Hendrickson.

Gaustad, Edwin S. 1993. Review of *The Churching of America, 1776–1990: Winners and Losers in Our Religious Economy. Journal of Religion* 73/4: 640–42.

Gelen, Ted G., ed. 2002. *Sacred Markets, Sacred Canopies: Essays on Religious Markets and Religious Pluralism.* Lanham, MD: Rowman and Littlefield.

George, Carol V. R. 1993. *God's Salesman: Norman Vincent Peale and the Power of Positive Thinking*. New York: Oxford University Press.

Gergen, Kenneth. 1991. *The Saturated Self: Dilemmas of Identity in Contemporary Life*. New York: Basic Books.

Gibbs, Eddie, and Ryan K. Bolger. 2005. *Emerging Churches: Creating Christian Community in Postmodern Cultures*. Grand Rapids, MI: Baker Academic.

Gibbs, Nancy, and Michael Duffy. 2007. "How the Democrats Got Religion." *Time*, July 12.

Gifford, Paul. 1998. *African Christianity: Its Public Role*. Bloomington: Indiana University Press.

———. 2004. *Ghana's New Christianity: Pentecostalism in a Globalizing African Economy*. Bloomington: Indiana University Press.

Giggie, John M. 2003. "'Preachers and Peddlers of God': Ex-Slaves and the Selling of African-American Religion in the American South." In *Commodifying Everything: Relationships to the Market*, ed. Susan Strasser, 169–90. New York: Routledge.

Gill, Anthony. 1998. *Rendering unto Caesar: The Catholic Church and the State in Latin America*. Chicago: University of Chicago Press.

Goff, Philip. 1999. "'We Have Heard the Joyful Sound': Charles E. Fuller's Broadcast and the Rise of Modern Evangelicalism." *Religion and American Culture* 9/1: 67–95.

Goldberg, Michelle. 2006. *Kingdom Coming: The Rise of Christian Nationalism*. New York: Norton.

Goodman, Ellen. 2008. "Americans Are Shoppers: That Goes for Religion, Too." *Houston Chronicle*, March 2, E3.

Grem, Darren E. 2008. "Selling a 'Disneyland for the Devout': Religious Marketing at Jim Bakker's Heritage USA." In *Shopping for Jesus: Faith in Marketing in the USA*, ed., Dominic Janes, 137–60. Washington, DC: New Academia Press.

Griffith, R. Marie. 2004. *Born Again Bodies: Spirit and Flesh in American Christianity*. Berkeley: University of California Press.

Gushee, David P. 2008. *The Future of Faith in American Politics: The Public Witness of the Evangelical Center*. Waco, TX: Baylor University Press.

Hall, David. D., ed. 1997. *Lived Religion in America: Toward a History of Practice*. Princeton, NJ: Princeton University Press.

———. 2003. "Review Essay: What Is the Place of Religious 'Experience' in Religious History?" *Religion and American Culture* 13/2: 241–50.

Hall, Timothy D. 1994. *Contested Boundaries: Itinerancy and the Reshaping of the Colonial American Religious World*. Durham, NC: Duke University Press.

———. 2002. "Migration, Choice, and the Development of the Religious Marketplace in America." *Historisch Tijdschrift Groniek* 156: 321–40.

Hall, Timothy D., and T. H. Breen. 1998. "Structuring Provincial Imagination: The Rhetoric and Experience of Social Changes in Eighteenth-Century New England." *American Historical Review* 103: 1411–39.

Hambrick-Stowe, Charles E. 1996. *Charles G. Finney and the Spirit of American Evangelism*. Grand Rapids, MI: Eerdmans.

Hangen, Tona J. 2002. *Redeeming the Dial: Radio, Religion, and Popular Culture in America*. Chapel Hill: University of North Carolina Press.

Harding, Susan Friend. 2000. *The Book of Jerry Falwell: Fundamentalism Language and Politics*. Princeton, NJ: Princeton University Press.

Harrell, David Edwin, Jr. 1985. *Oral Roberts: An American Life*. Bloomington: Indiana University Press.

———. 1993. "Oral Roberts: Religious Media Pioneer." In *Communication and Change in American Religious History*, ed. Leonard I. Sweet, 320–34. Grand Rapids, MI: Eerdmans.

Harrison, Milmon F. 2005. *Righteous Riches: The Word of Faith Movement in Contemporary African American Religion*. New York: Oxford University Press.

Hart, D. G. 2004. *Deconstructing Evangelicalism: Conservative Protestantism in the Age of Billy Graham*. Grand Rapids, MI: Baker Academic.

Hatch, Nathan O. 1989. *The Democratization of American Christianity*. New Haven, CT: Yale University Press.

Hedges, Chris. 2007. *American Fascists: The Christian Right and the War on America*. New York: Simon and Schuster.

Heinze, Andrew. 1996. "The First Mass Market Rabbi." *Midstream* 42: 14–17.

Hendershot, Heather. 2004. *Shaking the World for Jesus: Media and Conservative Evangelical Culture*. Chicago: University of Chicago Press.

Hulsehter, Mark. 1995. "Interpreting the 'Popular' in Popular Religion." *American Studies* 36/2: 127–37. Review Symposium on American Religion.

Hunter, Kent. 2004. *The Jesus Enterprise: Engaging Culture to Reach the Unchurched*. Nashville, TN: Abingdon Press.

Hybels, Bill. 1997. *Transparency*. Grand Rapids, MI: Zondervan.

———. 2002. *Honest to God: Becoming an Authentic Christian*. Grand Rapids, MI: Zondervan.

———. 2005. *Authenticity: Being Honest with God and Others*. Grand Rapids, MI: Zondervan.

Iannaccone, Laurence R. 1991. "The Consequences of Religious Market Structure: Adam Smith and the Economics of Religion." *Rationality and Society* 3/2: 156–77.

———. 1992. "Sacrifice and Stigma: Reducing Free-Riding in Cults, Communes, and Other Collectives." *Journal of Political Economy* 100/2: 271–92.

———. 1994. "Why Strict Churches Are Strong." *American Journal of Sociology* 99: 1180–1211.

———. 2006. "The Market for Martyrs." *Interdisciplinary Journal of Research on Religion* 2/4: 1–29.

Introvigne, Massimo. 2005. "Niches in the Islamic Religious Market and Fundamentalism: Examples from Turkey and Other Countries." *Interdisciplinary Journal of Research on Religion* 1/3: 1–26.

Jackson, John. 2003. *PastorPreneur: Pastors and Entrepreneurs Answer the Call.* Toronto: Baxter.

Jakes, T. D. 1993. *Woman, Thou Art Loosed: Healing the Wounds of the Past.* Shippensburg, PA: Destiny Image.

———. 1995. *Loose That Man and Let Him Go!* Minneapolis, MN: Bethany House.

———. 1996. *The Harvest.* Lanham, MD: Pneuma Life Publishing.

———. 1997. *So You Call Yourself a Man? A Devotional for Ordinary Men with Extraordinary Potential.* Tulsa, OK: Albury Press.

———. 1998. *The Lady, Her Lover, and Her Lord.* New York: Berkley Books.

———. 2001. *Naked and Not Ashamed: We've Been Afraid to Reveal What God Longs to Heal.* Shippensburg, PA: Destiny Image.

———. 2005. *Ten Commandments of Working in a Hostile Environment.* New York: Berkley Books.

———. 2006. *Not Easily Broken: A Novel.* Nashville, TN: FaithWords.

———. 2007. *Reposition Yourself: Living Life without Limits.* New York: Atria Books.

Jenkins, Philip. 2002. *The Next Christendom: The Coming of Global Christianity.* New York: Oxford University Press.

———. 2006. *The New Faces of Christianity: Believing the Bible in the Global South.* New York: Oxford University Press.

Jones, Tony. 2005. *The Sacred Way: Spiritual Practices for Everyday Life.* Grand Rapids, MI: Zondervan.

———. 2008. *The New Christians: Dispatches from the Emergent Frontier.* San Francisco: Jossey-Bass.

Karkabi, Barbara. 2006. "New Game Not Playing Well at Lakewood: Church OK with Intent of Product, but Didn't Officially Sanction Release." *Houston Chronicle,* December 2.

Kelley, Dean. 1972. *Why Conservative Churches Are Growing: A Study in Sociology of Religion.* New York: Harper and Row.

Ketchell, Aaron. 2007. *Holy Hills of the Ozarks: Religion and Tourism in Branson, Missouri.* Baltimore: Johns Hopkins University Press.

Kilde, Jeanne Halgren. 2006. "Reading Megachurches: Investigating the Religious and Cultural Work of Church Architecture." In *American Sanctuary: Understanding Sacred Spaces,* ed. Louis P. Nelson, 225–49. Bloomington: Indiana University Press.

Kimball, Dan. 2003. *The Emerging Church: Vintage Christianity for New Generations.* Grand Rapids, MI: Zondervan.

Kuhn, Thomas. 1962. *The Structure of Scientific Revolutions.* Chicago: University of Chicago Press.

Kyle, Richard. 2006. *Evangelicalism: An Americanized Christianity.* New Brunswick, NJ: Transaction.

Laing, Annette Susan. 1995. "All Things to All Men: Popular Religious Culture and the Anglican Mission in Colonial America, 1701–1750." Ph.D. diss., University of California, Riverside.

Lambert, Frank. 1993. "Subscribing for Profits and Piety: The Friendship of Benjamin Franklin and George Whitefield." *William and Mary Quarterly* 50/3: 529–54.

———. 1994. *"Pedlar in Divinity": George Whitefield and the Transatlantic Revivals*. Princeton, NJ: Princeton University Press.

———. 1999. *Inventing the "Great Awakening."* Princeton, NJ: Princeton University Press.

———, 2003a. *The Founding Fathers and the Place of Religion in America*. Princeton, NJ: Princeton University Press.

———. 2003b. "Virginia's Religious Revolution: From Established Monopoly to Free Marketplace." In *Britain and the American South: From Colonialism to Rock and Roll*, ed. Joseph P. Ward, 3–25. Jackson: University of Mississippi Press.

———. 2004. "Evangelical Revivals and Communicative Spheres in the Colonial Era." In *Atlantic Communications: The Media in American and German History from the Seventeenth to the Twentieth Century*, ed. Norbert Finzsch and Ursula Lehmkuhl, 15–44. New York: Berg.

Lamott, Anne. 1999. *Traveling Mercies: Some Thoughts on Faith*. New York: Anchor Books.

———. 2005. *Plan B: Further Thoughts on Faith*. New York: Riverhead Books.

Lang, Graeme, Selina Ching Chan, and Lars Ragvald. 2005. "Folk Temples and the Chinese Religious Economy." *Interdisciplinary Journal of Research on Religion* 1/4: 1–9.

Lawson, Steven. 1988. "John and Dodie Osteen: Their Oasis of Love Reaches a Troubled World." *Charisma*.

LeBeau, Bryan. 1995. "Why Upstarts Win in America: Religion in the Marketplace." *American Studies* 36/2: 111–17. Review Symposium on American Religion.

Lee, Shayne. 2005. *T. D. Jakes: America's New Preacher*. New York: NYU Press.

Levy, Bernard-Henri. 2006. *American Vertigo: Traveling America in the Footsteps of Tocqueville*. New York: Random House.

Liebman, Joshua Loth. 1946. *Peace of Mind*. New York: Simon and Schuster.

Lindsey, D. Michael. 2007. *Faith in the Halls of Power: How Evangelicals Joined the American Elite*. New York: Oxford University Press.

Lofton, Kathryn E. 2006a. "Practicing Oprah; or, the Prescriptive Compulsion of a Spiritual Capitalism." *Journal of Popular Culture* 39/4: 599–621.

———. 2006b. "The Preacher Paradigm: Promotional Biographies and the Modern-Made Evangelist." *Religion and American Culture: A Journal of Interpretation* 16: 95–123.

Lofton, Kathryn E. 2008. "Public Confessions: Oprah Winfrey's American Religious History." *Women & Performance: a journal of feminist theory* 18/1: 51–69.

Long, Carolyn Murrow. 2001. *Spiritual Merchants: Religion, Magic, and Commerce.* Knoxville: University of Tennessee Press.

Lynch, Christopher Owen. 1998. *Selling Catholicism: Bishop Sheen and the Power of Television.* Lexington: University Press of Kentucky.

MacDonald, G. Jeffrey. 2005. "Churches Seeking Market-Savvy Breed of Pastor." *Christian Science Monitor,* August 19. www.csmonitor.com/2005/0819/p01s03-ussc.html.

Marsden, George. 1993. Review of *The Churching of America, 1776-1990: Winners and Losers in Our Religious Economy. Church History* 62/3: 449-51.

Marti, Gerardo. 2005. *A Mosaic of Believers: Diversity and Innovation in a Multiethnic Church.* Bloomington: Indiana University Press.

———. 2008. *Hollywood Faith: Holiness, Prosperity and Ambition in a Los Angeles Church.* New Brunswick, NJ: Rutgers University Press.

Martin, Robert F. 2002. *Hero of the Heartland: Billy Sunday and the Transformation of American Society, 1862–1935.* Bloomington: Indiana University Press.

Martin, William C. 1991. *A Prophet with Honor: The Billy Graham Story.* New York: William Morrow.

———. 2005. "Prime Minister." *Texas Monthly,* August.

Marty, Martin. 1993. "Churches as Winners, Losers." *Christian Century,* January 27, 88-89.

Mattingly, Terry. 2005. *Pop Goes Religion: Faith and Popular Culture.* Nashville, TN: W Publishing.

McAdams, Dan P. 2006. *The Redemptive Self: Stories Americans Live By.* New York: Oxford University Press.

McDannell, Colleen. 1995. *Material Christianity: Religion and Popular Culture in America.* New Haven, CT: Yale University Press.

McKnight, Scot. 2007. "Five Streams of the Emerging Church." *Christianity Today* 51/2: 34–39.

McLaren, Brian. 1998. *Church on the Other Side: Doing Ministry in the Postmodern Matrix.* Grand Rapids, MI: Zondervan.

———. 2001. *A New Kind of Christian: A Tale of Two Friends on a Spiritual Journey.* San Francisco: Jossey-Bass.

———. 2002. *More Ready Than You Realize: Evangelism as Dance in the Postmodern Matrix.* Grand Rapids, MI: Zondervan.

———. 2003. *The Story We Find Ourselves In: Further Adventures of a New Kind of Christian.* San Francisco: Jossey-Bass.

———. 2004. *A Generous Orthodoxy.* Grand Rapids, MI: Zondervan.

———. 2005. *The Last Word and the Word after That: A Tale of Faith, Doubt, and a New Kind of Christianity.* San Francisco: Jossey-Bass.

McLaren, Brian. 2006. *The Secret Message of Jesus: Uncovering the Truth That Could Change Everything*. Nashville, TN: W Publishing.

———. 2007. *Everything Must Change: Jesus, Global Crises, and a Revolution of Hope*. Nashville, TN: W Publishing.

McLaren, Brian, and Tony Campolo. 2003. *Adventures in Missing the Point: How the Culture-Controlled Church Neutered the Gospel*. Grand Rapids, MI: Zondervan.

McRoberts, Omar M. 2003. *Streets of Glory: Church and Community in a Black Urban Neighborhood*. Chicago: University of Chicago Press.

Meyer, Joyce. 2003. *How to Hear from God: Learn to Know His Voice and Make Right Decisions*. St. Louis, MO: Joyce Meyer Trade.

Miller, Donald. 2003. *Blue Like Jazz: Nonreligious Thoughts on Christian Spirituality*. Nashville, TN: Thomas Nelson.

Miller, Donald E. 1997. *Reinventing American Protestantism: Christianity in the New Millennium*. Berkeley: University of California Press.

Miller, Douglas T. 1975. "Popular Religion of the 1950s: Norman Vincent Peale and Billy Graham." *Journal of Popular Culture* 9/1: 66–76.

Miller, Vincent J. 2005. *Consuming Religion: Christian Faith and Practice in a Consumer Culture*. New York: Continuum.

Moore, R. Lawrence. 1994. *Selling God: American Religion in the Marketplace of Culture*. New York: Oxford University Press.

———. 2003. *Touchdown Jesus: The Mixing of Sacred and Secular in American History*. Louisville, KY: Westminster John Knox Press.

Morgan, Timothy C. 2007. "Q+A with Rick Warren." *Christianity Today* 51/2: 21

Morton, Paul. 1999. *Why Kingdoms Fall: The Journey from Breakdown to Restoration*. Tulsa, OK: Albury.

Murley, Bryan. 2005. "The Mediahood of All Receivers: New Media, New 'Church,' and New Challenges." Paper presented at the conference "After Evangelicalism," Cornerstone University, Grand Rapids, Michigan, September 15–17.

Nelson, Marcia Z. 2005. *The Gospel According to Oprah*. Louisville, KY: Westminster John Knox Press.

Newbigin, Lesslie. 1986. *Foolishness to the Greeks: The Gospel and Western Culture*. Grand Rapids, MI: Eerdmans.

Noll, Mark A. 1992. *A History of Christianity in the United States and Canada*. Grand Rapids, MI: Eerdmans.

———. 2003. *The Rise of Evangelicalism: The Age of Edwards, Whitefield, and the Wesleys*. Downers Grove, IL: Intervarsity Press.

———. 2006. Review of *A Church of Our Own: Disestablishment and Diversity in American Religion*. *Journal for the Scientific Study of Religion* 45/3: 462–63.

Nord, David Paul. 1993. "Systematic Benevolence: Religious Publishing and the Marketplace in Early Nineteenth-Century America." In *Communication and Change in American Religious History*, ed. Leonard I. Sweet, 239–69. Grand Rapids, MI: Eerdmans.

Odunfa, Sola. 2005. "Miracles and Money." *BBC Focus: Africa* 16/3: 14–17.

Olds, Kelly. 1994. "Privatizing the Church: Disestablishment in Connecticut and Massachusetts." *Journal of Political Economy* 102/2 277–97.

Orsi, Robert. 2004. *Between Heaven and Earth: The Religious Worlds People Make and the Scholars Who Study Them*. Princeton, NJ: Princeton University Press.

Osteen, Joel. 2004. *Your Best Life Now: 7 Steps to Living at Your Full Potential*. New York: FaithWords.

———. 2005. *Your Best Life Now Journal*. New York: FaithWords.

———. 2007. *Become a Better You: 7 Steps to Improving Your Life Every Day*. New York: Free Press.

Osteen, John. 1968. *The Bible Way to Spiritual Power*. Houston: John Osteen Ministries.

———. 1978. *You Can Change Your Destiny*. Houston: John Osteen Ministries.

———. 1983. *Confessions of a Baptist Preacher*. Houston: John Osteen Ministries.

Pagitt, Doug. 2005. *Preaching Re-imagined: The Role of the Sermon in Communities of Faith*. Grand Rapids, MI: Zondervan.

Pagitt, Doug, and Tony Jones. 2007. *An Emergent Manifesto of Hope*. Grand Rapids, MI: Baker Academic.

Pappu, Sridhar. 2007. "In S.C. Obama Seeks Spiritual Reawakening." *Washington Post*, October 29, C01.

Peale, Norman Vincent. 1952. *The Power of Positive Thinking*. Englewood Cliffs, NJ: Prentice-Hall.

Percy, Martyn. 2000. "The Church in the Market Place: Advertising and Religion in a Secular Age." *Journal of Contemporary Religion* 15/1: 97–119.

Percy, Martyn, and Ian Markham, eds. 2006. *Why Liberal Churches Are Growing*. New York: T&T Clark.

Phillips, Kevin. 2006. *American Theocracy: The Peril and Politics of Radical Religion, Oil, and Borrowed Money in the 21st Century*. New York: Viking.

Pollock, John. 1985. *To All the Nations: The Billy Graham Story*. San Francisco: Harper and Row.

Powell, Milton B., ed. 1967. *The Voluntary Church: Religious Life, 1740–1860, Seen through the Eyes of European Visitors*. New York: Macmillan.

Prothero, Stephen. 2007. *Religious Literacy: What Every American Needs to Know—and Doesn't*. New York: HarperCollins.

Raschke, Carl. 2004. *The Next Reformation: Why Evangelicals Must Embrace Postmodernity*. Grand Rapids, MI: Baker Academic.

Ribuffio, Leo. 1981. "Jesus Christ as Business Statesman: Bruce Barton and the Selling of Corporate Capitalism." *American Quarterly* 33/2: 206–31.

Rieff, Philip. 1966. *The Triumph of the Therapeutic: Uses of Faith after Freud*. New York: Harper and Row.

Romano, Lois. 2005. "'The Smiling Preacher' Builds on Large Following." *Washington Post*, January 30.

Romberg, Raquel. 2003. *Witchcraft and Welfare: Spiritual Capital and the Business of Religion in Modern Puerto Rico.* Austin: University of Texas Press.

Roof, Wade Clark. 1993. *A Generation of Seekers: The Spiritual Journeys of the Baby Boom Generation.* San Francisco: HarperCollins.

———. 1999. *Spiritual Marketplace: Baby Boomers and the Remaking of American Religion.* Princeton, NJ: Princeton University Press.

Roozen, David A., and C. Kirk Hadaway. 1993. *Church and Denominational Growth.* Nashville, TN: Abingdon Press.

Sandler, Lauren. 2006. *Righteous: Dispatches from the Evangelical Youth Movement.* New York: Viking.

Sandras, Eric. 2004. *Buck-Naked Faith: A Brutally Honest Look at Stunted Christianity.* Colorado Springs, CO: Navpress Publishing Group.

Sargeant, Kimon Howland. 2000. *Seeker Churches: Promoting Traditional Religions in a Nontraditional Way.* New Brunswick: Rutgers University Press.

Scandrette, Mark. 2005. "A Week in the Life of a Missional Community." In *The Relevant Church: A New Vision for Communities of Faith*, ed. Jennifer Ashley, 131–48. Orlando, FL: Relevant Books.

Schlenther, Boyd Stanley. 1998. "Religious Faith and Commercial Empire." In *The Oxford History of the British Empire: The Eighteenth Century*, ed. Peter J. Marshall, 128–50. Cambridge: Cambridge University Press.

Schmidt, Leigh Eric. 1995. *Consumer Rites: The Buying and Selling of American Holidays.* Princeton, NJ: Princeton University Press.

———. 2005. *Restless Souls: The Making of American Spirituality.* San Francisco: HarperSanFrancisco.

Schultze, Quentin J., ed. 1990. *American Evangelicals and the Mass Media: Perspectives on the Relationship between American Evangelicals and the Mass Media.* Grand Rapids, MI: Baker Books.

———. 1991. *Televangelism and American Culture: The Business of Popular Religion.* Grand Rapids, MI: Baker Academic.

Seay, Chris. 2003. "I Have Inherited the Faith of My Fathers." In *Stories of Emergence: Moving from Absolute to Authentic*, ed. Mike Yaconelli, 75–84. Grand Rapids, MI: Zondervan.

Sheler, Jeffery L. 2006. *Believers: A Journey into Evangelical America.* New York: Viking.

Sherry, John F. 2005. "Brand Meaning." In *Kellogg on Branding: The Marketing Faculty of the Kellogg School of Management*, ed. Alice M. Tybout and Tim Calkins, 40–69. Hoboken, NJ: Wiley.

Shibley, Mark A. 1996a. "Contemporary Evangelicals: Born-Again and World Affirming." *Annals of the American Academy of Political and Social Science* 558/1: 67–87.

———. 1996b. *Resurgent Evangelicalism in the United States: Mapping Cultural Change since 1970.* Columbia: University of South Carolina Press.

Sider, Ronald. 2005. *The Scandal of the Evangelical Conscience: Why Are Christians Living Just Like the Rest of the World?* Grand Rapids, MI: Baker.

Simmons, Dale H. 1997. *E. W. Kenyon and the Postbellum Pursuit of Peace, Power, and Plenty.* Lanham, MD: Scarecrow Press.

Smith, Ashley, and Stacy Mattingly. 2005. *Unlikely Angel: The Untold Story of the Atlanta Hostage Hero.* Grand Rapids, MI: Zondervan.

Smith, Christian. 1998. *American Evangelicalism: Embattled and Thriving.* Chicago: University of Chicago Press.

Smith, Evan. 2007. "Texas Monthly Talks: Can Joel Osteen Get an 'Amen'?" *Texas Monthly,* November.

Smith, James K. A. 2006. *Who's Afraid of Postmodernism? Taking Derrida, Lyotard, and Foucault to Church.* Grand Rapids, MI: Baker Academic.

Smith, Warren. 2004. *Deceived on Purpose: The New Age Implications of the Purpose-Driven Church.* Magalia, CA: Mountain Stream Press.

Stark, Rodney. 2003. *For the Glory of God: How Monotheism Led to Reformations, Science, Witch-hunts, and the End of Slavery.* Princeton, NJ: Princeton University Press.

Stark, Rodney, and Roger Finke. 2000. *Acts of Faith: Explaining the Human Side of Religion.* Berkeley: University of California Press.

———. 2003. "The Dynamics of Religious Economies." In *Handbook of the Sociology of Religion,* ed. Michelle Dillon, 96–109. Cambridge: Cambridge University Press, 2003.

Stein, Stephen J. 1995. "'Buyer Beware!': Provocative Literature." *American Studies* 36/2: 119–25. Review Symposium on American Religion.

———. 2002. "American Religious History: Decentered with Many Centers." *Church History* 71/2: 374–79.

Steward, Stanley. 2003. "Where Sin Abounds: A Religious History of Las Vegas." Ph.D. diss., University of Nevada, Las Vegas.

Stolz, Jorg. 2006. "Salvation Goods and Religious Markets: Integrating Rational Choice and Weberian Perspectives." *Social Compass* 53/1: 13–32.

Stout, Harry S. 1977. "Religion, Communications, and the Ideological Origins of the American Revolution." *William and Mary Quarterly* 34: 519–41.

———. 1991. *The Divine Dramatist: George Whitefield and the Rise of Modern Evangelicalism.* Grand Rapids, MI: Eerdmans.

Strang, Stephen. 2002. "John Osteen." In *The New International Dictionary of Pentecostal and Charismatic Movements,* ed. Stanley M. Burgess and Eduard M. van der Maas, 951. Revised and expanded edition. Grand Rapids, MI: Zondervan.

Sullivan, Amy. 2008. *The Party Faithful: How and Why Democrats Are Closing the God Gap.* New York: Scribner.

Sundquist, James. 2004. *Who's Driving the Purpose Driven Church? A Documentary on the Teachings of Rick Warren.* Bethany, OK: Rock Salt Publishing.

Surratt, Geoff, Greg Ligon, and Warren Bird. 2006. *The Multi-site Church Revolution: Being One Church in Many Locations*. Grand Rapids, MI: Zondervan.

Sutton, Matthew Avery. 2007. *Aimee Semple McPherson and the Resurrection of Christian America*. Cambridge, MA: Harvard University Press.

Sweet, Leonard. 1993. "Communication and Change in American Religious History: A Historiographical Probe." In *Communication and Change in American Religious History*, ed. Leonard I. Sweet, 1–90. Grand Rapids, MI: Eerdmans.

———. 2000. *Postmodern Pilgrims: First Century Passion for the 21st Century Church*. Nashville, TN: Broadman and Holman.

Taylor, Steve. 2005. *The Out of Bounds Church? Learning to Create a Community of Faith in a Culture of Change*. Grand Rapids, MI: Zondervan.

Thumma, Scott. 2006. "The Shape of Things to Come: Megachurches, Emerging Churches, and Other New Religious Structures." In *Faith in America: Changes, Challenges, New Directions*. Vol. 1, ed. Charles H. Lippy, 185–206. Westport, CT: Praeger.

Thumma, Scott, and Dave Travis. 2007. *Beyond Megachurch Myths: What We Can Learn from America's Largest Churches*. San Francisco: Jossey-Bass.

Tocqueville, Alexis de. [1840] 2003. *Democracy in America: and Two Essays on America*. New York: Penguin.

Travis, Trysh. 2007. "It Will Change the World If Everybody Reads This Book." *American Quarterly* 59/3: 1027–51.

Turner, John G. 2006. "Selling Jesus to Modern America: Campus Crusade for Christ, Evangelical Culture, and Conservative Politics." Ph.D. diss., University of Notre Dame.

———. 2008. *Bill Bright and Campus Crusade for Christ: The Renewal of Evangelicalism in Postwar America*. Chapel Hill: University of North Carolina Press.

Tweed, Thomas A. 2006. *Crossing and Dwelling: A Theory of Religion*. Cambridge, MA: Harvard University Press.

Twitchell, James B. 2007. *Shopping for God: How Christianity Went from In Your Heart to In Your Face*. New York: Simon and Schuster.

Van Biema, David, and Jeff Chu. 2006. "Does God Want You to Be Rich?" *Time*, September 18, 48–56.

Vara, Richard. 2007. "He's Staying the Course: Israel Houghton Wasn't Looking for Success, but It Found Him." *Houston Chronicle*, February 10.

Voskuil, Dennis. 1983. *Mountains into Goldmines: Robert Schuller and the Gospel of Success*. Grand Rapids, MI: Eerdmans.

Wallis, Jim. 2004. *God's Politics: Why the Right Gets It Wrong and the Left Doesn't Get It*. San Francisco: HarperCollins.

———. 2008. *The Great Awakening: Reviving Faith and Politics in a Post-Religious Right America*. San Francisco: HarperCollins.

Walliss, John, and Wayne Spencer. 2003. "The Lost Aisle: Selling Atlantis in the 'Spiritual Supermarket.'" *Journal of Religion and Popular Culture* 3. www.usask.ca/relst/jrpc/.

Walton, Jonathan. 2006. "Watch This! Televangelism and Black Popular Culture." Ph.D. diss., Princeton Theological Seminary.

Waltz, Mark L. 2005. *First Impressions: Creating Wow Experiences in Your Church.* Loveland, CO: Group Publishing.

Ward, Karen. 2005. "The New Church: Artistic, Monastic, and Commute-Free." In *The Relevant Church: A New Vision for Communities of Faith,* ed. Jennifer Ashley, 79–88. Orlando, FL: Relevant Books.

Warner, R. Stephen. 1993. "Work in Progress toward a New Paradigm for the Sociological Study of Religion in the United States." *American Journal of Sociology* 98/5: 1044–93.

———. 2005. *A Church of Our Own: Disestablishment and Diversity in American Religion.* New Brunswick, NJ: Rutgers University Press.

Warren, Hillary. 2005. *There's Never Been a Show Like Veggie Tales: Sacred Messages in a Secular Market.* Lanham, MD: AltaMira.

Warren, Rick. 1995. *The Purpose-Driven Church: Growth without Compromising Your Message and Mission.* Grand Rapids, MI: Zondervan.

———. 2002. *The Purpose-Driven Life: What on Earth Am I Here For?* Grand Rapids, MI: Zondervan.

———. 2003. *The Purpose-Driven Life Journal.* Grand Rapids, MI: Zondervan.

Webber, Robert E. 1999. *Ancient-Future Faith: Rethinking Evangelicalism for a Postmodern World.* Grand Rapids, MI: Baker Books, 1999.

———. 2002. *The Younger Evangelicals: Facing the Challenges of the New World.* Grand Rapids, MI: Baker Books.

Weber, Max. 1930. *The Protestant Ethic and the Spirit of Capitalism.* New York: Scribner.

Weber, Timothy. 1994. Review of *The Churching of America, 1776-1990: Winners and Losers in Our Religious Economy. Fides et Historia* 26/1: 134–40.

White, Paula. 1998. *He Loves Me He Loves Me Not: What Every Woman Needs to Know about Unconditional Love, but Is Afraid to Feel.* Orlando, FL: Creation House.

———. 2004. *Deal With It! You Cannot Conquer What You Will Not Confront.* Nashville, TN: Thomas Nelson.

———. 2007. *You're All That! Understand God's Design for Your Life.* New York: FaithWords.

White, Randy. 1998. *Without Walls: God's Blueprint for the 21st Century Church.* Lake Mary, FL: Charisma House.

Wilkinson, Bruce H. 2000. *The Prayer of Jabez: Breaking through to the Blessed Life.* Sisters, OR: Multnomah.

Witt, Marcos. 2007. *How to Overcome Fear and Live Your Life to the Fullest.* New York: Atria.

Witten, Marsha G. 1993. *All Is Forgiven: The Secular Message in American Protestantism.* Princeton, NJ: Princeton University Press.

Wolfe, Alan. 2003. *The Transformation of American Religion: How We Actually Live Our Faith*. Chicago: University of Chicago Press.

Woodhead, Linda, with Paul Heelas and David Martin. 2002. *Peter Berger and the Study of Religion*. New York: Routledge.

Wuthnow, Robert. 1988. *The Restructuring of American Religion: Society and Faith since World War II*. Princeton, NJ: Princeton University Press.

———. 1994. *Producing the Sacred: An Essay on Public Religion*. Urbana: University of Illinois Press.

———. 2005. *America and the Challenges of Religious Diversity*. Princeton, NJ: Princeton University Press.

Young, Michael P. 2006. *Bearing Witness against Sin: The Evangelical Birth of the American Social Movement*. Chicago: University of Chicago Press.

Young, Richard. 2007. *The Rise of Lakewood Church and Joel Osteen*. New Kensington, PA: Whitaker House.

Zaher, Holly Rankin. 2005. "Connect, Experience, Live." In *The Relevant Church: A New Vision for Communities of Faith*, ed. Jennifer Ashley, 121–30. Orlando, FL: Relevant Books.

Index

About the Authors

SHAYNE LEE is Assistant Professor of Sociology and African Diaspora Studies at Tulane University and the author of *T. D. Jakes: America's New Preacher,* also published by NYU Press.

PHILLIP LUKE SINITIERE holds a Ph.D. in American History from the University of Houston.